The Only Guides You'll Ever Need!

THIS SERIES IS YOUR TRUSTED GUIDE through all of life's stages and situations. Want to learn how to surf the Internet or care for your new dog? Or maybe you'd like to become a wine connoisseur or an expert gardener? The solution is simple: just pick up a K.I.S.S. Guide and turn to the first page.

Expert authors will walk you through the subject from start to finish, using simple blocks of knowledge to build your skills one step at a time. Build upon these learning blocks and by the end of the book, you'll be an expert yourself! Or, if you are familiar with the topic but want to learn more, it's easy to dive in and pick up where you left off.

The K.I.S.S. Guides deliver what they promise: simple access to all the information you'll need on one subject. Other titles you might want to check out include: Living with a Dog, Playing Golf, the Internet, Microsoft Windows, and Astrology.

GUIDE TO PLAYING

Guitar

TERRY BURROWS

Foreword by Bill Wyman

A Dorling Kindersley Book

Dorling **DK** Kindersley

LONDON, NEW YORK, SYDNEY, DELHI, PARIS,
MUNICH AND JOHANNESBURG

Dorling Kindersley Publishing, Inc.
Editorial Director LaVonne Carlson
Series Editor Beth Adelman
Copyeditor Kristi Hart
Technical Consultant Matthew McCullough

Dorling Kindersley Limited
Project Editor David Tombesi-Walton
Editor Michael Downey
Senior Editor Bridget Hopkinson
Editorial Director Valerie Buckingham

Managing Art Editor Stephen Knowlden
Jacket Designer Neal Cobourne

Created and produced for Dorling Kindersley by
THE FOUNDRY, part of The Foundry Creative Media Company Ltd,
Crabtree Hall, Crabtree Lane, Fulham, London SW6 6TY

The Foundry project team
Frances Banfield, Lucy Bradbury, Josephine Cutts, Sue Evans, Karen Fitzpatrick,
Douglas Hall, Sasha Heseltine, Dave Jones, Jennifer Kenna, Lee Matthews, Ian Powling,
Bridget Tily and Nick Wells. Special thanks to Polly Willis.

Copyright © 2000
Dorling Kindersley Publishing, Inc.
Text copyright © 2000 Terry Burrows
2 4 6 8 10 9 7 5 3

Published in the United States by
Dorling Kindersley Publishing, Inc.
95 Madison Avenue
New York, New York 10016

Library of Congress Cataloging-in-Publication Data

Burrows, Terry.
    KISS guide to playing guitar / Terry Burrows. – 1st American ed.
      p. cm. -- (Keep it simple series)
      ISBN 0-7894-5979-5
1. Guitar--Methods--Self-instruction. I. Title. II. Series.
MT588 .B94 2000
787.87'193--dc21
                               00-008783
                                  CIP

Dorling Kindersley Publishing, Inc. offers special discounts for bulk purchases for sales promotions or premiums.
Specific, large-quantity needs can be met with special editions, including personalized covers,
excerpts of existing guides, and corporate imprints. For more information, contact Special Markets Department,
Dorling Kindersley Publishing, Inc., 95 Madison Avenue, New York, NY 10016 Fax: 800-600-9098.

Color reproduction by David Bruce Graphics
Printed and bound by Printer Industria Grafica, S.A., Barcelona, Spain

For our complete catalog visit

www.dk.com

Contents at a Glance

PART ONE

Simple Basics

PART TWO

Making a Noise

PART THREE

Music Theory Basics

PART FOUR

Getting into Style

PART FIVE

Sounds, Studio, and Stage

CONTENTS

PART ONE Simple Basics   24

CHAPTER 1 A Bit of History   26

CHAPTER 2 Guitar Music   40

Foreword

I WAS NOT ALWAYS a bass player or a Rolling Stone. My first guitar was a cheap Spanish acoustic, which I bought in 1956 when I was in the Royal Air Force, stationed in Germany. I was inspired to buy it after listening to Chris Barber's Jazz Band, featuring Lonnie Donegan. Casey Jones, a Liverpudlian, and I decided to start a skiffle group at the RAF camp. As fate would have it Casey would later have Eric Clapton in his group, for a short while.

In 1960 some friends and I started a group in southeast London, and called ourselves The Cliftons. Technology wasn't so good back then; I played my guitar through a tape recorder set to record/pause.

My decision to switch from lead guitar to bass came after going to a gig in Aylesbury, where I saw a band with a big bass sound – The Barron Knights. That was it; I scraped together £8 (about $12) to buy a second-hand bass. I took out all the frets, intending to replace them, but I liked the sound so much I kept it that way. I made my own speaker cabinet, which had an 18-inch Goodmans speaker, but the concrete block I put in the bottom made it almost too heavy to carry!

The first guitarist I played with who impressed me was Steve Carroll in The Cliftons. He could copy a Chuck Berry guitar solo, note for note, after just a couple of listens. In fact, that's how most of us learned: We listened to records and worked out what we needed to do. This K.I.S.S. Guide would have been a fantastic help to us back in the early sixties – there would have been far fewer worn out 45-rpm singles.

When I joined the Stones in 1962 they were impressed by "my gear" – at my audition I even had a spare Vox AC-30. Obviously playing with the Stones meant I got to watch some great guitar players close up. Keith Richards, Ronnie Wood, Mick Taylor and, of course, Brian Jones all have very different playing styles, and all have made a significant impact on rock guitar.

Later I got to play with other fantastic guitarists (and a few legends), including Eric Clapton, Hubert Sumlin, Buddy Guy, Muddy Waters, Stephen Stills, Andy Fairweather-Low, and Chris Rea. My new band, The Rhythm Kings, has three fantastic guitarists: Terry Taylor, my long time mate and writing partner; Martin Taylor, one of Britain's best jazz players; and the amazing Albert Lee. Albert is one of the greats, much admired by his peers.

I have learned from all of these guitarists, from watching them and playing with them – all the while admiring their talent. All of them practice now, just as they always have. They would all have bought a book like this when they started, some will buy it now; to be as good as they are, you never ever stop learning. As my wife said in 1960, "Once he started playing the guitar, you couldn't get him to put it down."

BILL WYMAN

Introduction

WELCOME TO A FRESH APPROACH *to learning the world's most popular musical instrument – the guitar. The K.I.S.S. Guide to Playing Guitar is different from other similar titles you may have read because many guitar tutorial books are written by teachers who want you to study the instrument while you may just want to strum the chords to your favorite Garth Brooks song or write your own tunes. Many of these tutors actively do not want you to play rock music. You'll find no such prejudices here – we make no claims to be arbiters of good taste. Whether it's classical, rock, jazz, folk, thrash, pop, avant garde, or metal that interests you, this book will get you on the path to success.*

So how does this all work in practice? In one word: flexibility. Some books assume that you will be prepared to spend time learning how to read standard printed music. Well, that's one way of doing it, but it isn't the only way. Let's face it, out of all the strummers and pickers on the face of the planet, most of them didn't learn to play from music academy teachers or even from books. Most of them simply sat down with their pals, worked out a few chords together, and then went on from there. And this is how the K.I.S.S Guide to Playing Guitar works. This book and its accompanying CD will teach you the basics of guitar playing in an informal and easy-to-follow manner, free from hard-and-fast rules!

Most importantly, we'll arm you with the tools that will enable you to think and play for yourself. Throughout the book, a variety of audio-visual aids enhance the lessons and techniques so they're easy to follow. You can study finger diagrams, photographs, charts, and listen to examples on the accompanying CD. But you won't see a single piece of written music until you are familiar with the most basic of chords. Remember, the ability to read written music is not necessary to enjoy playing the guitar (but those who want to learn to read music will have ample opportunity).

Jammin' *with John Lee.*

So, get ready for the fun ride that lies ahead. At first you may find it fairly challenging: The muscles in your fingers will ache, and you'll want to smash your guitar each time they refuse to obey your commands. And then one day you'll pick up your guitar and, without thinking about it or looking at the fretboard, you'll strum an open E-major chord. When you experience this magical moment, you'll feel a few inches taller, the sun will shine a little more brightly, and you'll stride down the block with a new-found spring in your step. Okay, maybe that's pushing it a bit, but you'll certainly be entitled to think to yourself: "Hey, I am a guitarist! Cool!"

Have fun.

TERRY BURROWS
London

What's Inside?

THE INFORMATION IN the K.I.S.S. Guide to Playing the Guitar is arranged from the simple to the more advanced, making it most effective if you start from the beginning and slowly work your way to the more involved chapters.

PART ONE

In Part One I'll give you information on the history of guitars, and take you on a quick guided tour of the different styles of guitar music. Buying your first guitar? My tips on selecting and maintaining your instrument should get you well on your way. I will also advise you on other vital points such as how to hold and how to tune your guitar.

PART TWO

In Part Two, we get down to the serious matter of playing your guitar. After learning how to tune your guitar, how to play the most basic chords, how to play in time (and tune!), and how to use a pick, you will be ready for anything.

PART THREE

While Part Two showed you how to play, Part Three will help you understand a little more about the music itself. After I have taught you the basics of reading music, and you have mastered the art of keys and scales, you will have the chance to put your new-found skills into practice by playing some tunes.

PART FOUR

Part Four is when you get to play real guitar. So far I have showed you how to play any style, but now I will teach you the techniques you need to play blues, rock, country, jazz, Latin, or classical. Take your pick.

PART FIVE

Now that you are an accomplished guitarist, in Part Five I will show you how to alter your guitar's sound with amplification and different effects, and how to record yourself in a studio or at home. And when you are ready to take your music to a paying public, I have the lowdown on how to promote yourself to a wider audience. Get strumming!

The Extras

THROUGHOUT THE BOOK, *you will notice a number of boxes and symbols. They are there to emphasize certain points I want you to pay special attention to, because they will help you become a better guitarist. You'll find:*

Very Important Point
This symbol points out a topic I believe deserves careful attention. You really need to know this information before continuing.

Complete No-No
This is a warning, something I want to advise you not to do or to be aware of.

Getting Technical
When the information is about to get a bit technical, I'll let you know so that you can read carefully.

Inside Scoop
These are special suggestions and pieces of information that come from my experience as a guitarist.

You'll also find some little boxes that include information I think is important, useful, or just plain fun.

Trivia...
These are simply fun facts that will give you an extra appreciation of guitars and guitar music in general.

DEFINITION
*Here I'll **define** words and terms for you in an easy-to-understand style. You'll also find a glossary at the back of the book with the guitar-related lingo.*

INTERNET
www.internet.com
I think that the Internet is a great resource for guitarists, so I've scouted out some of the best web sites for you to check out that will help all aspects of your playing.

PART ONE

NOT REALLY THE SAME WITH A CLARINET

SIMPLE BASICS

WOULD ELVIS PRESLEY have created a sensation gyrating his hips behind a Steinway grand piano? Would Keith Richards have been viewed as an icon of rebellion blowing a clarinet? And how many kids have you seen playing "air violin" in front of their bedroom mirrors? There is no question that the guitar is the *coolest* musical instrument of them all.

So let's take a quick journey through the guitar's colorful history, looking at how it has shaped different forms of music throughout the ages. You'll discover how they're made, how they produce sounds, and which type is most appropriate for the music you want to create.

We'll then get you prepared to play, with some *practical* tips on choosing your first guitar and amplifier, and end by showing you how to hold the guitar properly and how to get it in tune – you need to get these things straight before you play a note.

Chapter 1

A Bit of History

FROM THE MID-1950s, the guitar – especially in its electric form – became one of the hippest of modern icons, conjuring up notions of rebellion and freedom. Although it's true that its widespread popularity in classical and pop music has been relatively recent, the instrument has a history that can be traced back over 4,000 years.

In this chapter...

✓ When is a guitar not a guitar?

✓ Growing up

✓ Breaking away

✓ The guitar goes electric

✓ Going solid

✓ It's a rip-off

✓ Nothing new

ELVIS – THE LIP-CURLIN', PELVIS-THRUSTIN' KING OF ROCK 'N' ROLL

When is a guitar not a guitar?

THE ORIGIN OF *our favorite instrument is shrouded in a mystery that has been further confused by disagreement among music historians. The oldest closely recognizable ancestors of the guitar can be traced back as far as the 14th century. But how they evolved to this point, we can only really guess.*

What is clear from archeological discoveries made over the centuries is that stringed instruments designed to be played either by strumming or plucking certainly existed before those times. The story is complicated by the fact that some of these instruments bear only the most superficial resemblance to the guitar. Filling in the missing links is made that much harder, since we can't say with any certainty how these instruments were used or what they even sounded like.

The earliest widely accepted evidence can be seen in Babylonian clay reliefs discovered in Asia Minor. Dating back about 4,000 years, images depict groups of musicians playing instruments from which the guitar probably evolved. These instruments shared a number of important features with their modern forebears, such as a fingerboard, frets, the use of more than two strings, and a resonating body capable of projecting sound. It seems likely that the volatile cultural and political landscape of the region, as well as the movements of the early merchants and traders, are likely to have spread the use and popularity of these mysterious early "guitars."

■ **The Ancient Egyptians** *were keen strummers.*

Beginning with the ud

The guitar's direct precursors are generally believed to have found their way into Europe via the south of Spain, following the conquests by the Moors around 800 AD. The Moors' contribution to this saga was the introduction of an Arabic stringed instrument called the ud. The instrument evolved over the centuries that followed, gradually spreading throughout Central and Northern Europe and giving rise to instruments such as the lute and gittern.

■ **Many hearts** *were won (and lost?) to the sound of the lute.*

Well, they look like guitars . . .

The earliest true guitars, which appeared at the end of the 15th century, were closer in size to the much smaller lute. In fact, a now-extinct stringed instrument called the vihuela was more closely proportioned to the modern guitar.

Trivia...

During the guitar's early days, it was widely viewed as a crude relative of the popular vihuela. And yet, by the beginning of the 17th century the vihuela had all but died out. Although a substantial body of work still exists for the instrument, only a handful of vihuelas are known to have survived.

■ **The twelve-stringed** *vihuela was considered a superior instrument to the guitar in its 16th-century heyday.*

Fundamental differences

These guitars may have looked like their modern counterparts, but there were some striking differences. First, rather than having a series of individual strings tuned to different notes as they are now, the strings were grouped in pairs called courses. Each pair was tuned to the same note. More dramatically, the fingerboard did not have fixed metal frets permanently in place; the frets were made from pieces of gut, which the musician wrapped around the neck. The number and position of these frets depended on the nature of the music being played.

Trivia...

The standard modern-day guitar has six strings tuned from bottom to top to the notes E, A, D, G, B, and E. During the 16th century most guitars featured four courses of strings tuned to C, F, A, and D. Five-course instruments also existed, adding a lower G.

This meant that, before performing, the 16th-century guitarist would not only have had to ensure that each pair of strings was in tune, but that the frets were positioned for correct intonation. We should be very grateful that the guitar managed to evolve beyond this point!

■ **Guitar makers,** *such as the influential Matteo Sellas in 1614, turned instruments into works of art.*

■ **In the years** *after this guitar was made (by Jean Salomon in 1760), the double courses began to be replaced with single strings.*

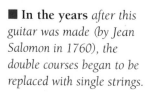

Growing up

BY THE 17TH CENTURY *the guitar was popular in the courts of Central Europe, replacing the vihuela as the instrument of choice and sending it into decline. Although Spain was home to the guitar's major developments, Paris and Venice were by then the two most important centers of activity. This period also produced the earliest recorded compositions for the guitar, such as the* Instrucción de Mœsica sobre la Guitarra Española *by the Spaniard Gaspar Sanz, which appeared in 1674 and was a considerably influential collection of pieces. You can still find some of these pieces in circulation today.*

From the middle of the 18th century, the guitar began a period of transition. The four- and five-course guitars gradually gave way to six-course instruments, courses were replaced by single strings, and the E-A-D-G-B-E tuning system was adopted. And, thankfully, the frets were finally fixed into the fingerboard.

■ **French guitar** *maker René Voboam constructed this instrument in 1641 out of materials including ebony, bone, and tortoiseshell.*

■ **The frets on** *this 16th-century classical guitar used to be made from gut and were wrapped around the fingerboard.*

Breaking away

THE 19TH CENTURY *was a revolutionary period for the guitar. In Spain, the work of Antonio de Torres Jurado (1817–92) turned the guitar into a serious and credible instrument. Torres experimented with the construction and dimensions, and created a template for the classical guitar that exists to this day. Torres became the maker of choice for the finest classical players of the second half of the 19th century. In particular Francesco de Tárrega, as a musician, brought respectability to the guitar among the European classical fraternity and, as a teacher, created the foundations of modern classical guitar technique.*

■ **Torres's guitars** *had much larger bodies than other instruments of the time, and produced a finely balanced sound; this one was made in 1860.*

As far as classical guitar goes, that's pretty much the whole story in terms of the development of the instrument. However, at that time, the guitar was looked down upon by the dowdy classical fraternity. It is largely through the efforts of one man – the self-taught Spanish virtuoso, Andrés Segovia – that the profile and respectability of the guitar escalated in concert halls throughout the world during the first half of the 20th century. Through his influence, some of the finest composers of the past century – Villa-Lobos, Ponce, Castelnuovo-Tedesco, and Rodrigo – have created seminal works for the guitar.

Although the last major developments in classical guitar occurred in the late 19th century, other radical moves were taking place across the Atlantic Ocean. Indeed, the vast majority of significant developments have taken place since then, in North America. The two most important figures in this process were C.F. Martin and Orville Gibson. It was here that two distinct styles began to evolve: C.F. Martin's flat-top guitar designs, and Orville Gibson's archtop models.

■ **Originally designed** *to carry 11 strings, including five bass strings, this 1876 Torres guitar has been restored to take only six.*

The Martin tradition

One of a long and eminent line of violin makers, Christian Frederick Martin was born in Germany. At the age of 15 he moved to Vienna to serve an apprenticeship to the great **luthier** Johann Stauffer. In 1833 he emigrated to the United States and set up business. The early Martin guitars were handcrafted to order and showed little in the way of standardization, apart from the unusual Stauffer-style **headstock** design, which featured all the tuning pegs on one side. A further unusual feature of the early Martin guitars was their adjustable neck, which was used until the 1890s; it went out of fashion when steel strings began to replace those made from gut, exerting greater stress on the joint between the neck and body.

After C.F. Martin's death, the company reins were successfully passed on to future generations. In 1916 the revolutionary large-bodied **dreadnought** style was developed. Intended to produce greater volume and bass response, it was seen as an ideal accompaniment for vocalists. It would later become extremely popular among folk and country singers. In 1929 Martin also introduced the 14-fret neck, intended to increase the guitar's range and make it a more versatile instrument. Dubbed the Orchestra Model, it quickly became a standard design feature among American guitars. Martin has continued to enjoy a worldwide reputation for its flat-top acoustic instruments.

> **DEFINITION**
>
> A **luthier** is a person who makes guitars.
>
> The top part of the guitar neck is called the **headstock**; it's where the machine heads that support the strings are fitted.

■ **An early example** by *master guitar craftsman C.F. Martin from 1838.*

> **DEFINITION**
>
> The **dreadnought** is large-bodied, steel-string acoustic guitar – first produced by the Martin company – and is popular in folk and country music.
>
> The **flat-top** is a steel-string guitar that has a flat soundboard.

■ **The Orchestra Model:** *With its 14-fret neck, this instrument was designed to have greater range.*

Orville Gibson and his archtops

The other major name in the early history of the American guitar is Orville Gibson. The son of a British immigrant, Gibson was not only a skilled wood carver, but also an accomplished mandolin player. During the 1880s he produced a new breed of guitar that used construction techniques more commonly employed with violins. His instrument designs eschewed the conventional flat-top approach in favor of a curved, arched top, called an *archtop*.

By the time of his death in 1918, Gibson guitars enjoyed a reputation second only to Martin.

Over the years that followed, Gibson played a pivotal role in a number of developments that would have a significant impact on the future of the guitar. During the 1920s Lloyd Loar, one of Gibson's engineers, began to experiment with the idea of electronic pickup devices. Loar was also behind the first of many legendary production guitars: the Gibson L5. By replacing the oval sound hole with violin-style f-holes, the L5 was able to project greater volume than other instruments. It quickly became a standard feature in early jazz bands, replacing the banjo and ukulele.

■ **The seminal Gibson L5:** *This archtop acoustic was to be heard on jazz stages all across the world for many years.*

The guitar goes electric

*IN SPITE OF THE SUCCESS of influential instruments like the Gibson L5, the guitar's naturally low volume meant that in most dance bands it could only be used to provide rhythmic backing. The answer to this problem came with the development of the **magnetic pickup***

Although Lloyd Loar had developed a basic magnetic pickup in 1924, the company failed to see its potential, leaving others to pave the way. In 1931 Paul Barth and George Beauchamp, who had been working on the same ideas for the Californian National Company, joined forces with Adolph Rickenbacker to form the Electro String Company. Together they produced a series of cast-aluminum lap-steel guitars referred to as Frying Pans because of their shape. Although they only barely qualify as guitars, Frying Pans were the first commercially produced electric instruments.

Although the Frying Pan was not a great commercial success, Rickenbacker applied the same horseshoe-magnet pickup to his production archtop acoustic guitars, creating the Electro Spanish series. Once again, however, Gibson took over, when in 1935, they created the famous Gibson ES-150. In the hands of pioneering jazz musician Charlie Christian, the electric guitar was demonstrated as a serious musical proposition for the first time.

■ This strange-looking *instrument is, in fact, the world's first electric guitar, the Frying Pan.*

Going solid

FITTING PICKUPS *to an acoustic guitar may have revolutionized music, but a number of serious problems also resulted. If the sound coming out of the loudspeakers was too loud, the body of the guitar would vibrate, creating a howling noise known as* **feedback***. A solution to this problem was to increase the body mass of the instrument so that it would not vibrate so easily. So it was that at the end of the 1940s, the first solid-body electric guitars were developed.*

There is considerable disagreement as to who actually invented the solid-body guitar, but there were clearly a number of like-minded individuals all working along similar lines. One claimant is the well-known country-jazz guitarist Les Paul, who created his own Log guitar using a Gibson neck attached to a solid piece of pine on which the pickups and bridge were mounted. He tried to sell the idea to Gibson, but they laughed at his "broomstick with pickups." Another pioneer was engineer Paul Bigsby, who designed an instrument with country guitarist Merle Travis. This was an important development, as the shape of the instrument clearly influenced some of the early Fender designs. Since around a dozen were produced, it could just about lay claim to being the first production solid-body electric guitar.

■ **The Fender Broadcaster,** *with its solid body and two pickups, was a milestone in guitar history.*

■ **Named after** *its inventors, the Bigsby Merle Travis, designed in the 1940s, was to have a great influence on other guitar makers, including Fender.*

At this point we can bring in the single most important name in the history of the solid-body electric guitar: Step forward Leo Fender. In 1950 the Californian radio repair shop owner created the first mass-produced production-line solid-body electric guitar — the Fender Broadcaster. A year later, when threatened with legal action, Fender was forced to rename his groundbreaking instrument — thus was born the Fender Telecaster.

Following the success of the Telecaster, the Gibson company invited Les Paul to take part in the development of its own first solid-body electric guitar. The resulting instrument, launched in 1952, was named in his honor.

Two years after the appearance of the Gibson Les Paul, Fender responded with the legendary Stratocaster, probably the most famous electric guitar of all. The two Fenders have remained in permanent production.

■ **The Gibson Les Paul** *Gold Top borrowed much from its archtop predecessors, and its design has barely changed since the early 1950s.*

■ **Identifiable by** *its single-layer, white scratchplate, this Stratocaster dates from the first period of the model's production in the late 1950s.*

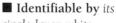

Trivia...

The Gibson Les Paul was not a huge hit when it first arrived, and in 1961 Gibson terminated production. However, during the early 1960s Les Paul guitars suddenly became popular with a new generation of electric blues guitarists, including Eric Clapton; they were prized for their unique tonal warmth. Demand for the Les Paul then soared to the point that Gibson was forced to reintroduce a new version in 1967. The Les Paul has remained hugely popular ever since. Many purists, however, still favor the originals. Indeed, the 1958 model is so highly valued that it's now more likely to be found in a bank vault than at a rock concert.

It's a rip-off

ONE PROBLEM FOR *fledgling electric guitar players during the 1960s and 1970s was the cost of the famous-name guitars. Most simply could not afford to get started. To fill this gap in the market place, Japan and Southeast Asia unleashed a never-ending supply of cheap imitations. But although they may have looked a bit like Telecasters, Strats, and Les Pauls, invariably they were hard to play and sounded terrible.*

This all changed in the 1980s when the Japanese company Tokai began to produce cheap copies. These came close to matching the quality of the originals, which, following the CBS corporate takeover of Fender, were felt by many to have gone into decline. Fender responded by launching a multi-tiered production system in which cheap alternatives of their own classic designs were built in places like Japan, Korea, and Mexico. This was a popular move that allowed novices, or those with little money, to own genuine well-made Fender guitars – it's just that they weren't the top-notch U.S. originals, which still retained their own market (and high prices).

■ **Although at first** *of poor quality, the guitars now produced by companies such as Tokai are good enough to pose a real threat to established makers.*

INTERNET

www.martin.com

www.gibson.com

www.fender.com

To this day, the Martin, Gibson, and Fender companies continue to make some of the finest and most popular guitars on the market. All three companies have excellent web sites that not only profile their current models, but provide in-depth histories of each company. Between the three of them they have the history of the modern guitar wrapped up.

Nothing new

OVER THE PAST 30 YEARS *there have been very few radical developments in the guitar world. Manufacturers have experimented with new shapes and materials, such as the Steinberg headless guitar. Attempts have also been made to integrate guitars and MIDI synthesizers, but these remain largely unpopular.*

■ **The Fender Telecaster**
is the longest-running solid electric guitar in history; this is the Deluxe model from the mid-1970s.

A simple summary

✓ Although the guitar as we know it only emerged during Renaissance Europe, its distant ancestors can be traced back almost 4,000 years ago to Ancient Babylon.

✓ The first guitars did not have six strings like their modern counterparts, but used four pairs of strings tuned in unison.

✓ The acoustic guitar was revolutionized by Antonio de Torres Jurado in the 19th century. His basic redesign of the classical guitar still stands today.

✓ The guitar in popular music has its roots in the United States, where companies founded by C.F. Martin and Orville Gibson dominated until the mid-20th century.

✓ The father of the modern guitar was Leo Fender, who launched the first solid-body electric guitars in the early 1950s.

Chapter 2

Guitar Music

NOW THAT YOU KNOW how the guitar evolved as a musical instrument, let's spend a few pages tracing how guitar music itself developed. Along the way, we'll be meeting the of the outstanding figures in the history of the guitar.

In this chapter...

✓ Classical guitar

✓ Country

✓ Blues and rock

✓ Jazz

Classical guitar

IN ITS EARLY DAYS, the guitar wasn't taken very seriously by "real" musicians. Most of the music played on the guitar consisted of simple strummed chords – or *rasgueado* – which gave the guitar a reputation as an instrument that could be mastered in a relatively short period of time.

Early history

The first printed music for the guitar appeared in 1546. Entitled Tres Libros, it was a collection of six pieces written by the Spanish composer Alonso de Mudarra for a four-string guitar. Within a hundred years, the guitar became more popular than the lute. Aided by teacher Francesco Corbetta, – one of the first guitarists to achieve international reputation – both King Louis XIV of France and King Charles II of England became enthusiastic players. This made the guitar rather fashionable, as was noted by the famed diarist Samuel Pepys… even if it was to say how much he hated the instrument! In 1677, Corbetta wrote Easie Lessons On The Guittar For Young Practitioners, a kind of 17th-century version of the book you're reading now.

■ **Would this manual** *teach you how to play like a 16th-century Hendrix?*

The early 19th century

■ **Fernando Sor** *advocated playing with the fingertips rather than the fingernails.*

By the early 19th century, the guitar had undergone a revolution that saw the four- and five-string instruments replaced by those fitted with six individual strings. It was also an era of experimentation. Posture, like other aspects of playing technique, had not yet been formalized. Although most players sat down while playing, some preferred to stand, wearing the guitar on a strap around their necks.

One of the great players of the period, Dionisio Aguado, went even further and built a special stand on which he would balance his instrument. In terms of playing, the use of the left thumb to fret the

lower strings was still commonplace, although by the turn of the century it was considered bad technique. Right-hand technique also varied a great deal. Aguado and others were known to have plucked at the strings with their fingernails, contrasting with the style of players such as Fernando Sor, who used the tips of his fingers.

In fact, Sor was the guitar's first great virtuoso, and a musician who made a major impact on the future of the guitar as a serious instrument. During the early part of the 19th century, he toured widely throughout Europe, thrilling audiences with the brilliance of his playing.

It was once rumored that Sor so inspired the great Niccolo Paganini that he briefly abandoned the violin in favor of the guitar. Sor's influence may be even wider, since Beethoven is thought to have lifted his main theme for the Moonlight Sonata from one of Sor's pieces. Indeed, Sor's book of guitar studies is still viewed as essential playing for fledgling classical players.

The late 19th century

The next great development came during the second half of the 19th century when the Spaniard Antonio de Torres Jurado modernized the guitar, improving its tone and, more significantly, its volume. Right away this meant that guitarists could play in larger concert halls.

These physical changes also led to new developments in the way the instrument was played. The man who led the way during this period was Francisco Tarrega. Not only was he the finest player of the period, he also developed new playing techniques that enabled single notes to be played with a richer tone and greater volume.

The increased size of the guitar's body sparked the formalization of the playing position in which the guitar was balanced on the left thigh. Tarrega also established a common practice in which compositions created for other instruments were transcribed for the guitar. This vastly enriched the relatively small repertoire of high-quality compositions for the instrument.

■ **Torres's newly** *designed guitar made the late 19th century one of the most important periods for the classical guitar.*

The early 20th century

It was during the early part of the 20th century that Tarrega's developments were honed into what is now standard classical technique. The musician responsible for this development in technique was the self-taught Andrés Segovia, — one of the most important figures in the history of classical guitar. Segovia established the practice of playing with a relaxed right hand and striking the strings with the left side of the fingernails.

■ **Andrés Segovia** is considered by many to be the evangelist of classical guitar.

One of the finest guitarists of the century, Segovia had an almost evangelical zeal to raise the profile of the guitar, and he inspired successive generations of players and composers alike. Several of the leading Spanish composers of the 20th century – Joaquin Turina, Federico Torroba, and Joaquin Rodrigo – composed for Segovia. In particular, Segovia's tours of South America helped to create a new tradition in guitar composition, and inspired the work of Brazilian Heitor Villa-Lobos and Mexican composer Manuel Ponce. Segovia, who died in 1987, can rest easy because his crusade to have the guitar afforded the same degree of respect as other traditional instruments of the orchestra has been well and truly achieved.

■ **Due to guitarists** such as Segovia, the classical guitar has become as highly regarded as other orchestral instruments.

Country

THE ROOTS OF COUNTRY music can be traced back to the various forms of folk music, such as blues and Celtic music, that found their way to the United States during the early part of the 19th century. Gradually evolving during the late 19th century, country music developed further into different guitar-based styles in the 20th century, with genres such as country and western, swing, bluegrass, Cajun, hillbilly, and rockabilly being the most popular.

Trivia...

Country music helped establish the guitar's popularity, particularly in the United States. In the 1930s, the widespread appeal of "singing cowboy" movie stars such as Gene Autry and Roy Rogers helped to sell millions of cheap acoustic guitars from Sears Roebuck – the starting point for many a great guitarist.

Jimmie Rodgers

The first country guitar player to reach a large radio audience was Jimmie Rodgers. As a kid, he'd been taught guitar by African-American railroad workers. He sang songs that told of the hardship of the working man – a baton later taken up more eloquently by Woodie Guthrie, the grandfather of the singing protest movement.

Fingerpicking giants

Also during the 1930s, Lester Flatt was instrumental in developing the famous western swing sound with a style that used the thumb to play a bass line while the other fingers played the chords and melodies. This style of picking was taken up by Merle Travis and, most importantly, by Chet Atkins, who added flourishes of incredible speed. Atkins remains the greatest and most influential country guitarist of all time, not only as a player but also for his influence within the RCA record label – a label that was influential in creating the sophisticated Nashville Sound in the 1950s.

Country crossover

Although variations on the Nashville Sound have dominated country music ever since, artists crossing over into the rock and pop mainstream have enjoyed considerable success. The late 1960s saw bands such as The Byrds pioneering the emergence of country-rock, a genre that peaked in popularity a decade later when The Eagles became one of the biggest-selling bands in the world. Today's top country stars such Garth Brooks and The Mavericks are among the most popular artists throughout the world.

■ **Chet Atkins** *mastered the art of fingerpicking and made it his own.*

Blues and rock

THERE IS A DIRECT LINE *that runs from the blues and ethnic music of the early part of the 20th century to the popular rhythm-and-blues bands of the 1940s. The first great star of ragtime blues guitar was Blind Lemon Jefferson. Between 1925 and 1929 he sold hundreds of thousands of records. Tragically, he received almost no reward for his success and was buried in a pauper's grave. Jefferson was a major influence on other blues players, such Leadbelly, Lightnin' Hopkins, Robert Johnson, and T-Bone Walker.*

Chicago blues

Until the 1940s, the popularity of raw acoustic blues was largely restricted to black audiences. This slowly changed with the new generation of Chicago-based rhythm-and-blues players, most notably Muddy Waters. The first great electric blues player, Waters' sound was a major influence on the first wave of young white rock musicians in the 1950s.

■ **Muddy Waters:** *the source of the blues.*

Rock 'n' roll

When rhythm and blues evolved into rock 'n' roll in the 1950s, traditionally black music began to reach a massive audience. Chuck Berry was one of rock's pioneers; his rhythm playing and unmistakable solos influenced a generation of budding guitarists. At the same time, white country musicians began to make a big impression. Although never a household name, Scotty Moore, Elvis Presley's guitarist, is considered by many to be the first true rock guitarist.

■ **Chuck Berry** *rocks!*

Blues into rock

By the start of the 1960s, the electric guitar-based pop group had become the standard form of ensemble. English bands such as The Beatles gained huge worldwide audiences. During the same period, the British blues boom turned out an endless stream of young virtuoso electric guitarists, and players such as Eric Clapton, Jeff Beck, and Peter Green are still revered decades later. These were among the first rock players to combine the raw emotion and energy of the great bluesmen with dazzling playing techniques.

■ **Electric genius:** *Jimi Hendrix.*

Heavy rock

VIP

The second half of the 1960s saw the birth of heavy rock. The English group Cream, featuring Eric Clapton, is often cited as being its pioneer. The sound consisted of loud, distorted guitar riffs played in unison with the bass, and accompanied by fast soloing. The late 1960s also turned up the single most significant electric guitar player of them all: Jimi Hendrix. Although barely four years passed between his first album and his death in 1970, Hendrix redefined the electric guitar. While his playing technique was formidable (if pretty unorthodox), he was among the first prominent guitarists to experiment with the sonic possibilities of the amplifier and electronic effects.

The 1970s and beyond

Heavy metal, a harder, faster, louder form of rock, dominated the first half of 1970s. Also popular in the 1970s was progressive rock, a form that saw serious young musicians taking a much more intellectual approach to rock music. Although considered to be pop music "growing up," progressive rock nevertheless faded in the late 1970s with the punk and new wave explosions in London and New York. Punk, in its many forms, managed to capture the raw energy of the 1960s' beat groups. The sheer thrashing noise and accompanying alternative attitudes have ensured that punk has remained popular with successive generations, most notably the grunge bands of the early 1990s such as Nirvana.

The influence of the past

Guitar-wise, rock and pop have not developed radically in recent years. Most notably, musical boundaries have gradually fallen, largely under the strong influence of dance music and DJ/VJ culture.

Modern digital technology has made many musicians and producers take a retrospective look at the appeal of old-fashioned, vintage sounds, many of which can be heard on the hippest sounds coming out of your MTV screen.

Jazz

JAZZ EMERGED *at the end of the 19th century as a genuine black American folk music; at that time it was mainly heard around the New Orleans area. The guitar played a very low-key role at first in jazz for a very simple reason: It just wasn't loud enough to compete with all those horns!*

■ **Eddie Lang** *was one of the most famous jazz guitarists of the 1930s.*

Jazz pioneers

The first great jazz guitarist was New York musician Eddie Lang. Active during the 1920s, Lang was widely credited with having pioneered the guitar as an instrument for playing solos. Although Django Rheinhardt made similar progress on the other side of the Atlantic, the guitar was still primarily heard in the background as a rhythm instrument.

Going electric

All this changed when the guitar went electric. During the early 1940s, Charlie Christian revolutionized not only jazz but guitar playing in general, establishing the instrument as a credible tool for his virtuoso soloing.

Christian was active for only four years before his death, and it would be almost 20 years before the jazz guitar world saw its next significant influence – Wes Montgomery.

■ **Charlie Christian** *was one of jazz's most influential players.*

Fusion and beyond

In the late 1960s, jazz was given a new direction and impetus as Miles Davis integrated elements of rock into jazz. This so-called fusion sound produced many fine guitarists, including figures such as John McLaughlin and Pat Metheny. Many of the most technically accomplished players have continued to inhabit this territory since, unlike rock, the jazz scene is less fashion driven. In fact, many of the different subgenres of jazz that have emerged over the past 60 or so years continue to thrive today.

■ **"The John Lennon"**: *The Rickenbacker 325's most famous player gave this instrument its name in the 1960s.*

INTERNET

www.GuitarSite.com

This site has everything, from profiles of bands to a weekly newsletter to discussion groups to links to the finest flamenco pages. Whatever style you think you're into, you'll find it here.

A simple summary

✓ In 1546, a collection of six pieces written by Alonso de Mudarra entitled *Tres Libros* became the first guitar music to appear in print.

✓ Andrés Segovia is generally credited as being the developer of modern classical-guitar technique.

✓ While at the RCA Records in the 1950s, Chet Atkins was highly influential in developing what became known as the Nashville Sound.

✓ Chicago-based blues singer, guitarist, and band leader Muddy Waters wrote and performed electrifying blues music that influenced a whole generation of white rock guitarists.

✓ Jimi Hendrix's astounding playing and sonic experimentation redefined the sound of the electric guitar.

✓ Vintage guitar sounds from the 1960s and 1970s are once again popular with many contemporary musicians and producers.

Chapter 3

How Guitars Are Made and How They Work

As you have no doubt seen, guitars come in many different shapes and sizes and can create a wide variety of distinct sounds. They can be conveniently classified into three broad categories: electric guitars, which require amplification to be heard; acoustic guitars, which require no additional amplification; and electroacoustic guitars, which can be used either with or without an amplifier. In the coming pages we'll take a look at how each type is constructed and how they make their sounds.

In this chapter...

✓ Acoustic guitars

✓ Electric guitars

✓ Bass guitars

✓ Strings

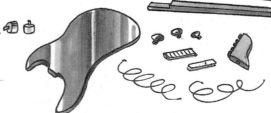

Acoustic guitars

THERE ARE TWO DISTINCT TYPES *of acoustic guitar, those with a flat soundboard (flat-tops) and those with a curved soundboard (archtops). But all acoustic guitars work along the same basic principles.*

You strike the string, which causes it to vibrate, and these vibrations are converted into audible soundwaves by the guitar's acoustic chamber — the soundbox — which vibrates in sympathy with the strings. By altering the length of the strings, achieved by pressing down on the fingerboard, notes of different pitches can be produced.

INTERNET

www.jps.net/kmatsu/

This is Kathy Matsu's guitar page, where she explains how she became an amatuer luthier. There's information here on tools you will need, building from kits, and everything else involved in building your own guitar.

Trivia...

It was thought to have been the good old Pythagoreans — they of the famed mathematical theorem — who first deduced that altering the length of a vibrating string by specific ratios would create different but related pitches. For example, halving the length of the string doubles the frequency of the vibrations, which has the effect of creating a note of the same pitch but one octave higher. The Pythagoreans liked music almost as much as they liked math — they saw the two disciplines as being closely linked. This idea was later summarized neatly by the philosopher Leibniz, who wrote "music is unconscious arithmetic." If you get into programing MIDI keyboards, you'll find out how true that is!

■ **Martin's top-of-the-line** *model; the 1929 O-45 flat-top displays many decorative features.*

Materials

The soundbox is the body of the acoustic guitar. The way it's designed and built, and the materials used, largely defines the volume and tonal characteristics of the instrument. Put simply, any decent acoustic guitar should be capable of producing a good, audible volume; it is the tonal aspect that is much harder to define. The tone is also a subject that can easily have guitarists and luthiers coming to blows. If you play any two guitars, they will not sound *quite* the same. Some will have an indefinable warmth; some will have greater clarity over certain ranges of notes. This is not surprising since guitars are made from wood – a natural "living" resource – and no two pieces of wood are the same.

Many different types of wood can be used in guitar manufacture. The main consideration is that it is treated, either by being *kiln-dried* or, in the case of the most expensive models, *seasoned*. These terms refer to the way in which the newly cut wood is dried out.

> **DEFINITION**
>
> *Seasoned wood is carefully stored in strict conditions for a period of several years until it has dried out.* **Kiln-dried** *wood, as the name suggests, has the moisture removed using a massive kiln – this process only takes a few months.*

■ **The Beatles** *played a major role in popluarizing the guitar's sound in the early 1960s.*

Acoustic exploded anatomy

On the opposite page you can see the different elements that go to make up a flat-top, steel-string acoustic guitar. Although there are certain differences in the making of classical and archtop instruments, the basic components are the same.

1. **Headstock:** *Tuning pegs attached to this; often faced in contrasting wood to rest of instrument*
2. **Fretwire:** *Made of nickel silver, these are hammered into slots in the fingerboard*
3. **Fingerboard:** *This is glued onto the neck after the truss rod has been fitted*
4. **Position dots**
5. **Soundboard:** *Usually made of close-grained spruce*
6. **Bracing:** *Named "X-brace" due to its shape, this type of bracing was devised by C.F. Martin in the 1850s*
7. **Bindings:** *A protective edging that lessens vibrations within soundboard and back panel*
8. **Saddle:** *Connected via the soundboard to the bridge; determines the length of the strings*
9. **Bridge:** *Spreads the strings, affecting the intonation, and supports the saddle*
10. **Bridge pins:** *Used to anchor the strings*
11. **Struts:** *Transverse struts are usually found on the back of the instrument*
12. **Cleats:** *Two pieces of back joined and strengthened with small pieces of wood (as here), or with one strip*
13. **Strap peg:** *Strap is attached to this device*
14. **End block***: Ties the ends of the sides, front and back*
15. **Ribs:** *Pieces of wood that form the sides are bent into shape by being soaked then heated*
16. **Lining:** *Strips of wood that hold the back and belly of the instrument to the ribs*
17. **Neck block:** *Ties the body and houses the neck joint – usually a tapered dovetail*
18. **Strings:** *Made from steel, the four lower strings are wrapped in bronze, brass or nickel-steel wire*
19. **Nut:** *Separates and gives height to strings at the top of the fingerboard*
20. **Truss rod cover:** *Covers the slot in the headstock*
21. **Tuning pegs:** *Strings are attached to these pegs; shaft passes through the holes in the headstock*
22. **Truss rod slot:** *The truss rod is fitted into this channel*
23. **Truss rod:** *Fitted into the neck to correct bending caused by string tension*

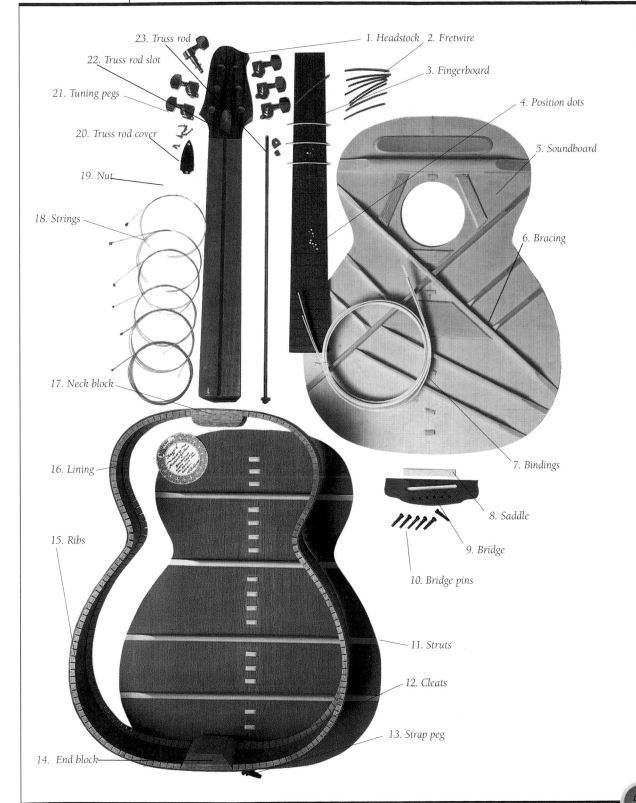

23. Truss rod

22. Truss rod slot

21. Tuning pegs

20. Truss rod cover

19. Nut

18. Strings

17. Neck block

16. Lining

15. Ribs

14. End block

1. Headstock   2. Fretwire

3. Fingerboard

4. Position dots

5. Soundboard

6. Bracing

7. Bindings

8. Saddle

9. Bridge

10. Bridge pins

11. Struts

12. Cleats

13. Strap peg

The body

The body of an acoustic guitar is made up of three sections: the soundboard (the top), the ribs (the sides), and the back. A selection of woods has been used in their construction, including pine, spruce, cedar, and redwood.

For a top-quality sound, the soundboard needs to be made from the finest materials. In an ideal world, that means using book-matched timber — two pieces sawn from the same piece of wood — so that the grain of the two pieces matches. Cheaper instruments use laminated plywood.

The soundboard is supported from the underside by a series of struts and braces. These are carefully positioned to give maximum strength without interfering with the sound. The soundboard shown in the exploded view (on page 55) uses an "X-brace" — the type popularized by the famous Martin company. Some other manufacturers use fan bracing, as shown below.

The soundboard and back are joined to the ribs using a continuous piece of ribbed (or kerfed, to use the language of the luthier) wood known as the *linings*. On the outside of the body, the edges are protected by decorative *purfling*. Not only is this an integral part of the guitar's look, but it has the practical value of concealing the joints, sealing the wood, and generally making sure that your precious instrument doesn't fall apart too easily.

■ **The soundboard** is here supported by fan bracing; other instruments use "X-braces" for support.

> **DEFINITION**
>
> The **linings** in an acoustic guitar is the continuous piece of ribbed wood that joins the soundboard to the back. Many string instruments, especially violins, are decorated with ornamental edging known as **purfling**.

The neck

Traditionally, guitar necks were sculpted from a single piece of hardwood – typically mahogany, rosewood, maple, or walnut. The increasing scarcity and costs of wood over the years has made this more and more impractical, and they are now usually a composite of three or more smaller pieces of timber. The neck is attached to the body at the heel (part of the neck that is curved for extra strength) which slots into the guitar's top block.

When steel-string guitars became the norm, they placed greater tension on the neck, so luthiers were forced to find ways of preventing the neck from buckling under the pressure. Their solution was to fix a truss rod in a central groove running the length of the neck. Later these became adjustable, so that the player could control the curve of the neck to his own needs.

The fingerboard (or fretboard, if you like) is a separate piece of wood glued to the top of the neck. It is on here that the frets are cut and fitted. Traditionally, ebony was the wood of choice for most serious guitars, but like many other woods, scarcity has made it unfeasibly costly for all but the most expensive guitars.

■ **The neck** *of this instrument is made from a single piece of mahogany.*

■ **Resonator guitars** *were invented by the Dopyera brothers to enhance volume and sustain.*

THE DOBRO RESONATOR GUITAR

One other type of acoustic guitar is also worth a mention because it played a noteworthy role in the history of the instrument – the so-called "resonator" guitar.

During the 1920s, over the period that directly preceded amplification, the main aim of guitar manufacturers was to create louder instruments, one of the most innovative of which was the Dopyera Brothers' resonator guitar. Their Dobro guitars (the name came from DOpyera BROthers) integrated the acoustic principles that drive a loudspeaker. A floating aluminum cone was fitted into the top of the guitar's body and fixed to the bridge. Vibrations from the strings were passed through the bridge saddles and transferred to the cone, which resonated back and forth in a similar way to a loudspeaker. The sound it created was a distinctive metallic jangle which, to be honest, you either love or hate. The first resonator guitars were built for the National Guitar Company in 1926 – they are still produced today.

Electric guitars

AS YOU CAN IMAGINE, electric guitars work on the same basic principle as their acoustic brothers. The only real difference is that, because the body is made of solid wood, there is no soundbox as such, so if you strum a chord it's barely audible. There's no way around it: If you want to hear your electric guitar, you have to plug it into an amplifier.

The anatomy and terminology used to describe the parts of an electric guitar are quite similar to those used for acoustic guitars, the one major difference being the appearance of the electronic circuitry.

Fixing the neck

One topic of conversation guaranteed to get guitar makers hot under the collar is how the necks should be fitted to the body. There are three different approaches used: The glued-in approach is favored by some, including Gibson; Fender famously prefers to bolt the necks on their Strats and Telecasters; and a small minority use the "straight-through" principle, in which the neck extends through the center of the body and incorporates the bridge – fanatics of this system claim that it allows for greater levels of sustain.

1. **Machine heads:** *Screwed to the headstock individually or in threes or sixes*
2. **Truss rod:** *A steel rod fitted inside the neck to counter any bending of the wood*
3. **Position markers:** *Used to indicate specific notes on the fingerboard*
4. **Fingerboard**: *This is glued to the neck, and is made from wood, such as rosewood, or synthetic material*
5. **Pickup:** *Formed of a coil of copper wire wound around six magnetic polepieces*
6. **Pickup covers:** *Used to protect the delicate windings*
7. **Scratchplate:** *Protects the body; made from metal, wood, or, more commonly, plastic*
8. **Pickup selector switch:** *Used to give series of combinations on guitars with more than one pickup*
9. **Bridge:** *Feeds the strings over individual saddles from the back of the body; each is height and length adjustable*
10. **Volume and tone controls:** *Used to adjust output of sound*
11. **Tremolo arm:** *This rocks the bridge, altering the tension and pitch of the strings*
12. **Bridge unit:** *This protects the bridge*
13. **Jack socket:** *Connects the guitar to the amp*
14. **Finish:** *Electrics come in a variety of finishes: natural, solid or metallic colors, even graphic designs*
15. **Body:** *Solid electrics are made from hardwood: maple, mahogany, alder, and ash are popular*
16. **Neck/body joint:** *The fingerboard is bolted or glued on to the neck*
17. **Nickel frets:** *Edges are smoothed and bound to ensure the player's hand is not injured*
18. **Neck:** *This is separate from the body and is bolted on to it*

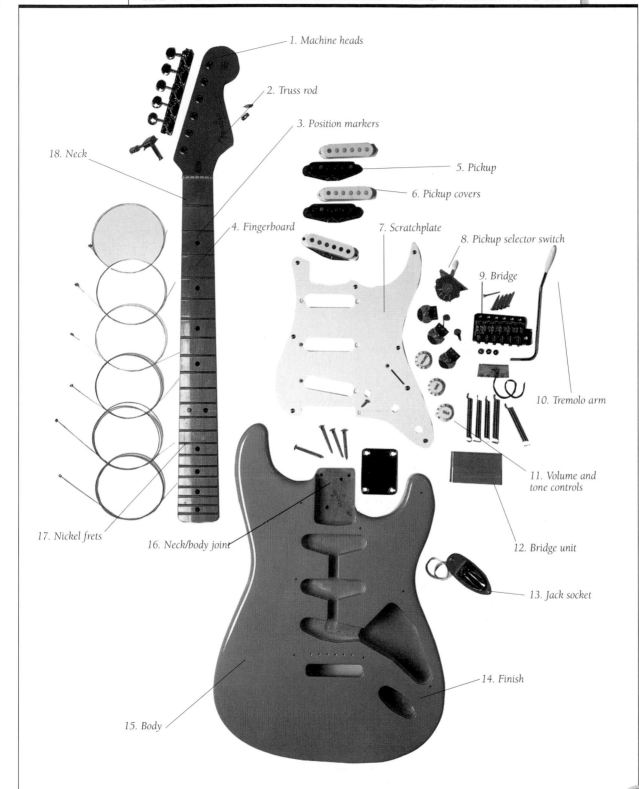

1. Machine heads

2. Truss rod

3. Position markers

18. Neck

5. Pickup

6. Pickup covers

4. Fingerboard

7. Scratchplate

8. Pickup selector switch

9. Bridge

10. Tremolo arm

11. Volume and tone controls

12. Bridge unit

13. Jack socket

17. Nickel frets

16. Neck/body joint

14. Finish

15. Body

How an electric guitar works

Electric guitars are amplified using magnetic pickups fitted beneath the strings.

At its simplest, a magnetic pickup is a magnet with thin copper wire wrapped around it hundreds of times. The magnet and windings create a magnetic field. When the steel strings vibrate, they disturb this magnetic field, creating small pulses of electrical energy that are passed to the amplifier.

The amplifier boosts the signal and this is then passed on to a loudspeaker, which converts the pulses into sound waves, making the signal audible.

If you were to hold a pickup over one of the strings while it was vibrating, and moved the pickup along the length of the string, you would hear how the tonal characteristics change. This is why most electric guitars have more than one pickup. One usually sits directly in front of the bridge: this is called the back or lead pickup because it has a harder, trebly, cutting sound better suited to lead playing. A second pickup is usually placed close to the join with the neck. This is usually called the rhythm pickup. Some guitars, like the Stratocaster, also have a middle pickup. You can choose which one you want to use by flicking a selector switch on the body.

The kind of magnetic pickups fitted to guitars come in two basic forms: single pole and twin pole. The classic Fender single-pole pickup uses six individual magnets with a coil passing around them as a group. Each magnet is aligned to a string.

In practice, the two pickups sound very different. Single-pole pickups tend to be brighter and more cutting, whereas twin-pole pickups create a warmer, fatter sound.

The circuitry for most electric guitars is very simple. The output of the pickup passes through a volume control and a tone control to the guitar's output socket. This is connected via a cable to an amplifier. As you can probably guess, the volume control regulates the loudness of the signal; the tone control usually acts as a way of cutting the treble signal.

A PAIR OF PICKUPS

Whammy bars

One other piece of hardware often found on solid-body electrics is a whammy bar, or tremolo arm. These are mechanical devices fitted to the bridge. By pressing down on a bar, the player reduces the tension of the string and hence the pitch of the note; when the bar is released, the string returns to its original position. Whammy bars have been used over the years to create vibrato effects or more dramatic pitch bends.

The trouble with the original whammy bars was that they were not terribly reliable. If overused, they tended to put the guitar out of tune. To the rescue came a New Zealander named Dave Storey, who developed the locking whammy bar system, whereby the strings were clamped in place at the bridge and the nut – meaning that whatever you did to them, they couldn't go out of tune. In the early 1980s, an American named Floyd Rose refined this system, which is now widely used.

■ **The whammy bar**
on the Gretsch 6120.

Trivia...

Gibson's twin-pole pickups – often called humbuckers (as they "buck the hum") – were created by Gibson in the mid-1950s. They were designed to prevent hum and other forms of electrical interference. Humbuckers have two sets of coils in each unit, wired up so that they are out of phase. This means that any interference reaches one coil as a positive signal and the other as a negative signal. The theory goes that when identical positive and negative signals are received at the same time, the one cancels the other out.

■ **Humbucking pickups** *with their twin coils are designed to cut out background interference.*

■ **The Floyd Rose**
tremolo arm is capable of greater pitch variation than traditional systems.

Bass guitars

THE BASS GUITAR isn't really a guitar in the conventional sense since it is essentially an amplified double bass – a stringed instrument that evolved from the older viol de gamba. Both the guitar and double bass have entirely unrelated historical paths. It was only when Leo Fender created the first electric bass in 1951 that the two stories began to converge.

1. **Frets:** *The standard is 24 frets, giving a two-octave range; older designs had 20 frets*
2. **Pickups:** *Each half of this classic "split" single-coil Precision-type unit serves two strings*
3. **Controls:** *Simple volume and tone arrangement*
4. **Scratchplate:** *Guitars without these have controls mounted from the rear*
5. **Bridge:** *This is often replaced with a sturdier bridge to withstand heavy string tension*
6. **Neckplate:** *This secures the neck and body joining screws*
7. **Joining bolts:** *Used to secure the neck with the body*
8. **Contoured body:** *Curve of the back and front improves comfort for players*
9. **Fingerboard:** *From bridge to nut, the fingerboard is usually 34 inches*
10. **Roundwound strings:** *These type of strings give a better quality of sound than the older flatwounds*
11. **Machine heads:** *Units are larger to cope with the bass's heavier strings*

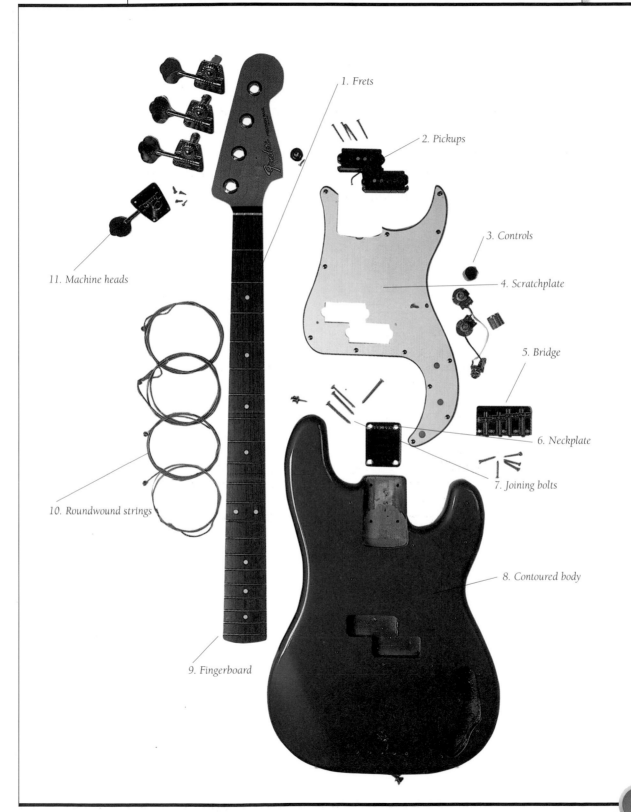

1. Frets

2. Pickups

3. Controls

4. Scratchplate

5. Bridge

6. Neckplate

7. Joining bolts

8. Contoured body

9. Fingerboard

10. Roundwound strings

11. Machine heads

The electric bass

Until the advent of amplified music in the late 1930s, the role and development of the double bass had changed little over the previous two centuries. There were, however, a number of reasons why the instrument was becoming more and more unsuitable for the increasingly popular small group ensembles that emerged after World War II. The major issue was that the acoustic volume produced by a double bass could never match the increasingly loud amplified electric guitar. Furthermore, the acoustic properties of the double bass made it extremely difficult to amplify. Also, as a member of the string family, the double bass had no fretted fingerboard, meaning that it required considerable technique to play in tune.

The first electric basses were actually solid-body double basses, but with a body of vastly reduced volume. Rickenbacker started to make t hese instruments – sometimes known as "stick basses" – in 1944. Variations on the idea can still be found today. This development may have solved amplification difficulties, but it still left the tuning question unresolved, as well as some less obvious problems. At this time, many bands had a guitarist who would also double on the upright bass when required. The problem was that he was also often required to sing backing vocals, which, when playing the double bass was somewhat challenging, especially with the microphones of the period.

Leo Fender again showed the way forward when he created the Fender Precision, in 1951. The first electric bass guitar, the Precision, solved all the problems associated with the double bass at once. Little wonder that the instrument was adopted with such speed. Indeed, throughout the 1950s, even though many other manufacturers were producing fine instruments, the generic term for the electric bass guitar was the Fender bass.

The first Fender bass was a simple but effective design. Fender named it the Precision because its fretted fingerboard allowed the musician always to play in perfect intonation (assuming, of course, that the instrument was in tune). The fretting of the Precision was the same as Fender's six-string Broadcaster, albeit with a longer, 34-inch, string length. The strings were tuned in the same way as the bottom four strings of the standard guitar – the notes E, A, D, and G. Although the first of its kind, the Fender Precision arguably still remains the most popular bass guitar still in use today

■ **Inspiration for** *a thousand variations: The Fender Precision of 1951.*

The Fender Jazz

Fender's idea was copied by other manufacturers, who all added their own refinements and variations to his simple design. Among these classic designs are the Rickenbacker 4001 (1957), the Gibson Thunderbird (1963), and the Hofner "violin" bass (1959), which was used by Paul McCartney. In 1960, Fender launched his second electric bass, the Fender Jazz. A more sophisticated instrument, the Jazz bass featured a narrower neck, a restyled body for greater comfort, and a second pickup for greater tonal variation.

■ **The Gibson Thunderbird** *from 1963.*

The modern bass

Like guitar players, bass guitarists have shown themselves to be a pretty conservative breed when it comes to taking new ideas on board. And although there have been plenty of new developments over the past 30 years, some of which have found high-profile users, none have really become part of the mainstream.

Arguably the most significant post-Fender name in the electric bass world is U.S. industrial engineer Ned Steinberger. In the late 1970s he began experimenting with both the shape and materials usually used. He fixed on the principle that an instrument's sound quality and capacity for sustain rested with its body mass. If something denser than a hard wood could be found, then these elements would be improved.

His experiments led him, in 1980, to create a prototype instrument built entirely from a molded epoxy resin strengthened by fiberglass and carbon fiber. As revolutionary as this was, it was the guitar's physical appearance that captured the imagination: Steinberger had taken the radical step of removing the headstock, fitting the machine heads to the base of a tiny body. When it first reached the outside world in 1982, although considerably more expensive than most mainstream bass guitars, the "headless" Steinberger became extremely fashionable. Although the novelty didn't last, Steinberger went on to produce a range of headless "graphite" instruments with more conventionally shaped bodies.

Fashions in modern music have also led to the extension of the range of notes available. In an effort to match the lower range of synthesizer basslines, basses with an additional low string were developed. Similarly, players with more space for melodic maneuvers called for an increased upper range, which could be achieved by an additional higher string. As a result, five- and six-string basses are now widely used, especially in jazz circles.

■ **Fashion is fickle:** *The headless Steinberger bass was once highly sought-after.*

OVATION ELECTROACOUSTICS

The most significant manufacturer of acoustic guitars to have emerged over the last 40 years is the American Ovation company. Ovation was founded in 1966 by wealthy industrialist Charles Kaman. A keen musician, Kaman used his engineering expertise to design an instrument that would revolutionize the way we think about steel-string acoustic and electroacoustic guitars.

Kaman completely overhauled the design of the traditional acoustic guitar body. The back and ribs were replaced by a single, one-piece "bowl," crafted using Lyrachord, a new type of fiberglass. With no corners or body strutting needed to support the top of the guitar, the sound could no longer be trapped in the corners of the soundbox and so created a purer tone and greater volume.

Although the first Ovation guitar – the Balladeer – was a revolution, Kaman didn't stop there. Taking on the problems of miking an acoustic guitar on stage, he created a generation of electroacoustic guitars featuring individual piezo-electric transducer pickups on the underside of the bridge saddle beneath each string. The effect was to create the most natural, amplified acoustic guitar sound ever heard. It also uaranteed a consistent sound irrespective of venue.

In simple terms: Just play one of these and you'll see why they feature on so many guitarists' wish-lists!

■ **Standing Ovation:** *the revolutionary Adamas guitar.*

■ **Formed entirely** *from fiberglass, the sound produced by the Ovation Adamas was truly incredible.*

Strings

STRINGS ARE A PRETTY *fundamental part of a guitar's anatomy – where would we be without them? Pretty quiet, that's where. Strings come in a variety of materials for specific kinds of guitars. Steel strings are used on electric, flat-top, and archtop acoustic instruments, and nylon is used for classical and flamenco guitars. But that's not the end of the story.*

String windings

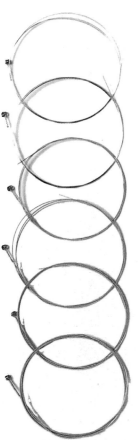

While each of the top two strings (and sometimes the third) comprise a single thread of wire, the remaining strings consist of a wire inner core with a second piece of wire wound tightly around the outside. The cores are usually made from steel, but nickel, bronze, and a variety of alloys can be used for the wrappings. There are three distinct types of winding: roundwound, flatwound, and groundwound.

■ **Nickel-wound** *strings are more commonly associated with electric guitars.*

■ **Bronze-wound** *strings are used on acoustic guitars and produce a bright sound.*

Roundwound strings are most commonly used on electric and acoustic instruments. The winding is made from conventionally shaped round wire, which gives a ridgelike feel when you touch it. These are generally thought to provide the best sound quality.

Flatwound strings are often used on archtop guitars. On these strings, the steel core is covered by a flat ribbon of metal. When tightly wound, these strings feel as smooth as a pure thread. Guitarists who use them like the fact that they help to eliminate the squeak of the fingers moving along the fretboard, which is often audible on delicate acoustic playing. On the downside, they produce a slightly dull tone and also crack easily. I'm not a fan, but try them out for yourself.

Finally, groundwound strings attempt to provide a compromise between the other types. They are essentially conventional roundwound strings with the surface slightly ground down so as to be partially flat.

String gauges

Guitar strings are produced in a variety of thicknesses — referred to as gauges. Strings are always measured and sold in decimal fractions of an inch.

■ **You must ensure** *that the end of each string is wound tightly and securely around the capstan on the head of your guitar.*

Deciding which gauge to use is very much up to you. The choice is essentially a balancing act between sound quality and playability. Lighter strings are easier to hold down and bend, and are less hard on the fingers. However, they also produce a lower volume and shorter sustain, and they are harder to keep in tune and break more easily. They also don't really sound as crisp.

You can buy strings in complete sets or individually. Sets are grouped into gauges from the thickest (usually called heavy) down to the thinnest ultralights. The sets are often referred to by the gauge of the top-E string. So if you go into your local music store and ask for "a set of 008s please," you'll be handed a set of ultralight strings.

The table below shows typical string gauges within the most commonly used sets:

	1	2	3	4	5	6
Ultralight	.008	.010	.014	.022	.030	.038
Extralight	.010	.014	.020	.028	.040	.050
Light	.011	.015	.022	.030	.042	.052
Medium	.013	.017	.026	.034	.046	.056
Heavy	.014	.018	.028	.040	.050	.060

Nylon strings

Classical and flamenco guitars always use nylon strings. The top three strings are always made from a monofilament nylon. The three bass strings are made from multifilament nylon and are usually roundwound with silver-plated copper or bronze.

■ **Nylon strings** *are found only on classical and amenco guitars.*

■ **Unlike the three** *treble strings, the bass strings on a classical guitar are wound around with bronze or a similar alloy.*

■ **Shortening the strings** *by pressing down on them produces different sounds.*

A simple summary

✔ Acoustic guitars create their sounds when the soundbox vibrates in sympathy with the strings.

✔ By pressing down on the fingerboard, the length of the string is altered, creating different notes.

✔ Electric guitars create amplified sounds using magnetic pickups fitted beneath the strings. When the steel strings vibrate they disturb the pickup's magnetic field, creating small pulses of electrical energy that are passed to an amplifier, which boosts the signal, making an audible sound.

✔ The position of the pickup alters the sound of an electric guitar.

✔ Although the double bass is not related to the guitar, the two instruments came together when Leo Fender created the first electric bass guitars in the 1950s.

Chapter 4

Choosing Your Equipment Wisely

STARTING OUT ON any new leisure pursuit can be a scary experience. You won't necessarily know what equipment you need or how to choose it. Whether to buy new or second-hand, or risk getting ripped off by unscrupulous music dealers? Fear not! This chapter will guide you through the daunting maze of technology and arcane terminology with which the modern guitarist needs to be conversant. With our help you'll be well equipped to take your first steps toward mastering the guitar.

In this chapter...

✓ What do I need?

✓ No compromise (unless you really must)

✓ Assessing a guitar's quality

✓ Choosing your first amplifier

What do I need?

NO SURPRISES TO BEGIN WITH – *you'll be needing a guitar of some sort. Whether you choose a steel-string acoustic, nylon-string classical, electroacoustic, or solid-body electric model depends entirely on the type of music you want to play.*

If you go electric, you'll need an amplifier and loudspeaker. Oh, and a cord to plug yourself in.

As you'll see when you set foot in any music store, there are also numerous other related items that can easily spirit away your hard-earned or ill-gotten cash. These are nice-to-haves rather than essentials. Below you can see some of the essentials – any guitarist who owns this lot doesn't need to ask for too much more. Although when the bug really bites, one guitar just won't be enough – you'll keep wanting more and more and *more*!

Your first guitar

Every guitar has a sound and feel of its own. Just as people are sometimes naturally drawn together, many guitarists would claim to have experienced a similar love at first sight with a guitar.

However dumb it sounds, you must feel happy with the instrument you choose – it's a relationship that will play an important role in your development as a guitarist.

Choosing a guitar can be a nerve-wracking experience, so it's a good idea to involve someone who knows their stuff.

Buying a used instrument can be an ideal way of starting out, as long as you take certain precautions. Here we give you some tips and potential pitfalls – if you follow the advice with care, you shouldn't go too far wrong.

■ **Some of the essential gear:** *strings; picks; and guitar plus amp and loudspeaker.*

No compromise (unless you really must)

SET YOUR BUDGET and buy the best quality that you can afford. When you are starting out, there is no greater motivation than hearing yourself succeed: The better your guitar, the more likely that is to happen. Any compromise here will be a false economy. A cheap model may save you money, but it's more likely to sound poor and be difficult to play.

INTERNET

www.harmony-central.com

For a list of everything you could possibly buy relating to a guitar, including amps, software, sound-effects boxes and much more, check out this site.

DEFINING QUALITY

But what constitutes quality? Look at these two guitars. The first one is a 1959 Gibson Les Paul Standard. This could set you back the same kind of price as a brand-new sports car. The second guitar is a Japanese Tokai Stratocaster copy – the sort that had Fender's lawyers tearing their hair out in the mid-1980s. You should be able to pick something like this up new for around $200.

Trivia...

When buying a Stratocaster copy, look for a Japanese copy – or Southeast Asian-produced "official" models. They're almost as good as the real thing!

■ **The Gibson** *Les Paul Standard 1959; Tokai TST50 1985.*

Assessing a guitar's quality

BEFORE YOU BUY a guitar, you should make sure that it passes a number of basic quality-control steps. Although for most new instruments this ought to be a formality, it's especially important when buying second-hand guitars. Use the following sections as a checklist of tips and potential pitfalls. If you follow them with care, you shouldn't go too far wrong.

Warping

If the fingerboard is curved or warped, the *intonation* – how "in tune" the guitar is with itself – will be poor, and the guitar will be difficult to play.

To test it out, hold the guitar as if you were aiming a rifle, and align your eye with the top surface of the fingerboard. It should appear perfectly even. If the top of the fingerboard appears to be twisted, put it right down and ask to look at another guitar. This problem can only be fully repaired by fitting a new neck.

You should also check the side of the neck in a similar way. You are likely to notice a very slight curvature half way down the neck between the 7th and 9th frets. This is normal and can be controlled using the *truss rod*. Be cautious if the curve is more extreme, though.

DEFINITION

To reinforce the neck against string tension, a metal **truss rod** *runs through the full length of the neck underneath the fingerboard.*

■ **Check the neck** *for any obvious curves (which should be not be there!).*

■ **Perfectly formed:** *If an instrument has any warps or kinks, forget it.*

Intonation

If you play any note on the 12th fret, it should always be exactly one octave higher than if you play the string without pressing on it. If the notes are not perfectly in tune, then the intonation will be poor. This means that the guitar will gradually go out of tune the farther you play along the neck. Although this can usually be rectified by adjustments (see pages 396–397 of the appendices), you should ask someone in the store to do it for you.

Action

The distance between the top of the fret and the bottom of the string is called the action. If the action is low, your fingers don't have to press down so hard on the fingerboard, which makes the guitar easier to play. If the action is too low, though, you may experience *fret buzz* when you hold down a note. Therefore, it's a good idea to play every single note on the guitar before you make a decision.

Sustain

The length of time a note lasts before it fades out is called sustain. As *Spinal Tap* fans will know, it is greatly prized by guitarists. Play every note on the fingerboard to ensure that the notes broadly sustain equally. On some instruments you will experience dead notes (or wolf notes as they are properly called) where the sustain is dramatically reduced. This is usually the result of a guitar's natural frequencies. Avoid guitars with these problems.

■ **Play each note** *to make sure they sustain properly before you buy a new instrument.*

Machine heads

The tuning mechanisms – known as machine heads – on the headstock at the top of the neck control the tension of each string. The mechanism should be firm enough to allow you to alter the tension and get the string precisely in tune.

Electrics

If you are testing an electric guitar, this final set of checks is for you. To test an electric guitar, you have to plug the guitar into an amplifier. The first rule is to make sure that the amplifier is not enhancing the quality of the guitar, so switch off any on-board effects or special features the amplifier may have. All you want to hear is the pure sound of an amplified guitar.

Begin by checking the relative volumes of each string on the guitar. If there are significant variations, the height of the pickups needs to be adjusted. This is easy to do if the pole of the pickup beneath each string has an individual height adjuster. Otherwise, the pickup may need to be replaced. Next, test the volume and tone controls to make sure that they work correctly and don't produce electrical crackle. Play a note, and, while the string is sustaining, turn the controls around fully. You should not hear any buzzing or popping noises.

Finally, give the guitar the silent treatment. Stand the guitar close to the amplifier and listen to the sound. It should be nearly silent. Whistling feedback may indicate that the pickups are not properly isolated, which may cause difficulties later if you are playing at high volumes.

■ **The sound of silence:** *The guitar should not whistle when stood next to an amp.*

Choosing your first amplifier

IF YOU HAVE AN ELECTRIC GUITAR, you'll need some form of amplification and loudspeaker. You can either buy the amplifier and speaker separately or as a combined unit, known as a combo. An amplifier not only boosts the guitar's volume, but it also affects the quality of the sound. So, try out a variety of amplifiers before you make your choice – the differences will quickly become apparent. You can read more about the different types of amplifiers in Part Five.

As a first-time guitarist, the further expense of an amplifier can easily push you over budget. A slightly unsatisfactory compromise is to use your stereo system as an alternative. To do this, you'll need to ensure that your system can take external connections – all-in-one systems will be of little use for this.

On older systems, you should use the magnetic cartridge input – the ones that would formerly have been connected to a turntable. Newer models usually have an auxiliary input that can be used for just about anything.

Since most stereo systems use mini-jack connections, you'll need a guitar cord that has a jack plug on one end and mini-jack on the other. Alternatively, you can buy a small combined plug and socket that converts a jack plug to a mini-jack.

Whatever you do, though, don't play at high volumes. Stereo speakers are much more delicate than guitar amp speakers. Some of us can't even begin to count the tweeters we blew in this way as kids. Our dads were never too pleased.

Although any amplifier will work with any guitar, some combinations work better than others. Therefore, it's always a good idea to take your own guitar along to the store when you test an amplifier. Here are some other tips to help you along the way.

■ **An alternative** *to an expensive amp is to play the guitar through your stereo.*

The most basic *set-up.*

Figure out your needs

Try to think ahead about what you may ultimately want to do with your amplifier, or at least how loud you intend to play. If you want to perform on stage, you'll probably need a capability of between 50 and 100 watts. A watt is a unit of measurement of an amplifier's loudness. High output doesn't necessarily guarantee high quality, though.

Size it up

If you are buying a separate amplifier head, you will need a separate loudspeaker. These can vary enormously in size from single 10-inch cones to enormous cabinets containing four 12-inch speakers connected together. If you take the latter route, make sure that you have sufficient room to store it in your home. Damp basements or garages are not ideal places to keep delicate electrical equipment. And give a thought to getting it in and out of your home: Do you really want to have to hump it up and down 12 flights of stairs every time you play a gig or go to a rehearsal room?

Look for signs of maltreatment

If you are buying a used amplifier and speakers, look out for signs that they might have been badly treated by a previous owner – like you would if you were buying a second-hand car. If the covering is filthy, battered, and covered in beer stains, who knows what demons might be lurking inside. If possible, remove the grill that covers and protects the loudspeaker to ensure that the cone is not worn, torn, or dented, since this will adversely affect the sound.

Test the electrics

Plug in the amplifier, turn it on, and start by listening out for excessive buzzing or hissing before you plug the guitar in. This may mean that some of the circuitry is worn or damaged. Next, test all the switches and the volume and tone controls. Make sure that they do all of the things they are supposed to without making unpleasant clicks or crackling noises.

As a final test, unplug the guitar but leave the amplifier switched on. Now stamp your foot on the ground right next to where the amplifier is standing. If you hear any electrical noises as a result, there may be loose valves or circuitry, which might eventually cause problems.

STARTING OFF WITH CLEAN SOUNDS

We've all heard the strange and exotic sounds that it's possible to conjure out of an electric guitar. This is invariably the result of electronic sound effects like distortion, reverberation, and echo. Although these play a major role in the sound of most modern guitarists, we'll be mildly controversial here and suggest that – whatever the latest music-technology-type magazines are urging you – you limit your use of these effects when you first start playing. For one thing, you'll find it hard enough getting your fingers to move to the correct positions without the distraction of multiple-flanged echoes coming out of the loudspeaker. For another, it's always a good idea to use the cleanest sound possible when you are practicing your basic playing techniques. It's the only way you can hear with absolute certainty how you are progressing.

■ **While it's fantastic** *to have an overdrive and wah-wah, don't be distracted from the aim of the game.*

A simple summary

✓ The type of guitar you choose will depend largely on the type of music you want to play.

✓ If you buy an electric guitar you'll need an amplifier and loudspeaker if you want to be heard.

✓ Buy the best equipment you can reasonably afford.

✓ Quality "name" guitars have good resale value and can represent good investments.

✓ If you are a novice looking for second-hand equipment, try to take an experienced player with you when you want to make a purchase.

Chapter 5

Strings 'n' Things: Maintaining Your Guitar

UNLIKE WITH CARS, electronic keyboards, and most other forms of new technology, you should find that a good quality brand name guitar of any kind will depreciate little in value over the years. It is sound sense, then, to take time out to make the effort to keep your investment well protected. That said, even if your guitar is a cheap and cheerful model crafted from Eastern European plywood, by taking a few simple measures like storing and transporting it in the safest possible way, regularly cleaning the components, changing the strings, and checking the way it's been set up, your guitar will play and sound better, and your enjoyment will be multiplied. So why not do it?

In this chapter...

✓ Keeping your guitar clean

✓ Storing your guitar

✓ Changing strings

SIMPLE MAINTENANCE IS NOT TIME CONSUMING

Keeping your guitar clean

You can keep your guitar in a reasonably good state simply by wiping the strings to get rid of the residue from your sweaty paws each time you've finished playing. Before you put it away (hopefully in its own case), give it a quick dust-down with a cloth. For a more thorough job, you can buy a wide variety of cleaning agents to deal with the different parts of the instrument.

Body hygiene

Since most modern guitars are finished in cellulose or other kinds of synthetic varnish, you can clean them with care using most regular household sprays or creams (although you may want to avoid those that contain silicone or wax, as they can sometimes cause discoloration or give the body an unpleasant sticky feel).

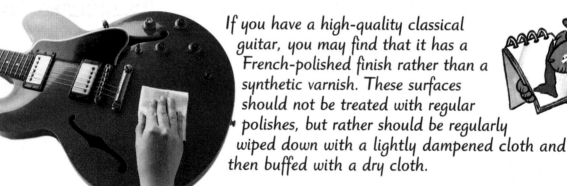

If you have a high-quality classical guitar, you may find that it has a French-polished finish rather than a synthetic varnish. These surfaces should not be treated with regular polishes, but rather should be regularly wiped down with a lightly dampened cloth and then buffed with a dry cloth.

■ **It's amazing** *what a bit of spit and polish can do!*

With acoustic instruments, dust tends to accumulate inside the body, especially if they are left out of their cases for long periods. In extreme cases, this can attract and trap moisture, which can also have an impact on the sound. You should be able to get rid of most of this by either blowing through the soundhole, or carefully using a vacuum cleaner with a suitable nozzle attached.

When cleaning the body of your guitar, never use abrasive cleaning fluids, since these will damage the surface. That is, unless you want your pristine glossy red Strat to take on a matte or an eggshell finish. If you are worried about using regular household cleaners, most music stores will sell you a specialized cleaning fluid that is guaranteed not to cause harm.

Cleaning the strings

There are two excellent reasons for keeping your strings clean: It makes your guitar feel more pleasant to play, and the strings will last a good deal longer. The best method is simply to take a dry, lint-free cloth, pass it between the strings and fingerboard, and drag it the full length of the strings between the bridge and the nut. You can also buy specialized string-cleaning fluids, although you shouldn't use these on guitars equipped with nonmetal strings.

■ **Don't wait for** *the grime on the strings to build up before you show them a cloth.*

Try to get into the habit of wiping down steel strings as soon after you finish playing as possible. This will prevent the salt that you naturally produce in your sweat from reacting with the strings. Salt creates discoloration and rust, and will make the strings sound duller and more liable to snap.

■ **Use only specialized** *cleaning fluids and cloths on your guitar.*

Cleaning the fingerboard and frets

Each time you change the strings on your guitar (see pages 88–89), you should take the opportunity to give the fingerboard a good wipe-down. Fingerboards that are treated with a synthetic varnish can be cleaned in the same way as the body, using standard household cleaning fluids.

For guitars that have oiled ebony or rosewood fingerboards, however, you should not use standard household cleaning fluids. For these guitars, apply some lemon oil to the wood, leave it on for around five minutes, and then clean it off using a dry cloth. Apart from cleaning the fingerboard and maintaining its feel, lemon oil also feeds the wood, preventing it from drying out. If the buildup of grime is especially deep, leave the lemon oil in place for a longer period of time, and then clean the fingerboard and frets using fine steel wool. Of course, if you keep your strings clean, then the build-up of dirt and grease on the fingerboard should never get to that state.

■ **Lemon oil** *and a clean, dry cloth are essential items for a sparkling fingerboard.*

Dirt can also build up along the edge of the frets. You can remove this carefully with any pointed object – a nail file or toothpick is ideal. The unpleasant substances should come away quite easily, but don't scratch too hard or you may damage the fingerboard.

Hardware

If the guitar's *hardware* is not kept clean, it can easily rust or tarnish. And, when that happens, there isn't much you can do to restore the parts to their original condition. A regular domestic chrome-cleaner will usually be sufficient for most of these items. Make sure that you follow the instructions on the label carefully.

> **DEFINITION**
>
> *A guitar's* **hardware** *refers to its metal parts, like the machine heads, pickups, bridge, and tremolo arm.*

■ **After all that** *contact with sweaty fingers, no wonder the frets can sometimes get a little grubby.*

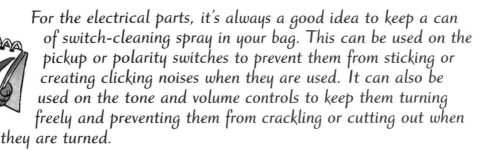

For the electrical parts, it's always a good idea to keep a can of switch-cleaning spray in your bag. This can be used on the pickup or polarity switches to prevent them from sticking or creating clicking noises when they are used. It can also be used on the tone and volume controls to keep them turning freely and preventing them from crackling or cutting out when they are turned.

Storing your guitar

STORING YOUR GUITAR *properly not only protects it from getting knocked around and scratched, but it also prevents wide variations in temperature or humidity, which can damage the performance and construction of the instrument. Before putting your guitar into storage, always detune the strings so that there is no tension placed on the joints between the neck and the body.*

Guitars should never be stored in attics or basements, or close to radiators or other hot water pipes. Dramatic variations in temperature can alter the action, distort the woods used, damage glue joints, and cause cracks in the finish.

It's invariably a good idea to store your guitar in a sturdy case. If you're lucky (or are a confident haggler), you may have managed to obtain a case when you first bought your guitar. Cases come in a variety of shapes and sizes. The most basic ones are made from padded plastic or fabric and zip up around the guitar. They are cheap and offer only the barest of protection, but they do keep the dust out.

■ **A hard case** *will ensure that your guitar is not damaged when it's being transported.*

A sturdier option is to use a case with a hard shell, usually made from plywood or a strong plastic, and this is known as a flightcase. The insides are padded to keep the instrument in place, and are lined with soft fake fur to protect the body finish. These cases are usually ideal for most everyday protection.

If you are handy, a simple plywood flightcase is not that difficult to make, and is likely to cost less than a quarter of the price of a shop-bought equivalent. For the serious gigging musician, a metal flightcase is a necessity.

■ **A flightcase** *is a good option if you will be doing a lot of traveling.*

Aluminum side panels and thick metal corner units offer the best protection short of a personal bodyguard. Be warned, though: They can be expensive – sometimes as costly as the guitar itself – and are very, very heavy. They will also destroy anything they accidentally come into contact with.

For everyday use, some players prefer to leave their instruments out in the open, where they are easily accessible. If you really don't want to keep putting your guitar away in a flightcase every day, it's best to either use a floor stand, or use special fixtures to attach it to the wall.

Whatever you do, never expose your guitar to long periods of direct sunlight – it will damage the bodywork, fading the finish and distorting the woods.

■ **A floor stand** *is ideal storage for your guitar if you use it every day.*

GETTING AROUND

If you are a gigging musician, your guitar is in peril every time you step outside your front door. If you are transporting a guitar in a car or by rail, you should *always* keep your instrument in a sturdy flightcase. Avoid placing heavy items like amplifiers and drum kits on top of it, too.

Transporting a guitar by air can be a major pain. Try to arrange in advance to take your guitar onboard as carry-on luggage – although be warned that some airlines may charge you for the privilege. Don't even consider putting it in the cargo hold without the sturdiest metal flightcase – anything less and you can guarantee that your precious guitar will be badly damaged. Some airlines offer a separate hold for delicate items, but the above warning still applies. If you do go down this path, make sure that the guitar is securely packed inside the case so that it can't move at all. You should also slacken the strings since the guitar will respond to the change in altitude and air pressure.

■ **Make special** *arrangements in advance if you plan to fly with your guitar.*

■ **While on the road,** *always transport your instrument securely in a hard case.*

Insurance

If your guitar never leaves your home, and is not considered to be a part of your everyday business, you should be able to cover your guitar as a part of your regular household-contents insurance policy. If you are a semiprofessional musician or above, the matter becomes more difficult. It's a well-known fact that the security systems in every insurance office in the world switch to Red Alert the moment a musician walks through their doors.

There are, however, a number of specialist insurance companies that deal with insurance for professional musicians. But be warned: this can be an expensive business. If you do gig regularly, though, you should think of it as an essential cost.

Changing strings

AT SOME POINT *you will have to change the strings on your guitar. Sometimes you'll be forced to change one when a string snaps. But more often than not, the old ones will simply lose their brightness and wear out. How often you change your strings is a matter of personal taste. Some professional players restring every time they perform or record. If you put on a new set of strings, they do need to be broken in. A few hours of play should do the trick.*

You can remove the old strings by simply detuning the machine heads until the tension becomes so loose that you can pull each string away from the headstock. A quicker method is to snip them using a pair of wire cutters. Take care if you do it this way, since the bare ends can easily start flapping around – not so great if they catch your eyes.

How you go about installing the new strings will depend on the type of guitar you have, as there are several alternatives available, all of which use slightly different methods. However, the strings are held in place at one end by fixtures behind or on the bridge, and at the other by turning the machine head on the headstock.

■ **Wire cutters** *are invaluable to have around when changing strings.*

If you don't keep a good supply of spare strings as a matter of course – which you really ought to – then it's a good idea to remove the old strings as carefully as possible and keep them in an empty packet. At least you have something to fall back on in the event of an emergency breakage. A simple tip for the most impoverished of guitarists – and one used over the ages – is to boil old steel strings.

INTERNET

www.glenbrook.k12.il.
us/gbssci/phys/Class/
sound/u1l15b.html

For a simple physics lesson on how guitar strings make sounds, try this page from The Physics Classroom.

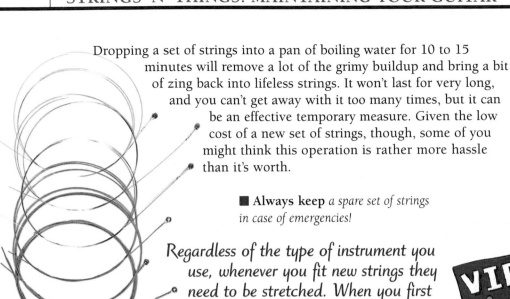

Dropping a set of strings into a pan of boiling water for 10 to 15 minutes will remove a lot of the grimy buildup and bring a bit of zing back into lifeless strings. It won't last for very long, and you can't get away with it too many times, but it can be an effective temporary measure. Given the low cost of a new set of strings, though, some of you might think this operation is rather more hassle than it's worth.

■ **Always keep** *a spare set of strings in case of emergencies!*

Regardless of the type of instrument you use, whenever you fit new strings they need to be stretched. When you first tune the guitar, put your hands under each string around the pickup area, pull the string a few inches away from the fretboard, and then release it. If the pitch has dropped, retune and repeat. Keep doing this until the string stays broadly in tune. Do this for all six strings.

■ **Always break** *new strings in before you really get playing on them.*

Standard electric guitars

On most electric guitars the strings are either secured at the bridge end by an independent tailpiece (as on most Gibson guitars), or are passed through the body of the instrument from the back into an all-in-one bridge unit (most Fender guitars).

At one end of every steel string, you will find a tiny disk of metal around which one end of the string is wrapped. This is known as the ball end. Take the opposite end of the string and thread it through the fixture at the bridge. Pull the string through until the ball end stops you from pulling any further.

THE HEADSTOCK

Most electric and steel-string guitars use a similar system for securing strings at the machine head. The capstan to which the string is attached stands out vertically from the headstock. Strings can be passed through a hole in the side of the capstan. The end is then passed around and under, trapping it in place when the machine head is tightened. Some capstans have vertical slots instead of holes. To use these, cut the string to length, and insert into the tip of the capstan. Then bend the string to one side and wind it around. This leaves the string endings neat and tidy.

The capstan

■ **A string-winder** *is the best option for the truly lazy.*

Slowly turn the machine head for each string, increasing the tension until the string becomes suitably tight. To save yourself time and energy, you can use a cheap plastic string winder, which simply fits over the machine head allowing you to crank it along more quickly.

For the bone idle (or sophisticated), why not take the end of the string winder — the piece that comes into contact with the machine head — saw it away, and fix it to the bit of an electric screwdriver, you can then wind on your strings at the press of a button.

LOCKING NUT SYSTEMS

When good old Floyd Rose launched his locking nut tremolo arm system in the early 1980s, he truly revolutionized the electric guitar, allowing heavy metal players to perform dive-bomb tremolo swoops without putting their instruments out of tune. It can be a bit of nightmare to change a complete set of strings for this system, though.

Because the strings are clamped in place at the bridge saddle using an allen wrench, the ball ends have to be removed first with a pair of pliers. The tension of all the strings alters when one string is removed, so it is a good idea to affix something like a block of wood or pack of cards in place beneath the bridge mechanism to prevent it from rocking back and forth while you work.

At the headstock, you wind the strings onto the machine heads in the conventional way. Once all the strings are all in place, remove the block supporting the bridge. It's important that you don't over-tighten the strings before this point – if the strings are too tight, they may snap when you move the block.

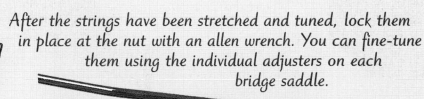

After the strings have been stretched and tuned, lock them in place at the nut with an allen wrench. You can fine-tune them using the individual adjusters on each bridge saddle.

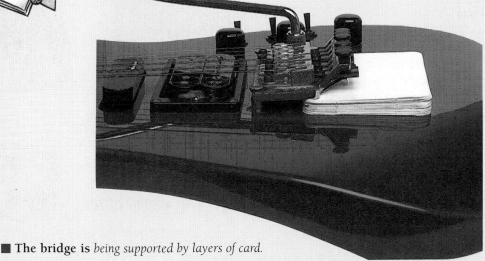

■ **The bridge is** *being supported by layers of card.*

Acoustic guitars

On most steel-string acoustic guitars, the strings are fitted using vertical bridge pins in the tailpiece. To change a string, simply remove the bridge pin from the bridge unit, pass the ball end of the string through the bridge-pin hole, and then reinsert the pin trapping the string in place. Fittings at the headstock are usually the same as for standard electric guitars.

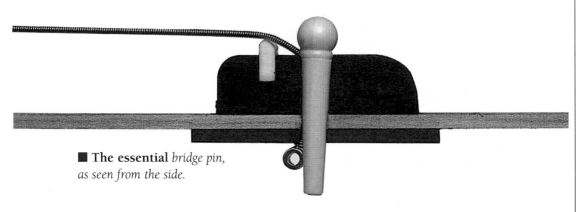

■ **The essential** *bridge pin, as seen from the side.*

Classical guitars are slightly different when it comes to restringing. Nylon strings do not have ball ends, but rather are fitted using a tied loop. The end of the string is passed through the bridge hole, passed back over the tailpiece, and knotted behind the bridge; the slack is then passed under the string on the tailpiece. When the other end of the string is pulled, the loop behind the bridge tightens, holding the string in place.

At the other end, on most classical guitars, the six capstans are fitted into slots cut into the headstock. To thread the string, simply pass it over the nut and insert it through the hole in the capstan. Bring the end of the string over the capstan and pass it underneath itself. When you tighten the machine head, the end of the string will be trapped in place.

■ **The new string** *is threaded through the capstan hole before being knotted, tightened, and tuned.*

**AN AMERICAN STANDARD
STRATOCASTER**

A simple summary

✔ Looking after your guitar will not only protect your investment but will make it play and sound better.

✔ Wipe down the strings at the end of every playing session – this will make them last longer.

✔ Clean the fingerboard and frets each time you change a set of strings.

✔ Never store your guitar in direct sunlight or where it will experience wildly varying temperatures – unless you want the neck gradually to resemble a banana…

✔ If you are a regular gigging or touring musician you should get an aluminum flightcase for your guitar.

Chapter 6

Posture and Fingering

You're probably getting a bit impatient by now given that five chapters have gone by without your playing a single note or strumming a chord. Hang on in there for a little while longer, because this chapter contains vital information that you really do need to know before you can get on with the serious business of making music. You need to consider the best ways to hold your guitar, and the correct way to hold down (or what we will term fret) the notes on the fingerboard.

In this chapter...

✓ Holding your guitar

✓ Choosing your posture

✓ Shapes

✓ Left-hand positioning

✓ Perfecting your posture and fingering

RICHARD THOMPSON MAY LOOK COOL, BUT IT IS NOT ALWAYS A GREAT IDEA TO COPY ROCK STARS' TECHNIQUES

Holding your guitar

IF YOU WATCH A VIDEO *or live performance of guitarists in action, you might be surprised at the variety of different approaches musicians take to holding their instrument. A lot of young indie or metal guitarists favor the low-slung look, with the body of the guitar close to touching their knees. The more studious players (strangely, often bearded with spectacles) can be seen almost clutching the guitar to their breasts. Most music teachers will tell you that the optimum position lies somewhere between those two extremes.*

■ **The low look** *is favored by many.*

There is no right or wrong way to hold a guitar. It's all simply a matter of personal preference. If an unorthodox method works for you, then use it — that's how progress is made. That said, before you settle on a style of your own, it's a good idea to weigh up the pros and cons of the conventional techniques.

A NOTE FOR SOUTH PAWS

Most of the world is right-handed. Although some left-handed players seem to be comfortable playing right-handed guitar, for many guitarists it just doesn't feel correct. Simply flipping over the guitar so that you pick the strings with your left hand and fret the notes with your right won't work because the six strings are then in reverse sequence.

There are two options open to you. You can buy a genuine left-handed guitar (most of the famous models are available in this form, even if you have to pay a premium for the privilege). Or you can take a standard guitar and re-string it in reverse. The latter option is fine as far as the fingerboard goes, but you may find that the shape of the body, or the positioning of the controls on electric models, can sometimes affect the positioning of your left hand around the bridge area, meaning that you may need to modify your posture.

Choosing your posture

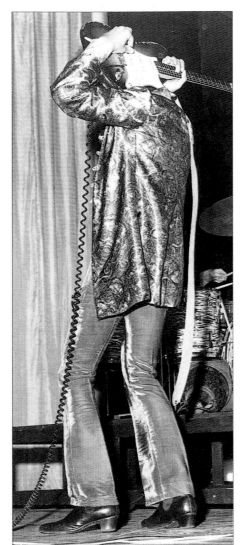

THERE ARE TWO BASIC alternative *postures for playing the guitar – you either stand up or you sit down. For the moment, we'll ignore the laying-flat-out-on-the-bed approach, the Keith Richards just-about-propped-up-against-the-studio-wall method, and the famous Hendrix resting-the-guitar-on-the-back-of-the-head technique. We don't want to make things any harder than necessary.*

The position you choose will often be dictated by the kind of music you play and the circumstances in which you are working. Classical and flamenco guitarists are invariably seated. In rock, pop, and country, performing on stage is nearly always a standing affair. Jazzers and folkies tend to favor a mixture. Away from the stage, many players seem to find it more relaxing to be seated, so practicing and a lot of studio work is often done in this way. To be honest, it's a pretty sound idea to get used to playing in both positions, since you're likely to use both at various times.

■ **Only try this** *when know what notes you should be playing!*

■ **It is more common** *to play classical guitar sitting down.*

Standing

If you want to play your guitar while standing up, you will need to get hold of a strap. This lets the guitar hang naturally against your body, with your shoulder taking most of the pressure. It also enables your hands to move around freely.

Padding on the strap stops it cutting into your shoulder

It is easier to reach the higher notes if you hold the guitar at waist height with the neck tilted

The two options you should think about are: The height at which the guitar hangs and the angle of the guitar's neck – each one will have an impact on the other. A good average height for novices is to have the bridge and tailpiece about the same height as your waist-line. A neck angle of somewhere between 30° and 45° will work best.

INTERNET

www.northwestern.edu/ musicschool/links/projects /guitar/elementaryGuitar Home.html

Maintained by the Northwestern University School of Music, Elementary Guitar Techniques explains in detail the correct playing posture for every part of your body, as well as basic stroke techniques.

■ **Attaching a strap** *to your guitar makes it much easier to play, since you have more freedom of movement.*

Aaaaaaaahhhhhhh!!

Like all major sports, learning the guitar has its own special pain thresholds that we've all had to work through before we can master "Smells Like Teen Spirit." We'll highlight these as we come up against each one. The first physical problem you are likely to face is muscle pains on the left wrist and left shoulder.

Unless you are used to carrying around a shoulder bag, you may find that your newly acquired guitar is surprisingly heavy. You may also find that the strap bites into your shoulder. You can ease this pressure by placing some padding between the strap and your shoulder until you get used to the weight.

■ **It may look easy,** *but holding your guitar for long periods of time takes some getting used to.*

Oddly enough, the wrist pain is more likely to be caused by the height at which your guitar is held. If it is too low, the angle at which the wrist of the your left hand needs to be held becomes unnaturally acute. Although your wrist will come around over time, playing in this way does tend to limit your flexibility and speed of movement – no matter how cool it looks.

■ **Don't get into** *bad guitar-holding habits by copying the way your favorite star does it!*

Sitting: the casual method

When you sit down to play, depending on your height, the guitar neck is more likely to assume a naturally horizontal position. The guitar sits with its waist – the inward curve at the bottom of the body – resting on your right thigh (if you're a right-handed player). This is the position to which most novices automatically gravitate, and it's good for both electric and acoustic guitars.

Not every seating surface is ideal for playing the guitar. Choose a sturdy stool or upright chair, as these provide good solid support. The surface on which your left foot is positioned also needs to be pretty firm. Desk chairs are not usually great since they often have arms, which will just get in the way.

Although most of us have spent hours playing in the following way, beds are especially poor to play on because they make it difficult to hold the guitar in the correct position. This can encourage bad habits, which can take a lot of effort to unlearn. In some cases, the shape and weighting of some solid-body electrics can cause the instrument to tilt awkwardly. If this happens, you can find additional support by using a shoulder strap.

Playing when seated results in less pressure on your shoulders, and is less tiring

Sleeves and cuffs can mute the strings at the bridge if you are not careful

■ **Adopt a good** *posture each time you play – sit up straight and don't slouch.*

Sitting: the classical method

The world of classical guitar has evolved its own very formal posture, and few noted concert performers have deviated from this method. Unlike in the casual approach shown above, the body of the guitar is placed between the legs, so that the waist rests on the left thigh (if you're a right-handed player). The guitar neck is always held at an angle of about 45°. To accommodate players of different statures, a small adjustable stool is used to support their left foot so that it can maintain the neck's proper angle.

An adjustable footstool enables the foot to be raised to different heights

Holding the neck at this angle allows for the optimum positioning of your left hand for movement along the fingerboard, and your right hand above the strings at the bridge. The classical posture is rarely used outside of the classical acoustic guitar performance.

■ **The correct way** *to play a nylon-stringed guitar is to angle the neck upwards so the fingerboard can be easily reached.*

CHOOSING THE RIGHT STRAPS

This may seem a little over the top, but it's worth putting a bit of thought into choosing the right sort of strap. Although almost any kind of strap will provide the necessary support – I guess you could even use a piece of thin rope if you really wanted – not all of them are sturdy or durable. For example, the commonly used plastic "leatherette" types have a tendency to tear around the strap buttons. This will always happen when you are "wearing" your guitar – and if you're really unlucky, when you're on stage playing. The best plan is to spend a little more money on a good-quality, adjustable leather strap. It's a worthwhile investment that should last a lifetime. A strap with additional shoulder padding is also a good idea, especially if you play heavier, solid-body instruments.

For the more paranoid player, an even safer option exists. Although most shoulder straps are perfectly adequate to support any guitar, many professionals choose to use locking straps. These are small metal fixtures that are clamped onto the shoulder strap and can then be "clicked" into place on the body of the guitar – rather like putting on a seatbelt in a car.

The strap lock is secured to the holes on either end of the strap by a simple nut, washer, and bolt mechanism. Manufacturers usually supply their own strap buttons that must be fitted to the guitar.

■ **Invest in the best** *strap you can afford – your shoulder is worth the cash!*

Shapes

AS YOU HAVE ALREADY SEEN *a few chapters earlier, guitars can come in all shapes and sizes. Many of the more exotic designs may look interesting, but spare a thought for their playability. The original classic solid-body electrics produced by Fender and Gibson evolved from the standard guitar shape and remain versatile regardless of whether the guitarist is standing or sitting.*

Guitars like the original Steinberger "headless" models were designed without waists – the inward curve on the body that is supported by the player's thigh. This may be fine when the guitar is strapped on, but less good in the sitting position where the guitar can easily slide off the thigh. It is always worth bearing these considerations in mind when choosing a guitar.

Choosing the right clothes

A final word that applies equally to every posture is to take care about the kind of clothing you wear when you play the guitar.

Thick or bulky clothing can restrict your movement, making it more difficult for you to play accurately. Sleeves that are too loose can easily drag against the strings, muting the sound. Large metal buttons, jewelry, or zippers can easily catch the body of the guitar; not only will this make an unpleasant noise, it can also scratch or damage your instrument.

Finally, as a good rule of thumb, never wear satin jump suits or capes like many bands did in the 1970s – it'll make you look so stupid.

Trivia...

The left-handed Jimi Hendrix – probably the most important player in the history of the electric guitar – managed to cope with a standard right-hand re-strung Fender Stratocaster. He even managed to take advantage of the controls being in the opposite position from usual – with the guitar re-strung, they were above the bridge – and was able to manipulate them with his thumb while playing.

Left-hand positioning

JUST IN CASE you're in any doubt, if you're a right-handed person, you have to pluck the string with the your right hand to get a sound out of your guitar. And it's the position in which you press down with the fingers of your left hand, on the top of the neck – onto the fingerboard – that determines the pitch of the note that you hear. Clearly, then, developing a suitable left- and right-hand positioning is vitally important. We'll come on to the different approaches to sounding the strings with the right hand over the next few chapters; for now we'll concentrate on the left-hand positioning. Pay special attention to this segment – if you get into bad habits at this stage of the game, they can be really hard to correct.

Thumb on the back or thumb on the side?

There are two distinct schools of thought as to how you should hold the guitar with your left hand. The standard classical technique – which unlike the classical posture is nonetheless used by guitarists of all kinds – positions the thumb against the back of the guitar neck at all times. This enables you to clasp the neck firmly, providing additional pressure when fretting notes along the fingerboard. For correct classical posture, your thumb must be kept straight.

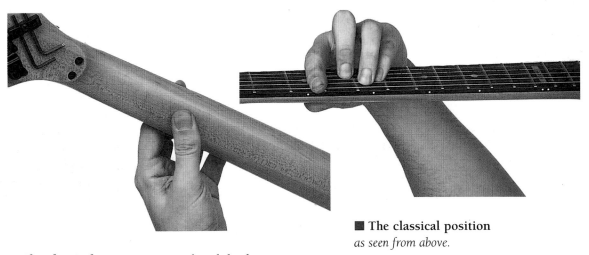

■ **The classical position** *as seen from above.*

■ **The classical position** *as seen from behind.*

In spite of this, many self-taught players can be seen sliding their left-hand thumb around the neck so that it rests along the edge of the fingerboard. When classical teachers see guitarists playing in this way, they often turn bright red and start trembling with rage, but let's think about this for a minute: Why is it such a bad thing? After all, many well-known players have used this method; many find it much more comfortable than the "correct" posture. Furthermore, if you have a wide enough fingerspan, it can enable your thumb to fret notes on the bottom two strings, which can be useful when playing certain types of chords (at this point, the classical teachers' veins usually begin to pop open).

There's no doubting that the classical technique is more versatile and that the alternative method can restrict your agility. But since there are clear virtues in both systems, we'll be controversial and recommend that you become conversant with both techniques.

■ **Alternative method from behind:** *note the position of the thumb on the edge of the fingerboard.*

Fretting a note

The way in which you use the fingers of your left hand to press down notes against the fretboard is absolutely central to mastering the guitar. If you don't fret the notes properly, your playing will always sound a bit off — end of story.

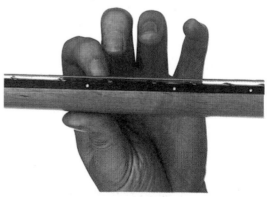

■ **Alternative method from above:** *the thumb is used by some to fret notes on the 5th and 6th strings.*

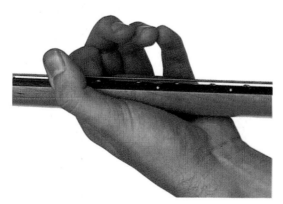

■ **Finger clearance** *in the alternative position.*

■ **Finger clearance** *in the classical position.*

To get the best sound, the tip of the your finger should be positioned immediately behind the fret. The center of the pad of the your finger should press securely down over the string, forcing it down against the fret. When you strike the string with the your right hand, you should hear a clear bell-like tone, not a buzz or dull thud.

To avoid muting the strings accidentally, you should keep all of the fingers of your left hand in as vertical a position as possible, with those that are not being employed kept away from the fingerboard. This is one clear benefit of using the classical left-hand technique, because if your thumb is resting on the edge of the fingerboard, it can be very difficult to keep those fingers vertical.

If you position your finger too far toward the headstock of the guitar when you are fretting a note, then the string is likely to buzz against the fret. If it is so close to the fret as to be covering it, then the string will be muted when you try to play. The perfect fretting position is to hold the your finger immediately behind the fret. You simply must get this right.

Fingernails!

One useful part of the guitarist's bag that we haven't mentioned so far is a pair of nail clippers. You just can't fret notes with the fingers of the your left hand if your fingernails are too long. The tip of the nail will dig into the fingerboard before the pad of the fingertip can hold down the string.

Here is a simple test for you to determine whether your nails are too long or not. Bring each finger down vertically in turn onto any firm horizontal surface. If the tip of the nail hits the surface before the pad of the your finger, then your nails are too long. This only applies to the fingers of the left hand (or the right hand if you are playing the guitar left-handed), since some classical or fingerpicking guitarists deliberately grow the nails of the opposite hand so that they can be used to strike the strings. Many prefer the tone of an acoustic guitar played in this way.

■ **Get your fretting** *hand familiar with the nail clippers.*

Perfecting your posture and fingering

HERE ARE A FEW *simple exercises to help you practice your posture and left-hand technique. These exercises are intended to get your left hand used to the idea of fretting different notes with different fingers.*

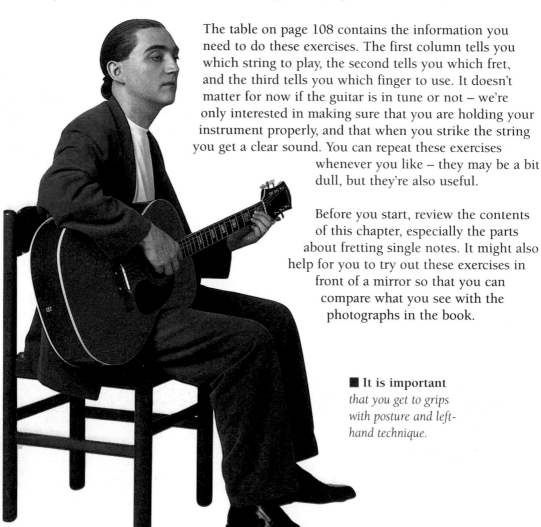

The table on page 108 contains the information you need to do these exercises. The first column tells you which string to play, the second tells you which fret, and the third tells you which finger to use. It doesn't matter for now if the guitar is in tune or not – we're only interested in making sure that you are holding your instrument properly, and that when you strike the string you get a clear sound. You can repeat these exercises whenever you like – they may be a bit dull, but they're also useful.

Before you start, review the contents of this chapter, especially the parts about fretting single notes. It might also help for you to try out these exercises in front of a mirror so that you can compare what you see with the photographs in the book.

■ **It is important** *that you get to grips with posture and left-hand technique.*

Stop practicing if your fingers get tired or it becomes too painful. Bear in mind that the soft pads on the tips of your fingers are rarely used for anything more demanding than holding a pencil or clicking on a mouse, so be patient — it may take a little time before they become hardened to persistent pressure on metal or nylon strings.

In each instance, you must press the finger down behind the fret and sound the string by striking it with one of the fingers of your right hand.

The fret numbering starts at the part of the neck farthest away from the body, and counts up towards the body of the guitar. Working out fret numbers is made easier by the dot markers that appear on the top and side of most guitar fingerboards. They can usually be seen on the 3rd, 5th, 7th, 9th, and 12th frets.

In normal circumstances, you don't use the your thumb to fret notes on the fingerboard, so the numbers one to four in the "Finger" column of the table indicate the first (index), second (middle), third, and fourth fingers, respectively.

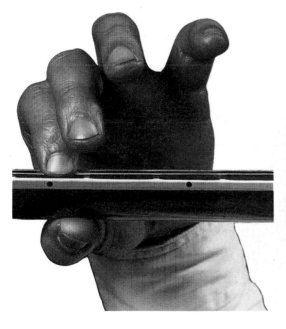

■ **Your fingertips** *may take a while to get used to pressing on the hard strings, so be patient!*

■ **Usually,** *your fourth finger is not used when you play.*

In the table here – as throughout the rest of the book – the strings are numbered from highest to lowest. The thinnest string – the one that produces the highest note – is called the 1st or top string; the fattest string – which produces the lowest-pitched note – is called the 6th or bottom string.

When you play throught this exercise, remember that the frets are numbered starting at the part of the neck that is furthest away from your body. If you get this vital piece of information sorted out here, you will have no problem understanding and playing the exerices later in this book.

String	Fret	Finger
1	7	1
2	10	2
3	4	1
4	5	2
5	1	3
6	3	1
1	9	3
2	6	2
3	3	4
4	7	1
5	8	2
6	11	3
1	4	4
2	3	3
3	8	1
4	9	2
5	12	4
6	2	2
1	4	1
2	2	2
3	2	4
4	9	3
5	10	4
6	9	3

■ **Everybody does it** *slightly differently: You will find the way that suits you best.*

■ **The oft-ignored** *classic left-hand position.*

A simple summary

✓ There are many different ways in which you can hold the guitar – which one you choose is a matter of personal preference.

✓ The sitting posture is used by most classical, folk, and flamenco players; most rock, jazz, and country players prefer to stand – at least when on stage.

✓ If you want to play while standing you'll need a guitar strap. (Doh!)

✓ For playing in the sitting position, always choose a firm surface.

✓ Classical left-hand technique positions the thumb firmly at the back of the neck – some modern players choose to ignore this.

✓ When fretting a note, to get the cleanest possible sound the tip of the finger should be positioned immediately behind the fret.

PART TWO

THE RESONATOR GUITAR

Making a Noise

BET YOU THOUGHT Part One was never going to end, didn't you? And how much noise did you make? But don't worry — it's time to pick up your guitar, plug yourself in, and start cranking out some *chords*.

The first rule of the guitar is always get in tune. To make your life easier, the sound of the open strings is on the CD in the back of this book. You'll be shown the nine most commonly used open-string chords; once you've learned these you'll be able to play along with many of your favorite songs. But there's more to playing the guitar than working out where to put your left hand on the fingerboard. There's the whole issue of playing in time, and here you'll learn the *fundamentals* of tempo and rhythm. We'll also look at pick technique and picking with the fingers. And, as good as our word, you still won't see a single piece of written music — yet.

Chapter 7

Getting in Tune

QUESTION: HOW DO YOU get two guitarists to play in perfect tune? Answer: You shoot one of them.

Segovia was probably wearing short pants when that lame joke was first uttered, but it nonetheless illustrates the very first rule of the guitar: You must get your instrument in tune. Each time you open up the case and reach for your guitar, the first item on your mental checklist must be to tune up. Tuning, it has to be said, can be pretty demanding stuff for the beginner. If you don't have a naturally musical ear (and the vast majority of people – musicians included – don't), then this is a new skill that you will need to acquire. But don't panic. There are numerous aids to help you along the way.

In this chapter...

✓ How to tune a guitar

✓ Using an electronic tuner

✓ Make it easy on yourself

✓ Using a single-note reference for tuning

LEARNING HOW TO TUNE IS A VITAL SKILL TO MASTER

How to tune a guitar

AS I THINK WE'VE ESTABLISHED *by now, the pitch of a guitar string is determined by its length, thickness, and tension. Each of the six open (unfretted) strings is adjusted by turning the machine head until it is at the correct tension. Each of the six strings is tuned to a different note according to a specific series of musical intervals. The notes are, from top to bottom (or 1st string to 6th string): E, B, G, D, A, and E. The interval between top E and bottom E is two octaves.*

There are two fundamentally different ways in which you can tune up: You can either tune each string to a strict reference pitch; or you can get one of the strings in tune and then set the other five in relation to that one.

A variety of fixed references are available for you to use. Pitch pipes, tuning forks, and piano keyboards used to be the conventional sources, but nowadays electronic tuners are more common. We have an alternative to offer you. On the first track of the CD that you'll find at the back of this book, you can hear the six strings of the guitar played in perfect concert pitch. So let's begin by using the CD to get your guitar in tune. Simply follow the steps on the next page.

On the CD you'll hear each of the six strings played five times. Use the first occurrence to get roughly in tune, and then each subsequent note can be used to get it closer and closer until you are perfectly in tune.

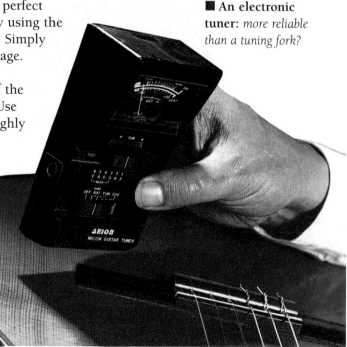

■ **An electronic tuner:** *more reliable than a tuning fork?*

Using an electronic tuner

THE GREAT THING ABOUT using an electronic guitar tuner is that you use your eyes rather than your ears. This can be most comforting for beginners.

To use an electronic tuner, you need a regular amplifier lead, which you connect between the guitar and the tuner. All you have to do is play the string and watch the meter on the face of the tuner. Turn the machine head until the needle points to the correct position, indicating that the string is in tune. Then repeat for the other five strings.

■ **Tune in a flash** *with an electronic tuner.*

If your guitar is fitted with a locking tremolo unit, such as the ubiquitous Floyd Rose system, the tuning process is slightly different. Begin by unlocking the clamp at the nut using an allen wrench (which is invariably supplied with the guitar). Tune the strings in the usual way by turning the machine heads to alter the string tension. When this has been done, lock the nut. After this, if you want to fine-tune the strings any further you need to use the hand-adjustable screws that sit at the back of the bridge unit.

■ **A locking tremolo unit** *makes the tuning process slightly more complex.*

Make it easy on yourself

HERE ARE THREE PITFALLS *that you should watch out for when you are tuning up:*

1 Don't pick the strings too hard with your right hand – it can cause the sound to distort, making the tuning process more difficult to control.

2 Don't fret notes too vigorously with your left hand by pressing too hard against the fret. If you are not careful, the string will go out of tune when you release your left hand – this is especially true if you use very light strings.

3 When you put on a new set of strings, always stretch them in first; otherwise, the guitar will not stay in tune (see pages 88–89 to see how this is done).

INTERNET

www.learn2.com/08/
0853/0853.php3

Step-by-step instructions on how to tune a guitar, and an explanation of what being in tune really means.

■ **Turning the** *machine heads counterclockwise increases string tension and raises the pitch of the strings.*

Using a single-note reference for tuning

THERE ARE MANY DIFFERENT WAYS *to tune your guitar. Every guitarist has his or her own preference. The next series of methods we'll look at requires just one reference note: When that's in tune, the other strings are tuned to one another.*

Top-to-bottom method

Not quite as common as the bottom-to-top method on page 121, top-to-bottom tuning may be easier to begin with. This method begins with the highest string.

1 You start off by tuning the 1st string (top E) to a concert pitch source (as we explained on pages 114–116) using the CD, a guitar tuner, keyboard, or anything else useful you happen to have at hand.

2 Place your finger on the 5th fret of the 2nd string and play the note E. While it's still ringing, play the open 1st string (E) so that the two notes can be heard together. Turn the machine head for the 2nd string until it is in tune with the open 1st string.

TUNING THE 2ND STRING

3 Now place your finger on the 4th fret of the 3rd string and play the note B. While it's still ringing, play the open 2nd string (B) so that the two notes can be heard together. Turn the machine head for the 3rd string until it is in tune with the open 2nd string.

TUNING THE 3RD STRING

4 Place your finger on the 5th fret of the 4th string and play the note G. While it's still ringing, play the open 3rd string (G) so that the two notes can be heard together. Turn the machine head for the 4th string until it is in tune with the open 3rd string.

TUNING THE 4TH STRING

5 Place your finger on the 5th fret of the 5th string and play the note D. While it's still ringing, play the open 4th string (D) so that the two notes can be heard together. Turn the machine head for the 5th string until it is in tune with the open 4th string.

TUNING THE 5TH STRING

6 Place your finger on the 5th fret of the 6th string and play the note A. While it's still ringing, play the open 5th string (A) so that the two notes can be heard together. Turn the machine head for the 6th string until it is in tune with the open 5th string.

TUNING THE 6TH STRING

Bottom-to-top method

This is probably the most commonly used method of all. It uses a similar principle to the method you've just seen, only this time you begin with the lowest note.

1 Tune the 6th string to a reference source.

2 Play the 5th fret of the 6th string and the open 5th string together. Tune the 5th string to the 6th string.

3 Play the 5th fret of the 5th string and the open 4th string together. Tune the 4th string to the 5th string.

4 Play the 5th fret of the 4th string and the open 3rd string together. Tune the 3rd string to the 4th string.

5 Play the 4th fret of the 3rd string and the open 2nd string together. Tune the 2nd string to the 3rd string.

6 Play the 5th fret of the 2nd string and the open 1st string together. Tune the 1st string to the 2nd string.

When in tune these open strings will sound the same note as the fretted strings of the corresponding numbers.

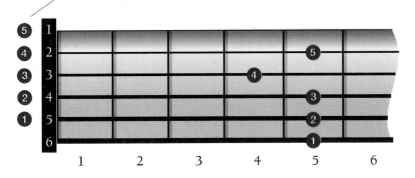

■ **Follow this diagram** *to master the bottom-to-top method of tuning.*

INTERNET

www.stagepass.com/ tuning.html

For an esoteric but interesting discussion of the limits of fine tuning, check out this article on Stage Pass.

Octave-intervals method

This tuning method uses pairs of notes played on different strings at octave intervals. Just follow the simple steps below.

1 Tune the 5th string to a reference source.

2 Play the 7th fret of the 5th string, and use this to tune the 1st and 6th strings.

3 Play the 7th fret of the 1st string, and tune the open 2nd string to that note.

4 Play the 8th fret of the 2nd string, and tune the open 3rd string to that note.

5 Play the 7th fret of the 3rd string, and tune the open 4th string to that note.

■ **Tune the adjacent** *strings in octave pairs, according to the numbers marked on the diagram and explained on the previous page.*

Another method of tuning

Here is a further alternative. Before you start following these steps you need to tune the 1st string to a reference source. This one needs the 1st string to be in tune before you can continue.

1 Play the 7th fret of the 1st string, and use this to tune the 2nd string.

2 Play the 3rd fret of the 1st string, and tune the open 3rd string to that note.

3 Play the 3rd fret of the 2nd string, and tune the open 4th string to that note.

4 Play the 2nd fret of the 3rd string, and tune the open 5th string to that note.

5 Play the 2nd fret of the 4th string, and tune the open 6th string to that note.

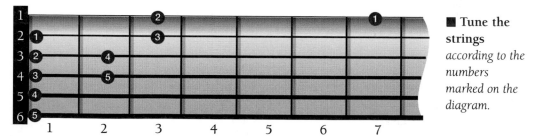

■ **Tune the strings** *according to the numbers marked on the diagram.*

Harmonics method

If you place your finger gently and directly over the 12th fret of the 1st string, and play the note, you should hear a bell-like tone. This sound is called a *harmonic*. We'll take a look at how these harmonics can be used in playing later on in the book. For now, though, you should know that harmonics can also be very useful when tuning the guitar using those found on the 5th and 7th frets.

DEFINITION

The upper parts of a note played by touching a string at certain points are called **harmonics**.

1 Tune the 6th string to a reference source.

2 Compare the harmonics on the 5th fret of the 6th string and the 7th fret of the 5th string. Tune the 5th string.

3 Compare the harmonics on the 5th fret of the 5th string and the 7th fret of the 4th string. Tune the 4th string.

4 Compare the harmonics on the 5th fret of the 4th string and the 7th fret of the 3rd string. Tune the 3rd string.

5 Compare the harmonics on the 7th fret of the 6th string with the open 2nd string. Tune the 2nd string.

6 Compare the harmonics on the 5th fret of the 2nd string and the 7th fret of the 1st string. Tune the 1st string.

The open strings marked with the numbers 4 and 5 are matched with their harmonic counterparts (which are within the diamonds in this diagram)

The harmonics marked 1, 2, 3, and 6 (in diamonds) on different strings are matched

■ **Play the harmonics** *on the 7th fret of the 1st string and the 5th fret of the 2nd string; adjust the machine head until it is in tune.*

RELICS

Although some classical musicians still use them, pitch pipes and tuning forks are no longer exactly the cutting edge for getting yourself in tune. However, if you happen to have either of these archaic items, they do the job perfectly well.

Pitch pipes act like any other reference source. They're kind of like having six whistles in one, with each separate mouthpiece providing concert pitch references for each of the strings. You can use them in much the same way as tuning to a keyboard or to track 1 of the CD.

■ **Pitch pipes are** *a useful reference note source.*

A tuning fork is especially popular with classical players. When you strike the fork against any surface, it begins to vibrate at a specific frequency. If you hold the vibrating fork against the body of an acoustic guitar, you will hear the note sounding loud and clear. You can get tuning forks that play at a variety of different pitches, but the most common is concert pitch A, which equates to the note you get by playing the 5th fret of the 1st string.

■ **A tuning fork** *is a convenient and reliable method of getting in tune.*

A simple summary

✓ Get into the habit of tuning your guitar *every time* you first pick it up to play.

✓ To play with other musicians, the guitar has to be tuned to "concert pitch."

✓ It's possible for your guitar to be in tune with itself but out of tune with other instruments.

✓ If you can tune one string to an external reference note you can tune the other five to that string.

✓ When you've tuned up, always check against your reference tone(s) to make sure that your guitar is still tuned to concert pitch.

■ **Making small adjustments** *to the strings of your guitar will make a big difference to its sound.*

■ **Make sure that** *your guitar is in tune before you play it – it will sound so much better!*

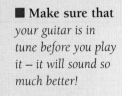

125

Chapter 8

Three Chord Tricks

FINALLY YOU CAN pick up your guitar and make your first vaguely musical sounds. You'll learn how to play three different chords, E, A, and D. That may not sound like much, but you'll be surprised at how many really famous songs you can play using just these three chords.

In this chapter...

✓ Picks

✓ Holding the pick

✓ Playing your first chord

✓ Playing your second chord

✓ Playing your third chord

✓ Make it perfect!

CARLOS SANTANA HAS A FEW CHORD TRICKS UP HIS SLEEVE

Picks

ACTUALLY, YOU WILL HAVE TO WAIT a bit longer, because before we play some chords, here are a few words about using a *pick*. Most modern players use a pick to hit the strings and hence make a noise. By contrast, classical and flamenco players pluck the strings with the thumb and fingers. Although you'll see many rock players use fingerpicking to achieve certain effects, even the likes of Joe Satriani would find it tough to play heavy-duty, high-speed solos without a pick.

Picks come in many different shapes, sizes, and materials. Take some time getting to know which ones you prefer, because they can seriously affect your playing. For example, soloists tend to favor small heavy-gauge picks that allow nimble movement; a thinner, flexible plectrum is well suited for strumming.

■ **Pick shapes** *and sizes are many and varied.*

Holding the pick

THE PICK should be held between your thumb and first finger so that it does not move when it hits the string.

If you hold the pick in such a way that it does move when you hit the string, then it will be in the wrong position when you are ready to strike the next note, so be careful. Whether you curl your remaining fingers toward your hand or away from your hand is up to you, but whichever you choose, take care that they don't accidentally muffle the strings.

For most types of playing, striking the string between 2 and 4 inches along from the bridge will sound great. But you can create interesting sounds playing closer to the fingerboard.

■ **Hold the pick** *firmly between your thumb and forefinger.*

■ **Grip the pick** *firmly to ensure that it does not slip.*

Playing your first chord

OKAY, YOUR GUITAR *is in tune, you're plugged in, and you're sitting or standing comfortably, holding the guitar just like we showed you. So let's make some music!*

Your first **chord** is called E – or E major to give its proper title. For now, you don't need to worry about why it's called that – just trust us, and follow these simple steps.

1 Place the first finger of your left hand on the 1st fret of the 3rd string. Make sure that the pad of your finger sits just behind the fret. Take care that it isn't positioned on top of the fret, or else the string will be muted and you won't hear it very clearly.

2 Position the second finger of your left hand on the 2nd fret of the 5th string.

3 Put the third finger of your left hand on the 2nd fret of the 4th string.

4 Are you ready? Are you ready? Now, with the pick in your right hand, strum it across all six strings, from the lowest-pitched string to the highest-pitched string.

Congratulations! You have just played your first chord. Bet that feels good.

DEFINITION

A **chord** *is three or more notes of a different pitch sounded at the same time.*

Track
2

THE E-MAJOR CHORD

Names of the notes that make up the chord

Strings are numbered, starting with the top E (1) and the bottom E (6)

E
B
G#
E
B
E

Numbers show which finger should be used

Make it perfect!

YOU KNEW THAT SOMEONE *was going to mention the dreaded P-word – practice – sooner or later, didn't you? So here you have it – harsh truth number one: You don't get to be good without practice. You've learned how to create the fingering (or voicings) for three simple chords. For them to be of any use, though, you need to be able to shift from one chord shape to another in as smooth a fashion as possible. This will be extremely difficult at first. Unless you have a prodigious talent, you're guaranteed to keep needing to stop to work out the finger positions. Don't worry about this – before too long, they'll become automatic.*

To help you on your way, here is a series of exercises aimed at getting you fluent in moving between the three chords. Your job is to move from one chord to another as smoothly as possible. For now, don't worry about timing – we'll be coming on to that in the next chapter. Just concentrate on getting the fingering right and moving smoothly from one chord to the next.

■ **A six-stringed legend:** *the Gibson Les Paul Gold Top.*

E	**E**	**D**	**A**
E	**A**	**D**	**A**
A	**D**	**E**	**A**
D	**A**	**E**	**E**
A	**E**	**D**	**E**
D	**E**	**A**	**A**
E	**D**	**A**	**D**
A	**D**	**A**	**D**

■ **Practice these exercises** *to help you remember the three chords.*

Track

5

A simple summary

✓ Most modern players strike the strings of the guitar with a pick (or plectrum as it's sometimes known).

✓ A chord is three or more notes of a different pitch sounded at the same time.

✓ Open voicings are chords based around the open strings of the guitar.

✓ Your first chords are likely to be accompanied by painful muscles in the left hand – don't worry, these will soon pass.

✓ Your first chords are also likely to sound a bit ragged. Again, don't worry: every guitarist from Segovia to Satriani has passed through this stage – you're in the best of company.

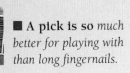

■ **A pick is so** *much better for playing with than long fingernails.*

Chapter 9

Timing and Rhythm

MASTERING THE GUITAR is not just about getting your fingers into the right positions on the fretboard – oh, no. There is that small matter of what you do with the other hand: namely, making your hand strike the strings in time.

In this chapter...

✓ Measuring speed

✓ Let's play music!

✓ Sustaining a chord

✓ Double speed

✓ Four strikes in the bar

✓ Strumming and chugging

✓ Note values

✓ Understanding rhythm

Measuring speed

THE TEMPO OF A PIECE OF MUSIC is usually measured in beats per minute – that's abbreviated as BPM. Many of you techno-savvy types will be familiar with BPM from using MIDI sequencers or drum machines.

The good thing about using BPM is that it provides an unequivocal standard to which you must play.

The same is not true for classical music, which uses a variety of Italian names (called tempo marks) to guide the player. You'll come across these terms if you look at a piece of written music. For example, if you read the instruction to play allegro, you should play it in a fast or lively manner – classical players generally interpret this as a tempo of between 120 and 150 BPM.

■ **Lento** as a... *snail?*

Other tempo marks include grave (very slow or serious); lento (slow); adagio (slow or at ease); andante (walking speed); moderato (moderate speed); vivace (lively); and presto (very fast).

Timing is made up of two different components: tempo and rhythm. The tempo is the speed at which a piece of music is played; rhythm refers to the way in which notes are played or accented. It is the rhythm that creates the feel of a piece of music.

■ **Or presto**, *like a sprinter.*

Let's play music!

WHAT YOU'RE GOING TO DO NEXT is use *the three chords you learned in the last chapter and play them over a real rock backing track that we've provided on the CD. In fact, you'll find eight of these backing tracks peppered throughout the CD that will enable you to practice the illustrated exercises by playing along with the backing track – it's kind of like karaoke for the guitarist.*

Trivia...

Even when you've become the master axeman you always knew you would be, you can use the backing tracks on this book's accompanying CD to jam over in any way you see fit. You can even write lyrics and sing over them if you feel inspired in that way.

Here, then, is a chord chart for the first backing track (CD track 6). As you can see, it is made up from 16 segments.

Each of these segments is called a bar. If you listen to the backing track, you can count up to four clicks or beats in each bar. This is because the track – like most pop and rock songs – is said to be in four-four or common time.

When you've counted through the 16 bars, the track returns to the first bar and begins all over again.

Track 6

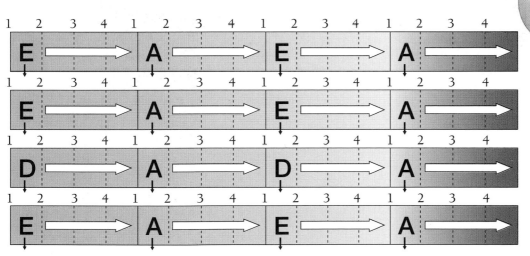

■ **This diagram will** *help you play to the backing track. The down arrows indicate that you should strike down across the strings (a downstroke).*

Sustaining a chord

WE'LL START YOU OFF BY PLAYING a very simple accompaniment that involves playing the first chord on the first beat of the first bar and letting it sustain (that is, allow it to continue to sound) until you play the second chord on the first beat of the second bar. This carries on until you reach the end.

Let's just take a look at what the different elements of each bar in the chord chart on page 141 actually mean. The numbers along the top tell you how many beats there are in the bar – you can count these numbers out aloud while you're playing. The letter at the start of the horizontal arrow gives you the chord name; the length of the arrow tells you for how many beats the chord has to be sustained. Finally, the downward- and upward-pointing arrows indicate the direction of pick stroke: a downward arrow instructs you to bring the pick downward from above and vice versa.

Track

7

To get you started, let's spell out exactly what you need to do for the first two bars – after that you should get the idea.

1 Set your CD player to track 7. You will hear a four-beat count-in of clicks. Count out loud along with the clicks.

2 Position the fingers of your left hand so that they form an E-major chord.

3 On the first beat of the first bar (the count of one), strum all six strings.

4 Hold the chord and continue counting through the second, third, and fourth beats without strumming again.

5 Between the count of four and the first beat of the second bar, stop the chord sustaining and position the fingers of the your left hand so as to form the A-major chord.

6 On the count of one in the second bar, bring the pick down across the strings.

■ **In most popular music,** *the percussion usually keeps the beat going.*

7 Hold the chord and continue counting through the second, third, and fourth beats without strumming again.

8 Continue working through the backing track, following the chord chart.

Track

8

To check if what you were doing was okay, you can listen to track 8 of the CD to hear the first two bars played as described above – without accompanying the CD yourself.

The most likely outcome of this exercise is that, because the fingers of your left hand haven't learned automatically to fret the chord positions accurately, by the time you managed to change chords the backing track was probably already on beat three of the bar. Don't despair: We can't say enough that this is *completely* normal at this stage. Simply keep practicing.

If you find it really unpleasant, work through the chords of the backing track on your own at a more leisurely pace. When you feel comfortable making the chord changes, pick up the tempo and then have another go at playing along with the CD.

INTERNET

www.dreamscape.com/ esmith/dansm/acoustic/ info/strumming.htm

Get into some basic strumming technique on this site.

■ **All guitars seem hard** *to play at first, but it gets easier with practice.*

Double speed

INSTEAD OF PLAYING THE CHORD only on the count of one, you're going to play it a second time – on the count of three. You'll play the first chord on a downstroke and the second chord on an upstroke. Simply follow these steps.

Keeping with our backing track, this time we'll work through it a little differently. Not only will you play the chord on the count of "one," but also on "three." Following the chord chart opposite, you play the first chord with a downstroke of the pick and the second chord with an upstroke.

1 Set your CD player to track 9. Count out loud along with the count-in clicks.

2 Position the fingers of your left hand so that they form an E-major chord.

3 On the first beat of the first bar (the count of one), bring the pick down (a downstroke) across all six strings. Continue counting through the second beat.

4 On the count of three, bring the pick back up (an upstroke) across all six strings.

5 Between the count of four and the first beat of the second bar, position the fingers of your left hand so as to form the A-major chord.

6 On the count of one in the second bar, use a downstroke across the strings. Continue to count through the second beat.

7 On the count of three, use an upstroke across the top five strings (remember, this is A major, so you don't play the bottom ([6th] string).

8 Continue working through the backing track, following the chord chart.

You can hear how that should have sounded by playing track 10 of the CD.

Track
O
10

Track
O
9

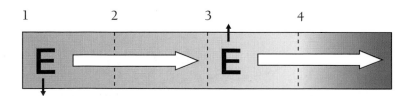

■ **The down arrow** *indicates that you should use a downstroke, up arrow that you should use an upstroke.*

PICK DIRECTION

Describing pick strokes as being either downstrokes or upstrokes is pretty self-explanatory: The former means that you push the pick down over the strings; the latter means that you pull in an upward direction. It's relatively rare to use upstrokes in isolation. In most situations, pick movement consists of either individual downstrokes or alternating strokes – where a downstroke is followed by an upstroke. This is a natural and economic way of moving the pick: because you can play single notes faster. When you play chords in this way, alternating strokes effectively becomes what is commonly called strumming.

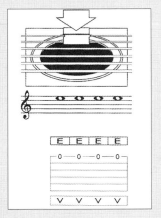

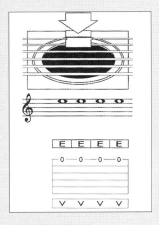

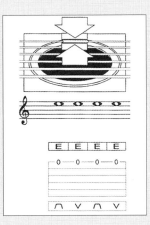

■ **Strumming the pick** *in the downstroke direction.*

■ **Strumming the pick** *in the upstroke direction.*

■ **Strumming the pick** *in an alternating direction.*

■ **Choosing your pick** *is important - the heavier and smaller picks are best for lead work or bass playing, the lighter, bigger picks are good for strumming. Harder picks give a good, crisp sound while the floppier ones produce a quieter effect. .*

Four strikes in the bar

FOR THIS EXERCISE, *you'll play on every beat of the bar.*
So if you are counting out the beat numbers, all you have to remember is that
your pick strikes the strings every time you count. We'll dispense with the
explicit steps now – we're sure you get the idea. Make sure that you follow the
pick directions on the diagram, so that you play the first and third beats as
downstrokes and the second and fourth beats as upstrokes. Listen to how it
should sound on track 11 of the CD.

Track

11

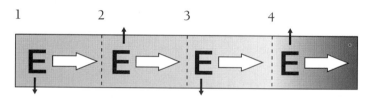

■ **Play every beat** *in the bar, using alternate down- and upstrokes.*

■ **Combining chord and single note runs,** *especially on an*
acoustic guitar, relies on good technique and endless practice.

INTERNET

www.music.indiana.edu/
som/courses/rhythm/
glossary.html

Sure, this Rhythm and Meter
Glossary from the University
of Indiana Music School is a
bit esoteric. But if you're
dying to know what
transformational grammar or
rhythmic stratification is, this
is the place.

Strumming and chugging

YOUR FINAL EXERCISE again doubles up the speed at which your right hand strikes the strings. This time the chord is played on every half-beat. A good way of dealing with this is simply to insert an extra word into your count. Like "one-and-two-and-three-and-four-and...".

The first time you work through the chords in this way, play them using alternating pick strokes. That means downstrokes on the beat and upstrokes between the beat (or on each "and" in the count).

After you've managed that, ignore the pick directions on the diagram and try playing the same chords as downstrokes on every half-beat. You'll notice that this kind of sounds like the crunching guitars recorded on the CD. It's far easier to get that chugging rocky guitar effect when you are playing downstrokes – you just can't get the same power or intensity from an upstroke. The difference between what you are playing and what you are hearing on the CD is that the chugging sound on the CD has been accentuated by deliberately damping the strings using the right hand. To do this, you gently rest the edge of the your right hand across the strings in front of the bridge. This creates a "muted" effect and stops the strings from resonating in the usual way, effectively shortening the length of the note.

Track

12

You can hear the three different ways of playing these chords if you listen to track 12 of the CD.

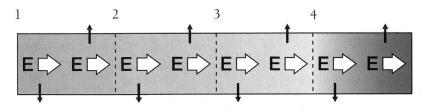

■ **Play twice for** *every beat in the bar, again using alternate down- and upstrokes.*

Note values

ANYONE WITH A VAGUE KNOWLEDGE of music notation will have probably figured out that successively halving the length of time that the chords were are sustained, mirrors the way in which note values are traditionally expressed.

Put simply, a chord or note that sustains for four beats (as in the first exercise) is called a whole note. A chord or note that sustains for two beats (as in the second exercise) is called a half note. A chord or note that last sustains for a single beat is a quarter note, and one that lasts a half a beat is called an eighth note.

We'll delve a little more deeply into this topic in Part Three (not too deeply, though – it's just not that kind of book!).

■ **Top to bottom:** *whole note, half note, quarter note, eighth note.*

Understanding rhythm

SO FAR, EVEN THOUGH IT NO DOUBT was extremely demanding, the music you've been playing (yes, you have been playing music!) has been very simple and consistent. But if every song plodded along so that chords were played on each beat of the bar, it would sound really dull – we'd soon get fed up and reach for our PlayStations.

What gives music its life and feel is the careful positioning of notes or chords within a bar – in other words, its rhythm. By varying the lengths of notes, or inserting silences (technically known as rests), it's possible to create a seemingly endless supply of unique musical statements. After all, how have so many millions of songs been written essentially using combinations of the same dozen notes?

Get exercising

Here are some exercises that develop things a few stages on from those simple rhythms you've just been playing. The first example effectively drags the chord used in the second bar back by half a beat into the first bar. It's as if the A-major chord has "stolen" half a beat from the last E-major chord so that it lasts for a beat and a half.

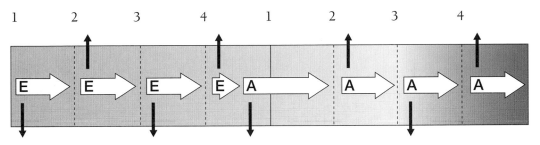

■ **This exercise will** *sound a bit more like music in that it includes a rhythm.*

The second exercise introduces a new idea – silence! This is the very essence of creating a rhythm. In the first bar, you don't play anything on the last half beat (the "and" that follows four if you're counting – and you should be counting). In the second bar, you don't play on the sixth half beat (the "and" after three).

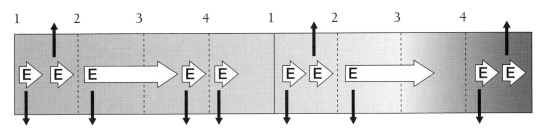

■ **Count out loud** *while you are playing this exercise – it will make things so much easier!*

Track

13

Try out the other two rhythms shown over the page: you can hear all four played on track 13 of the CD.

As the old song tells us, when you've got rhythm "who could ask for anything more?" (apart from a mint 1959 Les Paul, maybe). There are numerous ways in which you can develop your own sense of timing and rhythm.

DEFINITION

A metronome is a mechanical device that provides a clicking sound at a predefined tempo.

The oldest (and probably best) method is to play along with your favorite CDs. For pure tempo training, you can use a traditional metronome. MIDI sequencers and drum machines can do the job even more effectively. Keep in mind, though, the more you play strictly timed music, the more natural your sense of timing will get to be.

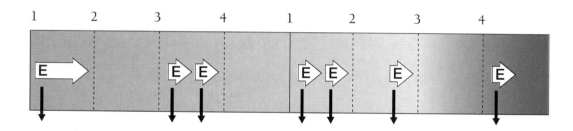

■ **Remember to keep** *to the rhythm of this exercise.*

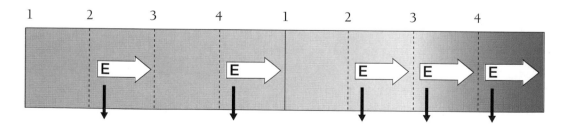

■ **This exercise will** *help you practice "playing" rests – keep counting!*

■ **Playing along with** *your favorite CDs is a great way to improve your rhythm.*

A simple summary

✓ Playing "in time" means performing a piece of music at exactly the right speed, only speeding up or slowing down if it is intended, and emphasizing the music correctly.

✓ The two components of timing are tempo and rhythm.

✓ Novice guitarists NEVER play in time at first. There are only three ways of mastering this art: practice, practice, and practice.

✓ Tempo is the speed of a piece of music; rhythm refers to the ways in which notes are grouped and emphasized.

✓ Playing with a pick can be described as using either upstrokes or downstrokes. An alternating stroke is an upstroke followed by a downstroke.

Chapter 10

More Chords, More Tunes

S O FAR YOU'VE LEARNED THREE SIMPLE CHORDS: E major, A major, and D major. In this chapter, you'll learn the other major open-string chords: C, G, and F. You'll also make your first acquaintance with a different type of chord, the "minor" series.

In this chapter...

✓ What's so major about a major chord?

✓ Introducing the minors

✓ More majors

✓ Putting the chords together

THE FIRST MODEL TO FEATURE TWO PICKUPS: THE GIBSON 1951 L5CES

What's so major about a major chord?

A CHORD IS MADE UP OF *at least three differently pitched notes played at the same time.*

The most basic chord types are called triads because they have exactly three notes. When used to describe a chord, the terms major and minor tell you the relationship or intervals between those notes. Although there are technical names for these intervals, we're going to leave that for later in the book. For now we'll put it more simply.

The lowest-pitched note of the triad is called the root note or tonic. This is the note name that prefixes the chord type – in E major, the root note is E. In a typical triad, the highest pitch in either a major or a minor chord is five notes higher than the root note.

It is the middle note that makes all the difference between a major and a minor chord. In both major and minor chords, the middle note is three notes higher. However, in minor chords, that middle note is lowered by a half-step.

INTERNET

www.djprince.net/ majorandminor.htm

What makes a chord major or minor? Find out from D.J. Prince.

Let's look at this in terms of a piano keyboard, where the distance between adjacent notes is the equivalent of one fret on the guitar fingerboard. In the following two figures, count the intervals between the notes to see how it works.

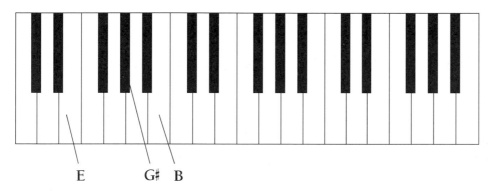

E   G♯ B

■ **It may be easier** *to count the intervals of this chord by looking at a keyboard.*

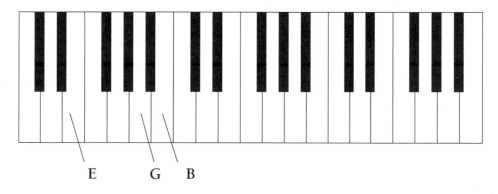

E   G   B

■ **E minor as played** *on a keyboard.*

E major has a low note of E, a middle note of G♯, and a top note of B.

E minor has a low note of E, a middle note of G, and a top note of B.

The same is true of keys other than E. Consider A major: If you count the same intervals between the notes, you'll see that A major is made from the notes A, C♯, and E, and that A minor consists of A, C, and E.

There are many types of chords other than these simple major and minor triads. However, they can always be described consistently by the way in which their notes are related to one another.

Introducing the minors

OK, ENOUGH TALK ALREADY – here are the minor equivalents of the three major chords that you've already played. These chords will give a new complexion to your playing.

Track

14

E minor

1 Place the second finger of your left hand on the 2nd fret of the 5th string.

2 Place your third finger on the 2nd fret of the 4th string.

3 Strum all six strings.

Ensure that you lift your first finger off the fingerboard, otherwise you will play E major

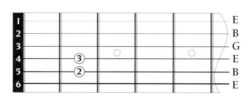

THE E-MINOR CHORD

Track

15

A minor

1 Place the first finger of your left hand on the 1st fret of the 2nd string.

2 Place your second finger on the 2nd fret of the 4th string.

3 Place your third finger on the 2nd fret of the 3rd string.

4 Strum across the top five strings.

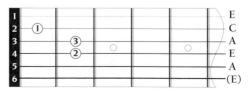

THE A-MINOR CHORD

Track
16

D minor

1 Place the first finger of your left hand on the 1st fret of the 1st string.

2 Place your second finger on the 2nd fret of the 3rd string.

3 Place your third finger on the 3rd fret of the 2nd string.

4 Strum the top four strings.

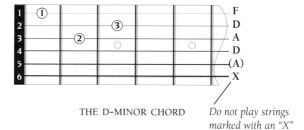

THE D-MINOR CHORD   *Do not play strings marked with an "X"*

Hearing the difference

To hear the effect of the two different chord types (major and minor) in action, try out this little exercise. Following the chord diagram below, play the eight bars; each major chord is always followed by its minor equivalent. You can hear how they should sound by listening to track 17 of the CD. You can repeat this sequence as many times as you like. Changing between major and minor chords in this way is an excellent exercise for getting your fingers to work automatically.

Track
17

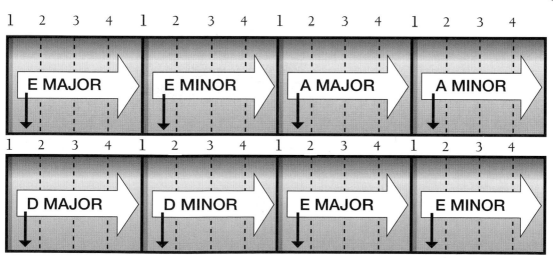

■ **Practice the major** *and minor chords using this exercise.*

More majors

CHORD ABBREVIATIONS

Major chords are often described simply by their key name – the name of the root note. So if you're asked to play an A chord, then you should play an A-major chord. Minor chords are always referred to with their unequivocal suffixes – if asked to play an A-minor chord, then you must be asked specifically to play an A-minor chord. When written down, minor chords are sometimes abbreviated – A minor can be shown as "Am."

Here are three more major chords to add to your rapidly expanding vocabulary. That makes a grand total of nine open-string chords so far. Too much! After that, we'll give you something useful to do with them.

G major

1 Place the first finger of your left hand on the 2nd fret of the 5th string.

2 Place your second finger on the 3rd fret of the 6th string.

3 Place your third finger on the 3rd fret of the 1st string.

4 Strum all six strings.

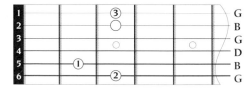

Track

18

THE G-MAJOR CHORD

> ### Trivia...
> Although that's the most common way to play an open G-major chord, you can get a much nicer sound by using all four fingers of your left hand. Fret the 5th and 6th strings as above, but this time place your third finger on the 3rd fret of the 2nd string, and your fourth finger on the 3rd fret of the 1st string. This voicing creates a fuller sound by bringing the interval between the highest two notes closer together.

C major

1 Place the first finger of your left hand on the 1st fret of the 2nd string.

2 Place your second finger on the 2nd fret of the 4th string.

3 Place your third finger on the 3rd fret of the 5th string.

4 Strum across the top five strings.

Track

19

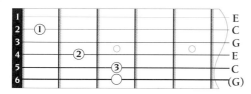

THE C-MAJOR CHORD

F major

This voicing is a little unusual in that your first finger has to fret two strings at the same time, which you haven't had to do before now. To do this, you need to position the top part of the first finger of your left hand so that it lays flat across the first two strings. Look at the photograph below to see how it works. This is a partial bar – in Chapter 12 you'll see how to create a full bar with the first finger.

1 Place the first finger of your left hand on the 1st fret of the 1st and 2nd strings.

2 Place your second finger on the 2nd fret of the 3rd string.

3 Place your third finger on the 3rd fret of the 4th string.

4 Strum across the top four strings.

Track

20

THE F-MAJOR CHORD

Putting the chords together

Track

21

BELOW YOU WILL SEE EIGHT chord exercises made up from the chords you already know. Use these sequences to accustom yourself to changing chords as fluently as possible. To check how they should sound, listen to track 21 on the CD.

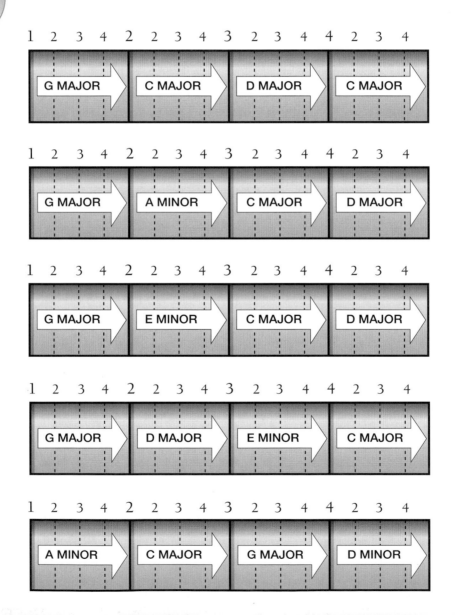

1 2 3 4 2 2 3 4 3 2 3 4 4 2 3 4

| G MAJOR | C MAJOR | D MAJOR | C MAJOR |

1 2 3 4 2 2 3 4 3 2 3 4 4 2 3 4

| G MAJOR | A MINOR | C MAJOR | D MAJOR |

1 2 3 4 2 2 3 4 3 2 3 4 4 2 3 4

| G MAJOR | E MINOR | C MAJOR | D MAJOR |

1 2 3 4 2 2 3 4 3 2 3 4 4 2 3 4

| G MAJOR | D MAJOR | E MINOR | C MAJOR |

1 2 3 4 2 2 3 4 3 2 3 4 4 2 3 4

| A MINOR | C MAJOR | G MAJOR | D MINOR |

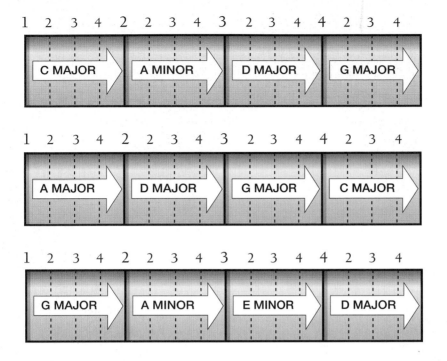

A simple summary

✓ A chord is made up of at least three different notes that are played at the same time.

✓ In a major triad, the middle note is always four frets above the root-note fret.

✓ In a minor triad, the middle note is always 3 frets above the root-note fret.

✓ There are many different chord types – major and minor chords are the most common.

Chapter 11

Picks or Fingers

LET'S MOVE AWAY from chord work for the moment and concentrate a little on some of the useful and interesting playing techniques for your right hand. You've already seen how to play simple chords using pick downstrokes, and also how to alternate them with upstrokes. Now it's time to let these strokes loose on single notes. Okay, this won't quite have you performing breakneck metal solos for the moment but hey, everyone has to start somewhere! We'll also take a first look at the alternative to using a pick – playing with your fingers.

In this chapter...

✓ Picking the open strings

✓ Fretting single notes

✓ Shifting up another octave

✓ Fingerpickin' good!

YOU'LL SOON BE PLAYING SOLOS BETTER THAN KEITH RICHARDS

Picking the open strings

ONE OF THE BEST WAYS to get used to practicing your pick technique when starting out is to concentrate on playing the open strings. This means that you don't have to worry about fretting notes with your left hand. You'll start with a simple series of exercises that echo those shown in Chapter 9 (see pages 141 and 145), but this time, instead of playing the E, A, and D chords, all you have to worry about are the open 6th, 5th, and 4th strings respectively. These are the notes E, A, and D, as if you hadn't already figured that out for yourself! Play through each of the exercises. When you know what you're doing (which shouldn't take you too long), you can play them over the top of the backing track, CD track 6.

(see pages 141 and 145)

DEFINITION

Tablature is a system for notating music. The advantage of using a "tab" system is that it tells you where to position your fingers on the fretboard, whereas conventional music notation doesn't. This can be handy for guitarists, as it's possible to play the same note at various places on the fretboard.

The diagrams in these exercises are an extended version of **tablature**, and provide a bar-by-bar schematic diagram of the fingerboard. As before, the bars are divided into beats. This time, however, there are six horizontal lines representing the six guitar strings from top to bottom. The number marked on the line represents the fret number you need to hold down for that string (in this example it's always 0, meaning the open string). The note name and pick direction are marked underneath.

Let's walk through the first exercise.

1 On the first beat of the first bar (the count of one), play the open 6th string using a downstroke.

2 Continue counting through the second, third, and fourth beats.

3 On the count of one in the second bar, play the open 5th string using an upstroke.

4 Continue counting through the second, third, and fourth beats.

5 Continue working through the remainder of the chord chart in the same fashion.

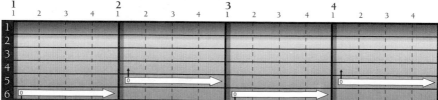

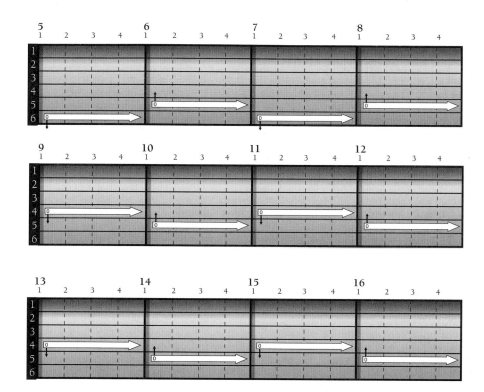

Listen to track 22 of the CD to check that what you were doing was OK. You can hear the notes played above a background metronome click on the CD.

When you bring your pick across all six strings to strum a chord, the speed and timing with which you play each string means that there is a relatively high margin of error that you can get away with. This is not so when you play single notes – especially when using fast alternating strokes.

Many beginners make the mistake of gripping the pick as if the fate of the planet depended on its safety. To play smooth pick strokes, you have to maintain a relaxed right hand to achieve the necessary accuracy. So relax and try not to tense up! Make the movements by swiveling your wrist and forearm rather than moving your thumb and finger – this will give you the greatest degree of control.

For the remaining three exercises, we'll just show the first two bars – you can figure out the rest for yourself. Don't worry, it's simple! Check your interpretation by listening to track 23 of the CD.

Track

23

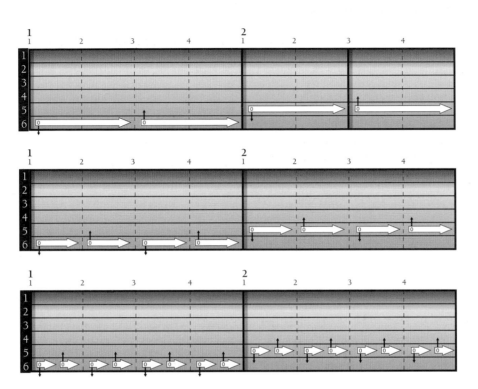

Fretting single notes

HERE'S AN EVEN MORE THRILLING TASK for you to perform. You can now work through what amounts to the same set of exercises, only this time you will have to fret the notes for yourself. Instead of using the open strings, you will play the same set of notes on different strings.

Begin by placing your first finger on the 7th fret of the 5th string. Play the note. For comparison, also play the open 6th string. As you can hear, the two notes have the same name, but they sound different – yet similar. This is because the note on the 5th string is higher in pitch than the open 6th string. The interval between the two notes is called an octave. If you now play the note on the 12th fret of the 6th string, you will hear that it is identical to the first note you played. All of the notes on the 12th fret are one octave higher than their open-string equivalents.

Because the exercise below will be the first time you'll have played single, fretted notes on the fingerboard, make sure that you have your left hand in the correct position. Remember that your thumb should be held at the back of the guitar neck and that the fingers you are not using should be clear of the strings.

If you feel inclined, you can also play this exercise over the backing track on CD track 6 as well as hearing it on track 24. Try sustaining the notes for different lengths of time as you did in the open-string exercises on pages 164–165.

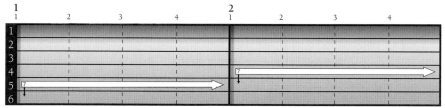

■ **This exercise will help** *you practice your first fretted notes.*

Track
24

Shifting up another octave

BEFORE WE MOVE ON to something a bit different, you'll complete this set of exercises by playing the same three notes two octaves above the open strings. Follow the example below, this time using the 4th, 3rd, and 2nd strings.

Notice in the diagram that this time you cannot use the same fret numbers for all three strings. The 14th fret on the 4th string is two octaves above open E, and the 14th fret on the 3rd string is two octaves above the open A. However, to play two octaves above the open D on the 4th string, you have to use the 15th fret on the 2nd string. The reason for this is simple: the pitch intervals between the open strings are all the same – the equivalent to five frets on the fingerboard – except between the 2nd and 3rd strings, which is the equivalent to four frets.

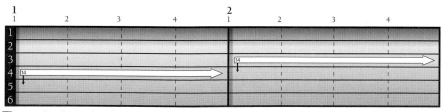

■ **Aim higher:** *this time the exercise is played two octaves higher.*

Track
25

Fingerpickin' good!

GETTING TO BE A MASTER *of the pick is an art form in itself. But in some types of music – classical and flamenco, for example – picks are almost never used. Instead, the strings are primarily struck by using the fingers or fingernails of the right hand in these styles. Although traditionally used on nylon-strung guitars, fingerpicking is widely used by rock, jazz, country, and folk guitarists on steel-string instruments. It's well worth learning this way of working since it enables you to create a wider variety of sounds and tones – and that can never be a bad thing, can it?*

> **DEFINITION**
>
> Fingerpicking is the right-hand playing technique where the strings are plucked by individual fingers rather than with a pick.

Naming the fingers

Classical guitar tutors usually begin by teaching their pupils the Spanish names for each of the fingers of the right hand. This is a system known as "PIMA."

The thumb is *P* (Pulgar); the first finger is *I* (Indicio); the second finger is *M* (Medio); and the third finger is *A* (Anular). The fourth finger is rarely used, but it can be referred to as C, X, or E. These letters can appear on written music to indicate which finger should be used to play a specific note. It may sound a bit weird and clumsy, but it's probably the most effective way of getting the idea across.

> **DEFINITION**
>
> The PIMA system refers to the names given to the thumb and fingers of the right hand: P is the thumb, I is the first finger, M is the second finger, and A is the third finger.

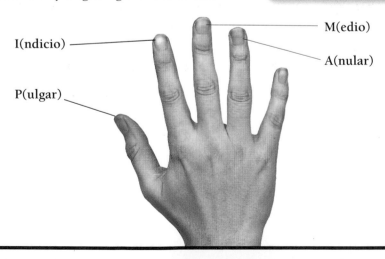

I(ndicio) — M(edio) — A(nular) — P(ulgar)

The clawhammer technique

To play any fingerpicking style, your right hand needs to be poised above the strings in front of the bridge so that the thumb and first three fingers can be used to pluck different strings.

The most common pop styles of fingerpicking have the fingers curled inward in a claw-like position – this is sometimes known as the clawhammer technique. The pad of your finger or thumb comes into contact with the string and gently pulls sideways before releasing the string.

■ **This is the correct** *wrist position.*

■ **Make sure** *your hand is in this position.*

169

Starting picking

For these first fingerpicking exercises, you'll play them using only open strings – simple!
Notice in the following diagrams that the pick directional arrows found in the previous
diagrams have been removed and are replaced by the letters P, I, M, or A – these tell you
which finger should strike the string. As a rule of thumb – if you'll excuse the pun – the
fingers play the treble strings (the top three), and the thumb plays the bass strings (the
bottom three). You can listen to the exercises by playing track 26 of the CD.

Track

26

■ **Dave Stewart** *demonstrating his right-handed technique.*

A simple summary

✓ Picking single notes requires you to play with greater right-hand accuracy.

✓ Single notes can be played with downstrokes or alternating strokes of the pick; or with fingers of the right hand.

✓ Normally, classical and flamenco do not use picks when playing strings.

✓ Pop, rock, and country players tend to curl picking fingers inward.

Chapter 12

Moving Around the Fingerboard

WHEN LEARNING the guitar it is hard making your fingers "remember" the open-string chord positions. But, by learning one basic finger position called the bar, you can play chords for any key. The second, third, and fourth fingers of your left hand form a chord shape, and you hold your first finger flat across all six strings (the bar). By moving this shape up and down the fingerboard, you can play the same type of chord in any key.

In this chapter...

✓ Mobile E major

✓ From E to eternity

✓ The bad bar

✓ Mobile A major

✓ Bar chords

✓ Picking out notes from a chord

DO YOU THINK THE CLASH PLAYED LIKE THEY DID WITHOUT LEARNING TO BAR?

Mobile E major

THIS EXAMPLE TAKES *the E-major chord, with which you are now reasonably familiar, and alters it so that it can be used away from the open-string position. The "E-type" bar is the most common type of bar chord. So you can see how it works in principle, here's how to convert E major into F major.*

1 Form a regular open E-major chord, but this time use your third, fourth, and second fingers to fret the 5th, 4th, and 3rd strings, respectively.

2 Keep your first finger poised above the nut but clear of the strings.

3 Carefully slide your left hand along the fingerboard so that your fingers move up toward the bridge by one fret.

4 Press down your first finger firmly behind the 1st fret. Simultaneously apply extra pressure from your thumb at the back of the neck. If you look at the neck from the side, it should almost appear to be gently "clamped" between your thumb and first finger.

■ **To prepare to bar,** *practice fretting the open-string chord shape, leaving your first finger free.*

5 Play all six strings. The chord you have just played is F major.

You can use the open E-minor chord shape shown in Chapter 10 (see page 156) as a bar chord in a similar way.

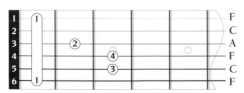

■ **Fingering for** *an F-major chord using the E-shaped bar.*

■ **Fretting an** *E-shaped bar to make an F-major chord.*

That troublesome fourth finger!

Practice is all-important when you first encounter bar chords.

One of the most frustrating aspects of learning the guitar is getting the fourth finger of your left hand to do as it's told. This is crucial when playing bar chords. Because the first finger is needed for the bar itself, the responsibility for fretting the notes has to shift down one finger, which means that the fourth finger takes over the notes previously held by the third finger.

As a consequence, within minutes of practicing bar chords, you're certain to discover pains in muscles that you didn't even know you had – especially at the side of your hand between your fourth finger and wrist. The main difficulty is making the fourth finger move in isolation from the other fingers. Don't despair, you will get there!

Suffering makes perfect

Also, depending on the contour of your fingers, you may well find your first finger in excruciating pain.

When you form a bar, your finger must be held completely straight and with equal pressure across the fingerboard, so expect the strings to dig into your joints and the softer parts of the skin – sounds great, eh?

That must be what they mean when they talk about suffering for the sake of your art.

The bad bar

Using a first-finger bar is not the only way you can create mobile chords by moving a basic shape up and down the fingerboard. Some guitarists can be seen bucking the classical thumb-behind-the-neck posture in favor of wrapping the thumb around the fingerboard to fret the 6th (and sometimes even 5th) string. Guitar teachers don't much care for this approach – to put it mildly. A point in its favor, though, is that it does give you access to a wider range of chord types and playing styles. However, without the support of the thumb at the back of the neck, changing chord shapes quickly may be a little tricky. An alternative F-major chord is shown below.

■ **Fretting an alternative** *E-shaped bar to make an F-major chord.*

■ **Fingering for** *an F-major chord using the alternative E-shaped bar.*

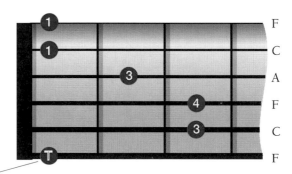

F
C
A
F
C
F

"T" indicates the use of the thumb

From E to eternity

LIKE ANY OTHER CHORD, *you get the key name of E major from the E-major chord's root note. In this case, it is E on the open 6th string.*

The beauty of the bar chord is that as long as you know the names of all the notes on the 6th string, you can identify and play a major chord in every key.

Track

27

The fingerboard diagram below shows the 12 different chords between open E and 12-fret E on the 6th string. As an exercise, play all of the E-shape bar chords on those frets. Start with an open E major, and move one fret at time up to the barred E major on the 12th fret. You can hear how this sounds by listening to track 27 of the CD.

You can probably now see the value of knowing the name of every note on every fret position on the 6th string. Your homework for today, then, is to learn each of their names so they are tattooed indelibly on your brain. Next time you pick up your guitar, you should know immediately that the 8th fret of the 6th string is the note C.

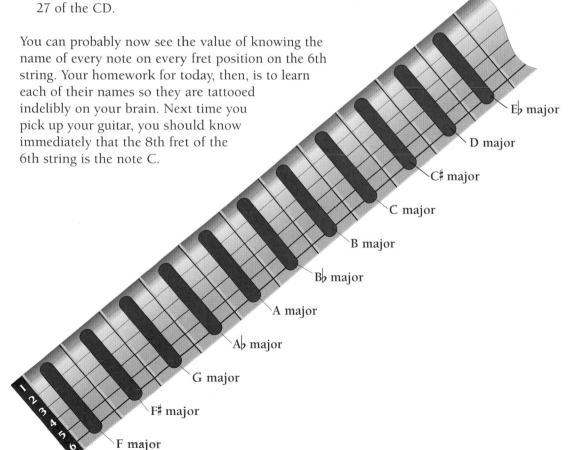

E♭ major

D major

C# major

C major

B major

B♭ major

A major

A♭ major

G major

F# major

F major

Mobile A major

YOU CAN ALSO TAKE *the barred approach with a basic open A-major chord shape. The following exercise shows you how to convert A major into a barred B-flat-major chord.*

1 Form a regular open A-major chord, but this time use your second, third, and fourth fingers to fret the 4th, 3rd, and 2nd strings, respectively. Keep the first finger poised above the nut but clear of the strings.

2 Slide your left hand along the fingerboard so that your fingers move up towards the bridge by one fret.

3 Hold down your first finger on the 1st fret.

4 Play across the top five strings. The chord you have just played is B♭ major. (You could also call it A♯ major if you wanted to, but that would be a bit weird.)

■ **Fretting a** *regular A-major chord.*

You can also play the sixth string in this chord, which will give you a bottom F

■ **Fretting an** *A-shaped bar to make a B♭-major chord.*

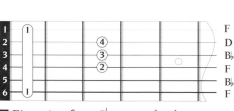

		F
		D
		B♭
		F
		B♭
		F

■ **Fingering for** *a B♭-major chord using the A-shaped bar.*

The fingerboard diagram below shows the 12 different chords between open A and 12-fret A on the 5th string. As an exercise, play all of the A-shape bar chords on those frets. Start with an open A major, and move one fret at time up to the barred A major on the 12th fret.

Because the root note of an A-major chord is on the 5th string, it follows that if you know the names of all the notes on the 5th string, you can play this type of chord in any key. So your next assignment is to learn the names of the notes on the 5th string by heart. Simple!

Play through the chords from open A major to the barred A major on the 12th fret. You can listen to them being played on track 28 of the CD.

You can use the A-minor chord shown in Chapter 10 (see page 156) to create a bar chord in the same way.

Track

28

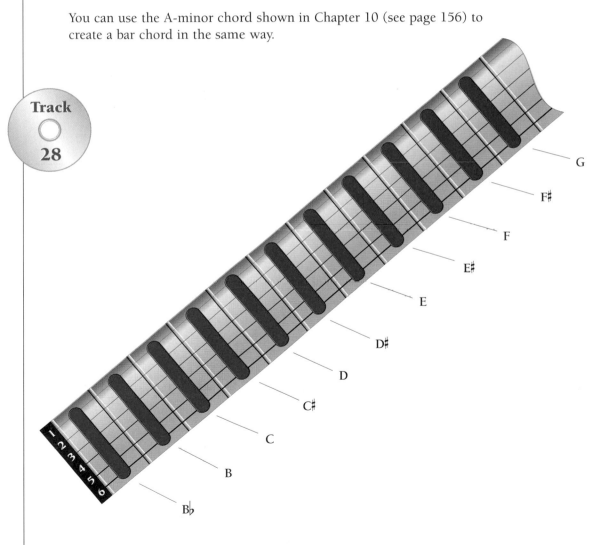

G

F#

F

E#

E

D#

D

C#

C

B

B♭

The double bar

IF YOUR FINGERS ARE NIMBLE ENOUGH, you can play a simpler version of the A chord that requires just two fingers – your first finger forms the bar over the first five strings; your third finger creates a smaller bar to cover the 2nd, 3rd, and 4th strings. To do this, you must be able to bend back the joint of your third finger so that it clears the first string; alternatively, you can play only the middle four strings, although that won't sound half as good.

INTERNET

www.guitar.about.com/
entertainment/guitar/
library/weekly/
aa022000a.htm

For more on playing the same chords in different places on the fingerboard, check out this site for the major chords. Then move on to

www.guitar.about.com/
entertainment/guitar/
library/weekly/
aa030800a.htm

for the minor chords.

■ **Fretting an** *alternative A-shaped bar to make a B♭-major chord.*

Do not use your second finger to play this chord – the first and third are the ones that matter here

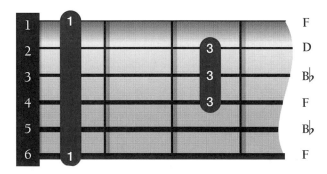

■ **Fingering for** *a B♭-major chord using the alternative A-shaped bar.*

Bar chords

NOW IS THE TIME TO put what you've learned about bar chords into practice. The second backing track, which you can hear (and accompany yourself with) on CD track 29, uses the chords G major, A major, C major, and D major.

Track

29

There are two ways you can approach playing this sequence. The first time, play the chords using only E-shaped bars – on the 3rd, 5th, 8th, and 10th frets. However, there's a more economical way of doing it, which you can use for the second time through. Play the first pair of chords as E-shaped bars on the 3rd and 5th frets, and the second pair as A-shaped bars on the same two frets. This way your hand can remain in the same position on the neck.

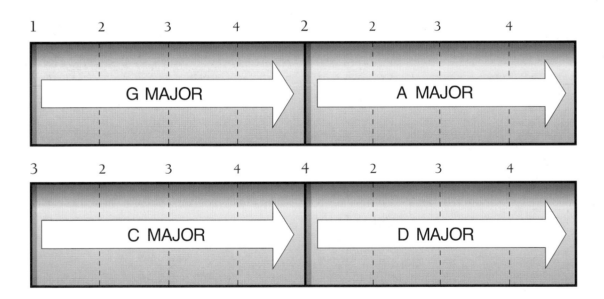

■ **Put the four bar chords** *you have just learned into practice.*

OTHER BAR SHAPES

Although the E and A shapes are used by nearly all guitarists, they are not the only bar chords you can play. Variations are also possible using open G and open C voicings. But both of these forms are really challenging to play – even experienced guitarists can have problems getting their fingers around them!

The G-shaped bar is formed from the 6th string. You can only play the bottom four strings since it isn't humanly possible to create a full voicing over six strings.

The C-shaped bar is formed from the 5th string. This can be played over the first five strings – just like an open-string C major, in fact.

■ **An example** *of a complex different-shaped bar.*

Picking out notes from a chord

Let's finish this chapter by further developing your right-hand technique, this time applying it to alternative ways of playing chords.

While highly effective, simply "chugging" out chords with a pick can be a rather dull way to play the guitar. A different, more interesting approach is to pick out notes of a chord and play them in rhythmic patterns to create a more tuneful effect. Chords played in this way are called arpeggios.

When you know the chord positions, it's your right hand that has to do all of the hard work. But be warned, picking in this way requires disciplined and accurate skills with a pick – one reason why many guitarists prefer to play in this way using their fingers instead.

Trivia...
The easiest bar chords to play are on open-tuned guitars, that is, when the unfretted strings are strummed and a chord is sounded. To change chords all you have to do is move your index finger up and down the fingerboard.

Try out the four examples below. These use the same chords as track 29 (backing track 2), so you can practice alongside. The diagrams show both pick direction and PIMA lettering to enable you to play using a pick or using your fingers. On track 30 of the CD, you can hear each example played through twice – once with a pick and once using fingerpicking. You can hear a clear difference between the two techniques. Playing with a pick tends to give a harder, more consistent tone.

Track

30

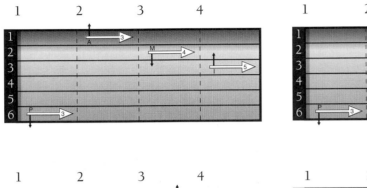

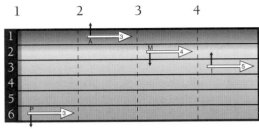

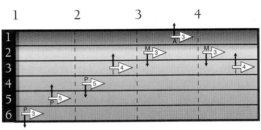

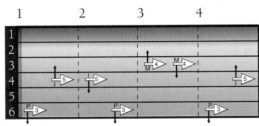

A simple summary

✓ Bar chords enable you to move basic chord shapes up and down the fingerboard to play in different keys.

✓ The most common bar chord uses the basic open-E shape.

✓ Bar chords based around the open-A shape are also commonly used.

✓ It's possible to form bar chords using C and G shapes, but they are a lot harder to play.

PART THREE

A METRONOME WILL GET YOU UP TO SPEED

Music Theory Basics

IN PART TWO YOU learned the very basics of music – rhythm and harmony – as well as many useful chords. Now it is time to get some simple *theory* under your belt. Part Three will kick off with a quick lesson on how to read music. It will only take you a short amount of time to become familiar with the *meanings* of the various symbols. If you're prepared to spend half an hour a day working through the examples in this book and looking at other printed guitar music, within a few months you should be able to comprehend even the most complex pieces of music. Guaranteed!

After practicing the basics through exercises, you will be rewarded with some real folk tunes to play. Understanding the major and minor scales in their various keys is *crucial* for all single-note lead guitar playing. Finally, you'll be introduced to some new chord types that will add a touch of sophistication to your playing.

pp
pp
cres
staccato
piu cresc
f
sf
sf
sf
dimin
p
piu piano
pp
cresc:
tr
fp
pp

Chapter 13

Reading Music

QUESTION: HOW DO YOU get a guitarist to stop playing?
Answer: You put some sheet music in front of him.
We had to touch on this subject at some stage, so here goes – to read or not to read? It's a vexing question. Anyway, here is a gentle introduction to the world of reading music.

In this chapter...

✓ Notes on the staff

✓ The smallest intervals

✓ The elements of the staff

✓ Notating rhythm

✓ Mixed note values

✓ Additional note values

✓ Rests

Notes on the staff

AS YOU'LL RECALL FROM CHAPTER 7, *each of the six strings of the guitar is tuned to a different note according to a specific series of musical intervals, and these notes are named from A to G. In written music, these pitches are shown by their position within a five-line grid called a staff (or staves in the plural). From bottom to top, the notes on the lines are E, G, B, D, and F; the notes in the spaces between the lines are F, A, C, and E. Below you'll see how the notes on the staff relate to the keys on a piano keyboard.*

If you want to master the art of sight-reading – the ability to read a piece of music as easily as the words printed on this page – you need to be able instantly to put a name to each note on the staff.

To help you learn these names, various mnemonic phrases have been used over the years: "Eat Good Bread Dear Father" and "Every Good Boy Deserves Fun" are just two of them.

The first letter of each word gives you the name of the note on each line of the staff; the names of the notes in the spaces between the lines are easy to remember – they spell the word "face."

As you can see from the keyboard diagram above, the notes A, B, C, D, E, F, and G are the white notes. There are also five other "in-between" notes, the black notes, each of which can have one of two names. It can either be a "sharpened" version of the white note to its left or a "flattened" version of the white note to its right.

So, the black note between F and G can either be called F sharp or G flat. The sharp and flat symbols are placed alongside the notes on the staff to indicate true state. These notes are referred to as being enharmonic.

Don't get too worried about which of the two names to use just now – that will become clearer as we move on.

F♯ AND G♭

TABLATURE

Okay, we know your brain maybe hurting by now, so we'll call a halt to this theoretical stuff in a moment, just after we've touched upon the subject of tablature. Tablature is an alternative (or complement, some may say) to regular musical notation. It is used to give string players – primarily guitarists and lute players – more specific fretting instructions.

In fact, you've already seen our own variation on "tab" used in some of the earlier chapters. In essence, it provides an overhead view of the fingerboard, where each of the six lines represents a string, and the number on the line tells you which fret or frets should be played. Although this approach is rarely used in classical music, it can be useful for us guitarists since – unlike the piano, for example – our chosen instrument provides us the luxury of being able to play the same note at different positions on the guitar. For example, open E on the 1st string can also be played on the 5th fret of the 2nd string, the 9th fret of the 3rd string, the 14th fret of the 4th string, the 19th fret of the 5th string, and the 24th fret of the 6th string (if your guitar has that range). Using good old tab, you can instruct the player precisely which version of E to play.

Tab can be found in many shapes or forms. In its simplest form, it merely shows fret numbers on each string with no instructions as to note values. This is perfectly adequate in some informal contexts. However, there is a growing trend towards integrating the explicit clarity of tab with the rhythmic facilities of standard notation, thus creating the hybrid form shown in the following diagram. Even this, it has to be said, is pretty simple to follow!

■ **This hybrid tab** *tells you which version of the notes to play*

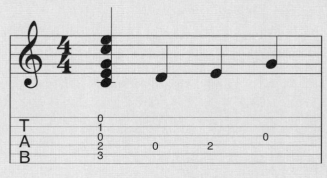

The smallest intervals

IF YOU STARTED WITH THE NOTE A *and worked through each of the 12 subsequent pitches, you would play the notes A, A#/B♭, B, C, C# /D♭, D, D#/E♭, E, F, F#/G♭, G, G#/A♭. The interval between each of these notes is called a half step. After you get to G#/A♭, the next note is again called A. If you play the two As separated by the 12 half steps, you'll realize that they sound like the same note, but one is higher in pitch than the other. This is what we call an interval of an* octave. *The two notes are said to be in different registers.*

The elements of the staff

IT SHOULD BE CLEAR TO YOU NOW *that the same note can appear in many different registers – a grand piano has a range of over seven octaves. So how do you compress all of those 80-odd notes into five lines of staff? There are two ways.*

First, a symbol called a clef is shown at the beginning of the staff. This determines the names of the notes that follow. There are several different types of clef, but the only one most guitarists need worry about is the treble clef.

■ **In terms of range,** *the grand piano is the winner.*

Ledger lines

That still doesn't tell us how to write down notes that are lower than E and higher than F – the two extremes on the bottom and top of the five-line staff. No problem! You just add single ledger lines to each note used above or below the staff. Look at the example below to see how simple this is.

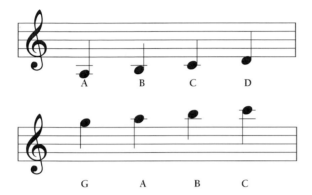

A   B   C   D

■ **Ledger lines** *below the staff.*

G   A   B   C

■ **Ledger lines** *above the staff.*

GUITAR'S RANGE

An electric guitar with a 24-fret fingerboard has a range of two octaves on every string. If you take the lowest possible note – open E on the 6th string – and the highest possible note – E on the 24th fret of the 1st string – that makes a total range of four octaves.

■ **Bottom E to top E:**
The guitar has a four-octave range.

INTERNET

www.datadragon.com/
education/reading/

This is a great step-by-step introduction to reading music.

Notating rhythm

WHEN WRITTEN DOWN ON THE STAFF, a note has two different attributes: pitch and duration. Figuring out the pitch is fairly straightforward – it's just a matter of getting acquainted with the note names. But the timing aspect may be a little harder to get your brain around.

If you listen to any piece of music, you'll hear a pulsing effect. If you try to clap along, you'll find yourself naturally drawn to a consistent beat – the time elapsed between each clap will be the same. The beat you'll hear the most frequently groups these pulses into fours: You can count them out loud in repeating cycles from one to four. This is known as four-four time. Try clapping out a four-four beat for yourself. Now gradually speed it up. This is called increasing the tempo.

The tempo of any piece of music is defined by how many beats can be played in the course of a minute and is referred to as beats per minute or BPM.

In four-four time, each grouping of four beats is defined as a bar, and each bar is a discrete unit on the staff. Vertical divisions called bar lines appear between each bar of notes on the staff. Of course, while the beat is fixed firmly, the notes played over that beat can be of different lengths of time.

Their specific durations are defined as fractions of the bar. Each duration is represented by a different note symbol so that you can tell how long each note being played should last.

Whole note, or semibreve

A note that sustains for four beats – the entire length of a bar in four-four time – is called a whole note. The following diagram shows what a whole note looks like on the staff.

■ Whole note.

Half note, or minim

A note that sustains for two beats – the length of half a bar in four-four time – is called a half note. The following diagram shows what a half note looks like on the staff.

■ Half note.

Quarter note, or crotchet

A note that sustains for one beat – the length of a quarter of a bar in four-four time – is called a quarter note. The following diagram shows what a quarter note looks like on the staff.

■ Quarter note.

Eighth note, or quaver

A note that sustains for half of one beat in four-four time is called an eighth note. The following diagram shows what an eighth note looks like on the staff.

■ Eighth note.

Sixteenth note, or semiquaver

A note that sustains for quarter of one beat is called a sixteenth note. It appears on the staff as a filled circle with a double-tailed stem.

■ Sixteenth note.

Relationship between notes

Each time the value of a note is halved, an additional tail is added to the stem. The diagram below should put this whole business into context, clarifying the precise relationship between the different types of notes.

■ **It's all about** *the stems.*

WHOLE NOTE

HALF NOTES

QUARTER NOTES

EIGHTH NOTES

SIXTEENTH NOTES

You can relax now. We're not going to get too much more complex than that. If you're still a bit confused about the theory you've just been reading, we're now going to put it into a practical context, which should help clear things up.

Mixed note values

THE WAY IN WHICH NOTES ARE GROUPED *within the same*
bar indicates a piece of music's rhythm. To create rhythm, notes of different
durations are used. The following exercise steps you through the four variations
on rhythms that are shown in the diagram below. To emphasize the point, the
same pitch has been used in each case. You can hear the examples being played
on track 31 of the CD.

1 Count out loud the
note values on every
beat. Remember that
a quarter note lasts
for one beat (a count
of one), a half note
for two beats (a count
of two), and a whole
note for four beats (a
count of four).

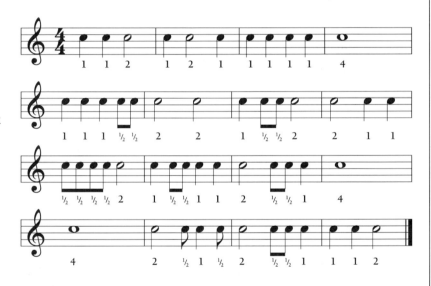

2 Clap the rhythm
according to those
note values. This
means clapping only
on the first beat of
the note – the other
numbers tell you how long the note should be sustained. Thus, the first sequence
will be CLAP-CLAP-CLAP-silence-CLAP-CLAP-silence-CLAP-CLAP-CLAP-CLAP-
CLAP-CLAP-silence-silence-silence.

3 Now put the two methods together, tapping out the rhythm and counting out the
beat values at the same time.

In the four examples above, regardless of what type of notes have
been used, the combined value of the notes in each bar always
adds up to four beats. The first two bars of the first exercise each
contain two quarter-notes and one half-note (1+1+2 beats = 4
beats). This rule always applies to any piece of music written in
four-four time.

Additional note values

THE BASIC NOTE VALUES *you've learned about so far, created by halving, provide a fairly limited palette for you to draw from. What, for example, would happen if you wanted to play a note that lasted for three beats? Although that's a perfectly reasonable desire, using the basic units of musical currency it would seem to be impossible. Similarly, what if you wanted a note to last longer than a bar, or start during one bar and end during another? Both of these questions can be answered using additional notations to the staff called dots and ties.*

Dots

This is an easy one! You can take a note of any value and place a dot immediately after the note on the staff. This has the effect of lengthening that note by half of its value. For example, to create a note that sustains for three beats, you would dot a note that lasts for two beats – a half note. This is called a dotted half note. Similarly, a dotted quarter note has the value of one-and-a-half beats; a dotted eighth note has the value of three quarters of a beat.

■ **Dotted notes** *on the staff.*

Ties

Another way of altering the length of a note is to use a curved line called a tie. A tie is used to link together notes of different values, creating a single note whose value is that of the two notes combined. Ties can be used to sustain notes across the bar line. In the staff shown below, the quarter note of the first bar is tied to the half note at the beginning of the second bar. This has the effect of giving the quarter note a value of three beats. The half note itself is not played separately.

Where two notes are linked by a tie, the second note is never played under any circumstances – its value is simply added to that of the first note.

■ **Dotted and tied notes** *on the staff.*

Rests

IMAGINE WHAT IT WOULD BE LIKE

if all music were a never-ending continuous sound – a relentless stream of notes.

Okay, that might sound like bliss to fans of some of the more arcane metal subgenres, but the point is that a vitally important element of any type of music is silence.

In written music, periods of silence are called rests. Each of the different note values has its own associated rest. A rest can be used in exactly the same way as a note, the only difference being that it represents an instruction not to play for a specific duration.

■ **Rests (top to bottom):** *whole, half, quarter, eighth, sixteenth.*

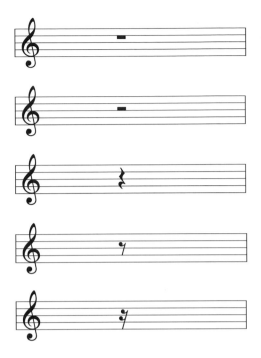

A simple summary

✓ Most electric guitars have a range of four octaves from the lowest E on the open E string to the E on the 24th fret of the 1st string.

✓ Tablature is very useful for guitarists since it shows exactly where on the fretboard a particular note or notes should be played.

✓ Dots and ties increase the duration of notes beyond their basic values.

✓ The time value of any note in music notation is indicated by its appearance, and its duration is defined as a fraction of the bar – for example, a quarter note.

■ **A fancy guitar** *will not make up for not knowing your notes!*

Chapter 14

Playing Some Tunes

I T'S NOW TIME for a bit of fun. In this chapter you'll work through a handful of traditional folk songs. As all the songs are on the CD, you can either strum out the chords, pick out the tune, or (if nobody else can hear you) flex your vocal chords! Before you start, though, you'll need to become familiar with an important new set of chords – the dominant sevenths.

In this chapter...

✓ Dominant sevenths

✓ Banks of the Ohio

✓ He's Got the Whole World in His Hands

✓ John Henry

✓ The Yellow Rose of Texas

Dominant sevenths

AFTER THE MAJORS AND MINORS, *the dominant-seventh chords – mostly referred to simply as the sevenths – are the most common chords. Sevenths are different from majors and minors in that four notes are needed to create the chord (the major and minor triads you know only require three notes). To play a seventh chord, you have to add a minor-seventh note to the major chord. Don't worry about the theory behind that just now – that'll become clear in the next chapter. For now, here are the principal dominant-seventh chords.*

Although the dominant-seventh chords are invariably referred to as sevenths, there are many other, less common types of seventh chords. You'll encounter some of these in Chapter 16.

■ **C7** *(C seventh).*

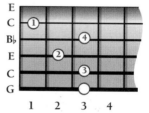

■ **D7** *(D seventh).*

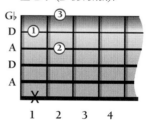

■ **E7** *(E seventh).*

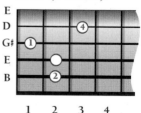

■ **G7** *(G seventh).*

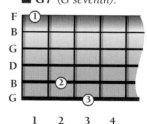

■ **A7** *(A seventh).*

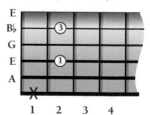

■ **B7** *(B seventh).*

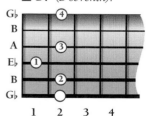

You can play seventh chords in all of the keys at different positions on the fingerboard by using the E- and A-shaped bar chords you learned in Chapter 12. Both versions played on the 1st fret are shown in the following diagram: F7 and B♭7.

■ **F7** *(F seventh).*

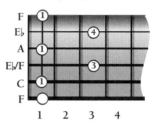

F
E♭
A
E♭/F
C
F
1   2   3   4

■ **B♭7** *(B♭ seventh).*

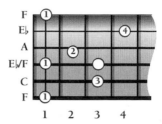

F
E♭
A
E♭/F
C
F
1   2   3   4

Banks of the Ohio

AS WITH ALL OF THE SONGS IN THIS CHAPTER, *the identity of the original composer has been long forgotten in the mists of time.*

The miniature chord charts above the tune are often found in informal written music where the main purpose is to show the tune, leaving the player to create his or her own backing arrangement.

You will find this on the CD (track 32). The tune has been recorded solely for the left speaker and the chords for the right. This enables you to hear each part independently by running the sound through one speaker. To hear them together, of course, you should balance the sound between both speakers. The lyrics are shown opposite the music.

INTERNET

www.teoria.com/books/
chords/chSevenths.htm

For the lowdown on dominant seventh chords, check this site out.

■ **The following songs**
would sound great played on the Hohner TWP.

Banks of the Ohio

Track

32

This traditional American folk song uses the chords C major, F major, and G7.

1 I asked my love to take a walk,
To take a walk, just a little walk,
Down beside where the waters flow,
Down by the banks of the Ohio.

Chorus

And only say that you'll be mine,
In no others arms entwined,
Down beside where the waters flow,
Down by the banks of the Ohio.

2 I held a knife against his breast
As into my arms he pressed
He cried, "My love don't you murder me
I'm not prepared for eternity."

Chorus

And only say that you'll be mine,
In no others arms entwined,
Down beside where the waters flow,
Down by the banks of the Ohio.

3 I wandered home 'tween twelve and one,
I cried, "My God, what have I done!
I killed the only man I love."
He would not take me for his bride.

Chorus

And only say that you'll be mine,
In no others arms entwined,
Down beside where the waters flow,
Down by the banks of the Ohio.

He's Got the Whole World in His Hands

This traditional gospel song uses the chords F major, F7, and C7.

Track

33

Chorus

He's got the whole world in his hands,
He's got the whole wide world in his hands,
He's got the whole world in his hands,
He's got the whole world in his hands.

1 He's got the earth and the sky in his hands,
He's got the night and the day in his hands,
He's got the sun and the moon in his hands,
He's got the whole world in his hands.

Chorus

He's got the whole world in his hands,
He's got the whole wide world in his hands,
He's got the whole world in his hands,
He's got the whole world in his hands.

2 He's got the land and the sea in his hands,
He's got the wind and the rain in his hands,
He's got the spring and the fall in his hands,
He's got the whole world in his hands.

Chorus

He's got the whole world in his hands,
He's got the whole wide world in his hands,
He's got the whole world in his hands,
He's got the whole world in his hands.

3 He's got the young and the old in his hands,
He's got the rich and the poor in his hands,
He's got everyone in his hands,
He's got the whole world in his hands.

Chorus

He's got the whole world in his hands,
He's got the whole wide world in his hands,
He's got the whole world in his hands,
He's got the whole world in his hands.

John Henry

This song is the first example that isn't in the key of C. John Henry is in the key of D, which means that every time you see the notes C and F in the music, you have to play the notes C# and F#. This is indicated by the two sharps shown after the treble clef at the beginning of the music. We'll explain more about this shortly. For now, get sharp with the chords D major, A7, D7, and G7.

1 When John Henry was a little baby,
Sittin' on his Pappy's knee,
Well he picked up a hammer and a piece of steel and
Said: "This hammer'll be the death of me, oh Lord,
This hammer'll be the death of me."

2 Well the captain said to John Henry,
"Gonna bring that steam drill 'round,
Gonna bring that steam drill out on the job,
Gonna whup that steel on down, oh Lord,
Gonna whup that steel on down."

3 John Henry then told the captain,
"Bring that thirty-pound hammer 'round,
Gonna beat that steam drill down, oh Lord,
Gonna beat that steam drill down."

4 "And I can tell you, captain,
A man ain't nothin' but a man,
But before I let that steam drill beat me down,
I'd die with a hammer in my hand, oh Lord,
I'd die with a hammer in my hand."

5 John Henry drove on down twenty feet,
The hammer only drove nine,
He drove so hard that he broke his heart,
He laid down his hammer and died, oh Lord,
He laid down his hammer and died.

6 They carried him off to the graveyard,
And buried him in the land,
And every engine that goes racin' by,
Says: "There's a real steel-drivin' man, oh Lord,
There's a real steel-drivin' man."

The Yellow Rose of Texas

As you can see in the following figure, this song has three sharps at the start of the staff.

This indicates that the song is in the key of A and that the notes C, F, and G should be played as C#, F#, and G#.

Track
35

1 There's a yellow rose in Texas that I am goin' to see,
No other fellow knows her, no other, only me.
She cried so when I left her, it almost broke my heart,
And if I ever find her, we never more will part.

Chorus

She's the sweetest rose of Texas this fellow ever knew,
Her eyes are bright as diamonds and sparkle like the dew.
You may talk about your dearest maids and sing of Rosalie,
But the yellow rose of Texas beats the belles of Tennessee.

2 Where the Rio Grande is flowing and stars are shining bright,
We walked along the river one quiet summer night.
She said: "If you remember, we parted long ago,
You promised to come back to me and never leave me so."

Chorus

She's the sweetest rose of Texas this fellow ever knew,
Her eyes are bright as diamonds and sparkle like the dew.
You may talk about your dearest maids and sing of Rosalie,
But the yellow rose of Texas beats the belles of Tennessee.

3 So I'm going back to meet her because I love her so,
We'll sing the songs together that we sang so long ago.
I'll play the banjo merrily and we'll sing the songs of yore,
And the yellow rose of Texas will be mine for evermore.

Chorus

She's the sweetest rose of Texas this fellow ever knew,
Her eyes are bright as diamonds and sparkle like the dew.
You may talk about your dearest maids and sing of Rosalie,
But the yellow rose of Texas beats the belles of Tennessee.

A simple summary

✔ Dominant-seventh chords are made up of four notes.

✔ Major or minor chords only require three notes.

✔ The key of D includes the notes C♯ and F♯.

✔ The key of A includes the notes C♯, F♯, and G.

Chapter 15

Getting to Know Keys and Scales

Y OU ALREADY KNOW a little about keys and scales in music, but in this chapter you'll expand that knowledge and discover what is meant by "third," "fifth," and "seventh." This is not more music theory without a purpose – you know enough now to strum out the chords or pick out the tunes to your favorite songs, but the stuff in this chapter will help you understand the musical basis behind what you are doing.

In this chapter...

"DOE, A DEER" FEATURES A BASIC SCALE

What is a scale?

A SCALE IS A SERIES OF RELATED *notes that follow a set pattern of intervals when played in sequence from a specified note to the octave above. Is that clear? If not, that's the kind of definition you'll find in music theory books. We'll try to make it a bit easier to understand.*

Almost everyone knows a scale – even if they don't know that they know it. Think of the famous tune from *The Sound of Music* – the one that starts off "Doe, a deer, a female deer . . ." As corny as this song may be, it very neatly teaches the essence of the most important scale used in nearly every form of music. When you sing the sequence of notes "do-re-me-fa-sol-la-ti-do," you are singing the notes of the major scale. It's such a familiar sound, isn't it? You can hear exactly the same relation between notes by playing the white notes on a piano keyboard from C to C.

There are many different types of scales, but the most common is the major scale. Others you'll come across are the minor series (later in this chapter) and the pentatonics (in Chapter 17). As you will hear, each type of scale has its own unique character. Remember that the first note of the scale – the root note – signifies the key of the scale.

KEY SIGNATURES

We've talked a bit about keys, but what does the term really mean? In effect, the key tells you the principal notes that are used in a composition.

If a song is in the key of C major, you know that it will revolve primarily around the notes of the C-major scale. However, that does not mean that notes from outside the scale won't be used in the song.

To discover the key of a written piece of music, look at the beginning of the staff. In all other keys apart from C, you will see an arrangement of sharps or flats directly in front of the time signature. This is known as the key signature. For example, a single flat symbol placed on the third line of the staff tells you that the music is in the key of F. The reason for this is simple: If you follow the pattern of intervals that make up the major scale starting from F, the notes you use are F (I), G (II), A (III), B♭ (IV), C (V), D (VI), E (VII), and F (I) – think "do-re-me-fa-sol-la-ti-do" starting on the note F. Each time a note appears on the third line of the staff as you play the music, you play the note B♭ rather than B (which is not part of the F-major scale).

Similarly, music with a single sharp symbol on the top line of the staff is in the key of G. The notes that comprise a G-major scale are G (I), A (II), B (III), C (IV), D (V), E (VI), F♯ (VII), and G (I). Each time a note appears on the top line of the staff, you play the note F♯ instead of F.

Here, we show you the different configurations of sharps and flats in most of the commonly used keys.

C major

G major

D major

A major

E major

B major

F major

B♭ major

E♭ major

A♭ major

D♭ major

■ **The last note** *in this diagram shows how F natural is written in a G-major scale.*

But what do you do if, for example, you need to play an F in a piece of music written in G major? Simple: Just as you can use sharp and flat symbols to raise or lower the pitch of a note, you can use a "natural" symbol to return sharps and flats to their original notes. Be aware, though, that the natural, like the other **accidentals**, is only effective for the duration of a bar; thereafter the music returns to the key signature defined at the start of the piece.

> **DEFINITION**
>
> *An* **accidental** *is a symbol like the sharp and flat that is placed alongside a note to alter its pitch.*

The major scale

Track
36

EVERY TYPE OF SCALE FOLLOWS *a strict sequence of intervals from root to the next root note. In the case of the major scale, the interval will either be one fret on the fretboard (a half-step) or two frets (a whole step). The major-scale intervals are:*

Step • Step • Half-step • Step • Step • Step • Half-step
In the key of C, the notes are C, D, E, F, G, A, B, and C.

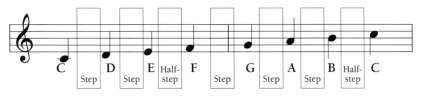

Each note of the scale is given its own Roman numeral, from I to VII. Each of these notes is referred to as a degree. The degrees are named below (and don't worry if you can't remember them at first!):

I	Tonic/Root	V	Dominant
II	Supertonic	VI	Submediant
III	Mediant	VII	Leading tone
IV	Subdominant		

Playing major scales

LET'S PUT THESE IDEAS into *practice now. Play the C-major scale using the fingering shown right. It can be played from a number of positions on the fretboard. The open-string version shown here uses only the first, second, and third fingers.*

■ C

■ G

■ D

■ A

■ E

■ B

■ F

■ C

Major scales from the 5th string

To play any major scale at positions other than the open position, you will have to use the fourth finger of your left hand. When using the correct fingering, you should be able to play all of the notes of a scale without having to move your left-hand position at all. This introduces the important "one-finger-per-fret" rule. This simply means that every finger on your left hand plays just one of the frets across all six strings.

To see how this works, look at the two examples below. You can play the C-major scale starting from the 3rd fret of the 5th string. In this case, the first finger frets the notes on the 2nd fret; the second finger frets the 3rd fret; the third finger frets the 4th fret; and the fourth finger frets the 5th fret.

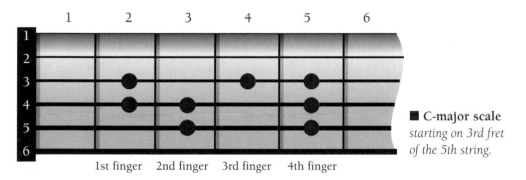

1st finger   2nd finger   3rd finger   4th finger

■ **C-major scale**
*starting on 3rd fret
of the 5th string.*

Major scale from the 6th string

Alternatively, you can play a C-major scale starting on the 6th string. In this case, the first finger frets the notes on the 7th fret; the second finger the 8th fret; the third finger the 9th fret; and the fourth finger the 10th fret.

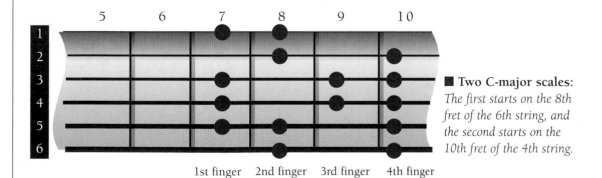

1st finger   2nd finger   3rd finger   4th finger

■ **Two C-major scales:**
*The first starts on the 8th
fret of the 6th string, and
the second starts on the
10th fret of the 4th string.*

Playing scales over a backing track

If you learn the two patterns shown on the previous page, you can easily play major scales in any key.

To show you how easy it is, here is another backing track (37 on the CD) for you to work through. This is a simple, repeating sequence containing the chords C major, D major, F major, and G major. Your task is to play a major scale over each chord (in the correct key, of course).

Track

37

■ **Play this** *with CD track 36.*

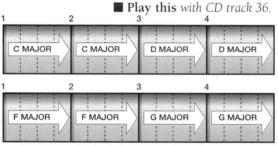

To play a D-major scale, use either of the two fretboard patterns shown above. When beginning from the 5th string, your starting note is D on the 5th fret. Since D is two frets above C, to play the complete D-major scale, you must shift the whole pattern up by two frets.

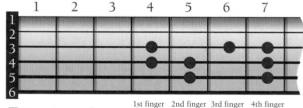

■ **D-major scale**
from 5th string.

Try playing the scale from the 6th string. Again, since D is two frets above C, your starting note is on the 10th fret, so you must shift the entire pattern up by two frets.

Now you should get the idea. To play scales over F major, you can start from the 8th fret of the 5th string or the 13th fret of the 6th string. You could also play an F-major scale from the 1st fret of the 6th string, although that would involve playing the 3rd and 6th notes on the open strings – not that that's a bad thing . . . .

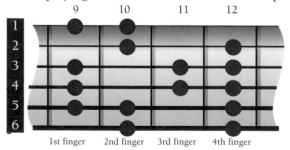

■ **D-major scales** *from 6th string, and from 4th string.*

■ **F-major scale** *incorporating open 4th and 5th strings.*

Finally, G major on the 5th string starts on the 10th fret; on the 6th string it starts on the 3rd or 15th fret.

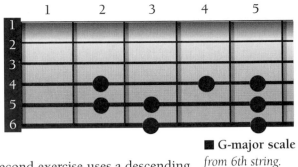

■ **G-major scale** *from 6th string.*

Here are four exercises, all of which can be played over track 36 on the CD (the backing track). The first uses the major scales shown above – these are called ascending major scales because they are played in order from the lowest note. The second exercise uses a descending major scale, in which the notes are played in reverse order, from the highest pitch to the lowest pitch.

The third and fourth exercises are broken scales in which all the notes of the scales are played, but not in order of their pitch. Practicing broken scales is an extremely effective way of improving not only your knowledge of the scales, but your pick dexterity.

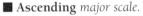

■ **Ascending** *major scale.*

■ **Ascending** *broken major scale.*

The importance of scales

THERE'S NO DENYING IT – *learning to play scales can be more than a little bit on the dull side. That said, it is very useful to have at least a rudimentary knowledge of how they work. When you understand scales, and the way in which notes are related to one another, you also begin to understand how harmony and melody work and why certain combinations and sequences of notes work better than others. It's invaluable knowledge not only for songwriters and composers, but also for the soloing guitarist, as scales are at the very heart of all lead playing. So there you have it: Love 'em or hate 'em, you can't live without 'em. Scales rock!*

INTERVALS

You already learned the names of the degrees of the major scale at the start of the chapter, but knowing the names of the intervals between different notes is even more useful. You know already that an interval of one fret on the fretboard is a half-step and that two frets is a whole step. In fact, every half-step between a root note and its octave equivalent can be given a name. The table below names all of the notes, and their relationships, between a root C and an octave C.

■ **Terminology** *behind chord structures and their names.*

Symbol	I	ii	II	iii	III	IV
Interval number	1st	♭2nd	2nd	♭3rd	3rd	4th
Interval name	Root or Unison	Minor 2nd	Major 2nd	Minor 3rd	Major 3rd	Perfect 4th
Degree	Tonic	Supertonic		Mediant	Subdominant	
Notes in C	C	C♯/D♭	D	D♯/E♭	E	F

Playing minor scales

THE MINOR SERIES *is the other significant scale system used in most musical genres. The principal difference between a major scale and a minor scale is the interval between the 1st and 3rd notes. In a major scale, the interval is a major third (four frets on the fretboard). In a minor scale, it is a minor third (three frets on the fretboard). There are three types of minor scale: natural minor, harmonic minor, and melodic minor.*

The natural minor scale

The most common minor scale is called a natural minor scale. You can hear it on track 38 of the CD. It contains the following intervals from the root:

Step • Half-Step • Step • Step • Half-Step • Step • Step

In the key of C, the notes are C, D, E♭, F, G, A♭, B♭, and C.

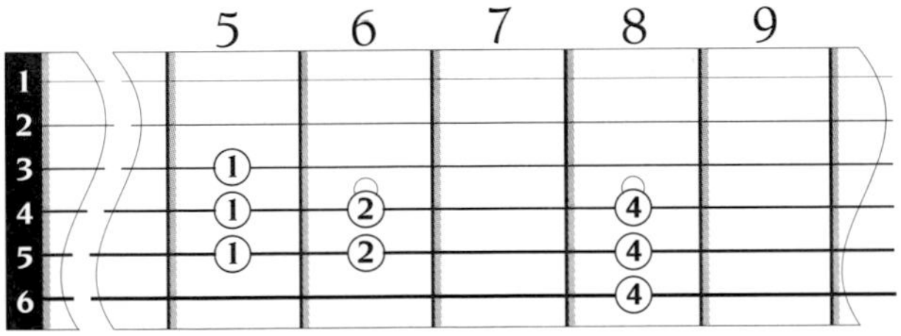

Track

38

C NATURAL MINOR

Play the C natural-minor scale using the fingering shown above. As with the major scale, once you know the basic pattern you can play this minor scale in any key by moving up and down the fretboard.

IV+ or V°	V	V+ or vi	VI or vii°	vii	VII	I
♯4th or ♭5th	5th	♯5th or ♭6th	6th or ♭♭7th	♭7th	7th	1st
Aug 4th or Dim 5th	Perfect 5th	Aug 5th or Minor 6th	Major 6th or Dim 7th	Minor 7th	Major 7th	Octave
Tritone	Dominant	Submediant		Subtonic	Leading note	Tonic
F♯/G♭	G	G♯/A♭	A	A♯/B♭	B	C

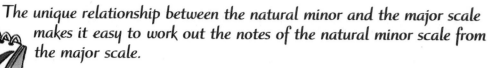

The unique relationship between the natural minor and the major scale makes it easy to work out the notes of the natural minor scale from the major scale.

Each major scale has its own "relative" natural minor scale. This minor scale takes the sixth note of the major scale as its root and then uses the same notes. Let's try it out with C major where the notes are C, D, E, F, G, A, B, and C. The relative minor scale begins from the sixth note of the C-major scale (A) and contains the sequence A, B, C, D, E, F, G, and A.

Although both scales use the same notes, don't get confused into thinking that they are the same scale.

Play them one after the other, and you'll hear that the tonal characteristics produced by each scale are very different. This is because the pattern of intervals that make up each scale is different.

The harmonic minor scale

The second minor scale is the harmonic minor. It differs from the natural minor in that the seventh note of the scale is sharpened – or raised by a half-step. This change creates a significant alteration to the flavor and flow of the sound.

The notes on the harmonic minor scale have the following intervals from the root to the octave:

Step • Half-Step • Step • Step • Half-Step • Step+Half-Step • Half-Step

In the key of C, the notes are C, D, E♭, F, G, A♭, B, and C.

Track

39

Play the C harmonic minor scale shown below. You can hear it on track 39 on the CD. Notice this time that the fingering requires a four-fret stretch between the 6th and 10th frets, which can be a bit of a challenge.

C HARMONIC MINOR

The melodic minor scale

The final member of the minor scale series is the melodic minor. You can hear it on track 40 of the CD. It differs from the natural minor in that the sixth and seventh notes are raised by a half-step. The melodic minor scale is created using the following set of intervals:

Step • Half-Step • Step • Step • Step • Step • Half-Step

In the key of C, this the notes are C, D, E♭, F, G, A, B, and C.

To play this scale, the one-finger-per-fret rule has to be compromised. You have to use the first finger to cover the notes on the 6th and 7th frets.

C MELODIC MINOR

Track
40

When you are playing a descending melodic minor scale, the intervals always revert to those of the natural minor scale. If you descended with the same ascending notes of the melodic minor, the "minor flavor" of the sequence would be lost.

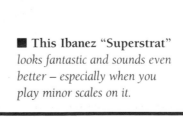

■ **This Ibanez "Superstrat"**
looks fantastic and sounds even better – especially when you play minor scales on it.

Contrasting the four scales

Track 41

TO HEAR THE DIFFERENCES between the major scale and the three minor scales, play the following exercise and listen for the contrast. The exercise is in the key of G. You can use the same fingering patterns shown for the scales in C, but you must transpose them to G by moving from a root note on the 9th fret of the 6th string down to the 3rd fret of the 6th string. It is on track 41.

G MAJOR   G NATURAL MINOR

G HARMONIC MINOR   G MELODIC MINOR

■ **Melody**
Blue Sage.

INTERNET

www.looknohands.com/
chordhouse/

The Chord House offers plenty of chord charts for beginners and advanced players. in the Advanced Guitar Room, you'll also find lots of scales to practice.

■ **This Jim Burns** *Scorpio is named after its distinctive shape.*

■ **A Hutti Star** *is born.*

A simple summary

✓ The major scale is the most common type of scale; other frequently used scales are the minor series and the pentatonic scales.

✓ Scale types are derived from the intervals between the notes in the scale.

✓ The one-finger-per-fret method enables you to stay in the same left-hand position when playing certain scales.

✓ A knowledge of scales is relatively important for the guitarist who wants to solo creatively and understand what he or she is doing.

✓ Each major scale has its own relative minor, is derived from the 6th note of the major scale.

Chapter 16

Building Chords

MOST OF THE CHORDS you've learned so far are combinations of the 1st, 3rd, and 5th notes from the major and minor triads. We added to these chord types in Chapter 14 by introducing the dominant-7th chord. An extra note was added to the major triad – a minor 7th – to create the new chord. Although these chord types (major, minor, and seventh) are the most common in popular music, there are dozens more.

In this chapter...

✓ Seventh chords

✓ Suspended chords

✓ Sixth chords

✓ Going beyond the octave

✓ Ninth chords

✓ Eleventh and thirteenth chords

✓ Playing the chords

JUST AS WITH A HOUSE, IT IS IMPORTANT TO LAY SOLID FOUNDATIONS FOR CHORDS

Seventh chords

SEVENTH CHORDS ARE FORMED *by adding a 7th note to a triad.*
There are three types of 7th note: The major 7th is a half-step below the octave;
the minor 7th is two half-steps (one whole step) below the octave; and the
diminished 7th is three half-steps below the octave. In the key of C, these 7th
notes are, respectively, B, B♭, and A.

Track

42

The four most commonly used 7th chords are the
dominant 7th, which you've already met, the minor
7th, the major 7th, and the diminished 7th. There are
several other more complex 7th chords shown in the
Chord dictionary starting on page 368. You can hear
those four chords played on track 42 of the CD.

To understand the way chords are created
and named, you need to know about
two other forms of triads: augmented
and diminished.

The augmented triad differs from the major triad in
that the 5th note is raised by a half-step; in the key of C,
the augmented triad would consist of C, E, and G♯. The
diminished triad has both the 3rd and 5th notes lowered by a
half-step; in the key of C, the diminished triad would consist
of C, E♭, and B♭. By taking the four triads and different notes
related to the root, you can create any number of alternatives.

Trivia...

Technically speaking, the
diminished 7th in the key of
C should be referred to as B♭♭
(that's "B double flat"), since
it is effectively a flattened
flat. However, since B♭♭ has
the same pitch as A, it is
referred to as A. This means,
however, that it becomes
possible for otherwise
seemingly impossible notes
such as C♭ or E♯ to exist.

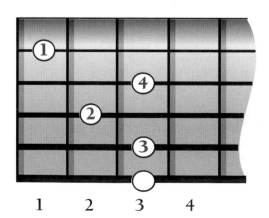

1   2   3   4

Dominant-7th chord

Add a minor 7th note to a major triad, and
you have a dominant-7th chord. In the key of
C, the notes are C (root), E (major 3rd), G
(perfect 5th), and B♭ (minor 7th). This chord's
abbreviation is C7.

■ C7 *(C seventh).*

Minor-7th chord

Add a minor-7th note to a minor triad, and you have a minor-7th chord. In the key of C, the notes are C (root), E♭ (minor 3rd), G (perfect 5th), and B♭ (minor 7th). This chord's abbreviation is Cm7.

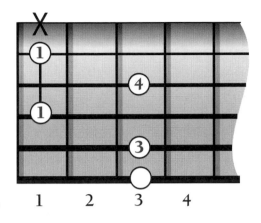

■ **Cm7** *(C minor seventh).*

1   2   3   4

Major-7th chord

Add a major-7th note to a major triad, and you have a major-7th chord. In the key of C, the notes are C (root), E (major 3rd), G (perfect 5th), and B (major 7th). This chord's abbreviation is Cmaj7 or CΔ.

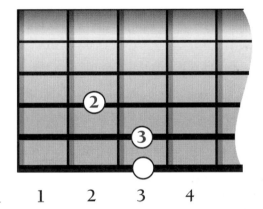

■ **Cmaj7 or CΔ** *(C major seventh).*

1   2   3   4

Diminished-7th chord

Add a diminished 7th to a diminished triad, and you have a diminished-7th chord. In the key of C, the notes are C (root), E♭ (minor 3rd), G♭ (diminished 5th), and A (diminished 7th). This chord is usually referred to simply as a "diminished chord." Its abbreviation is Cdim or C°. This chord can be played in this formation in various ways: Position the second finger on the 2nd, 5th, 8th, or 11th fret.

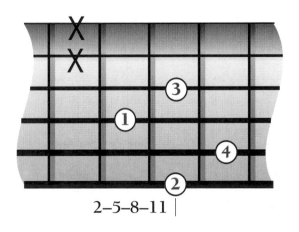

2–5–8–11

■ **Cdim or C°** *(C diminished).*

Suspended chords

Track
43

IF YOU TAKE A MAJOR TRIAD and replace the major 3rd with a perfect 4th, you get what is called a suspended-fourth chord. In the key of C, the notes are C (root), F (perfect 4th), and G (perfect 5th). This chord's abbreviation is usually written as Csus4.

A suspended four is nearly always used in conjunction with the major chord. Play this sequence that is on track 44 of the CD to see how it works:

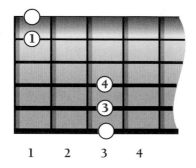

■ **Csus4** (*C suspended fourth*).

Track
44

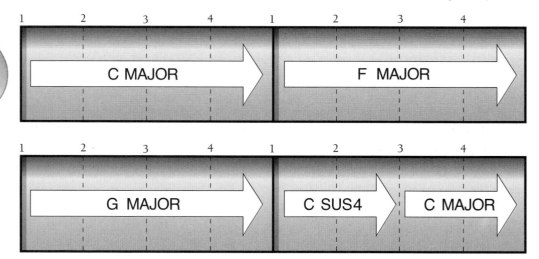

C MAJOR

F MAJOR

G MAJOR

C SUS4

C MAJOR

The same idea can also be applied to a dominant-7th chord, creating a "seventh suspended fourth" (7sus4). In the key of C, the notes are C (root), F (perfect 4th), G (perfect 5th), and B♭ (minor 7th).

 The opening chord of The Beatles' "A Hard Day's Night" is one of the most dramatic and famous uses of the 7sus4 chord.

Track
45

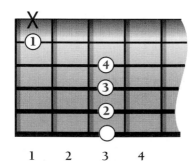

■ **C7sus4** (*C seventh suspended fourth*).

Sixth chords

Track
46

YOU CAN ADD A MAJOR-6TH
*note to a major triad to create a major-6th
chord. The notes are C (root), E (major 3rd),
G (perfect 5th), and A (major 6th), and the
abbreviation is C6.*

You can also add a major 6th to a minor triad to
create a minor-6th chord. The notes are C (root),
E♭ (minor 3rd), G (perfect 5th), and A (major
6th), and abbreviation is Cm6.

X

1   2   3   4

■ **Cm6** (*C minor sixth*).

Going beyond the octave

INTERVALS CAN BE SURPRISING. *Adding 2nd, 4th, and 6th notes to a
triad can create unusual and sometimes not terribly pleasant sounds. And yet, if
you add these notes beyond the octave, you can create a whole new series of
what are called* **extended chords.**

Consider the major 2nd note in C as an example. When this note is played
beyond the octave, it becomes a major 9th. The reasoning is simple. There are
seven different degrees of the major scale before it reaches the octave. If we
take two major scales played one after the other, we could think of the
octave note not as the first degree of the scale, but as the eighth
degree. Thereafter, the second degree of the second scale could be
called the ninth degree. Get the idea? Counting on in this way, you
can see that adding a major 4th beyond the octave
could be called an 11th, and adding a major
6th could be called a 13th.

So let's take a look at the 9th, 11th, and 13th
chords. Some of these rank among the most
difficult to play on the guitar.

INTERNET

www.eskimo.com/~ogre/
lessons/19961011.html

*This is a very thorough
introduction to chord theory,
written for beginners, from
the Online Guitar College.*

DEFINITION

*Chords using additional notes
that are over an octave higher
than the root note are referred
to as* **extended chords.**

Ninth chords

THE MOST COMMON 9TH CHORDS *are created by adding a major-2nd note an octave beyond the root note to dominant, minor, or major-7th chords.*

Dominant-ninth chords

The dominant-9th chord is usually referred to simply as a nine. To play a nine, you add a major-2nd note above the octave to a dominant-7th chord. In the key of C, the notes are C (root), E (major 3rd), G (perfect 5th), B♭ (minor 7th), and D (major 9th). This chord's abbreviation is C9.

■ **C9** *(C ninth).*

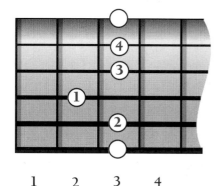

1   2   3   4

Track

47

Minor-ninth chords

Add a major-2nd note beyond the octave to a minor-chord, and you have a minor-9th chord. In the key of C, the notes are C (root), E♭ (minor 3rd), G (perfect 5th), B♭ (minor 7th), and D (major 2nd/major 9th). This chord's abbreviation is Cm9.

■ **Cm9** *(C minor ninth).*

1   2   3   4

Major-ninth chords

Add the major-2nd note above the octave to a major-7th chord, and you have a major-ninth chord. In the key of C, the notes are C (root), E (major 3rd), G (perfect 5th), B (major 7th) and D (major 2nd/major 9th). This chord's abbreviation is Cmaj9 or CΔ9.

■ **Cmaj9 or CΔ9** *(C major ninth).*

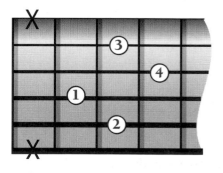

1   2   3   4

Eleventh and thirteenth chords

ELEVENTH AND THIRTEENTH CHORDS *are formed using the same principles as the chords you've learned so far in this chapter.*

Track 48

Elevenths are created by adding a perfect-4th note beyond the octave to an existing 9th chord of any type. Thus, dominant-9th, minor-9th, and major-9th chords can each produce their own equivalent 11th chords. Similarly, 13th chords are created by adding a major-6th note beyond the octave to any of the 11th chords. You can hear the dominant, minor, and major 11ths followed by their equivalent 13ths on track 48 of the CD.

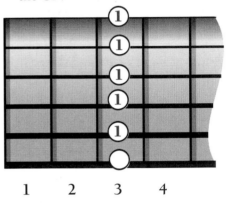

1   2   3   4

■ **C11** *(C eleventh)*.

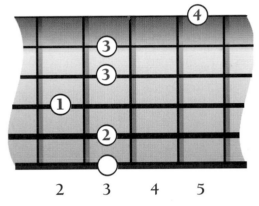

2   3   4   5

■ **C13** *(C thirteenth)*.

The challenge of big chords

Some of you might have already noticed a potential problem here. To play a "full" 13th chord in the key of C requires a root note, a 3rd, a perfect 5th, a 7th, a 9th, an 11th, and a 13th. You don't need to be too smart at math to see that this means you need to get seven different notes out of your six strings. Although you could buy a seven-string guitar – they do exist – the more orthodox approach is to leave out some of the notes, creating chords that retain a "flavor" of the full version.

■ **Playing on this** *12-string Washburn would really complicate matters!*

You're on fairly safe ground leaving out the 5th notes or 9th notes from 11th chords, or 5ths, 9ths, or 11ths from 13th chords. It's not such a good idea to leave out the 3rds or 7ths as these notes play a major part in defining the sound of the chord.

In fact, for some keys, even 9ths – which only require five notes – these chords are difficult to play in their full-voiced versions. So we're not cheating here, honest!

Playing the chords

Track

49

LET'S FINISH UP THIS CHAPTER with an exercise. By playing along with a backing track (track 49 on the CD), you can try out some of the new chord types you've learned in this chapter. The chords you need to use are shown in the following chord chart.

INTERNET

www.drsdigital.com

You can obtain a neat piece of computer software called "ChordBook" by logging onto www.drsdigital.com. The free demo version gives you chords in the keys of C, D, and G; you'll have to pay if you want the rest.

1	2	3	4	1	2	3	4	1	2	3	4	1	2	3	4

A MAJOR 7 → F# MINOR 7 → B9 →

1	2	3	4	1	2	3	4	1	2	3	4	1	2	3	4

B MINOR 9 → E7 SUS 4 → E7 →

1	2	3	4	1	2	3	4	1	2	3	4	1	2	3	4

A6 → C DIM → B MINOR 7 →

1	2	3	4	1	2	3	4	1	2	3	4	1	2	3	4

DM6 → F MAJOR / G MAJOR → A13 →

A simple summary

✓ Apart from the major, minor, and dominant-7th chords, there are many other possible chords that can be played on the guitar.

✓ A suspended-fourth chord is usually used in conjunction with a major chord.

✓ Extended chords are created by adding notes an octave higher than the root note of the chord.

✓ When playing a chord that contain more than six notes, it is typical to leave out some of the notes of the chord to make it easier to play – though preferably not the 3rd or the 7th note.

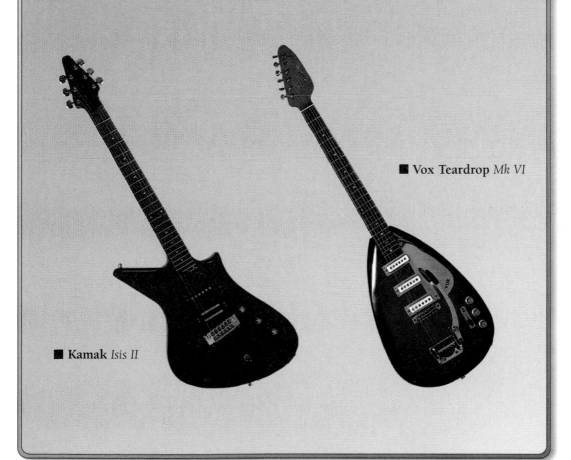

■ Vox Teardrop *Mk VI*

■ Kamak *Isis II*

PART FOUR

KING OF THE BLUES: BB KING

GETTING INTO STYLE

ALL THE IDEAS you have encountered so far can be applied pretty much to any style of music you care to name. In this part, which covers the practical aspects of playing the guitar, some *techniques* will be introduced that are closely associated with specific musical styles.

As you learn about blues in Chapter 17, you'll also learn about pentatonic scales. These scales will prepare you for Chapter 18, which is on rock playing, and also includes advice on techniques such as string bending. You'll get to try your hand at country and folk techniques, which are more likely to be used with steel-string acoustics rather than with electric guitars. The final two chapters present a series of jazz, Latin, and classical pieces for you to play. Although not overly difficult, these pieces are designed to challenge you and help you *develop* your skills.

Chapter 17

A Touch of Blues

ASK ANYONE UNDER THE AGE of 25 about rhythm and blues, and they'll probably point you toward any of the numerous sampled, synthesized, swing-beat, pseudo-soul sounds that sell by the truckload these days. Chances are they won't mention the likes of Muddy Waters, Howlin' Wolf, and B.B. King – the first generation of electric bluesmen to whom the term rhythm and blues was originally applied in the late 1940s. But while the influence of the blues is less immediately obvious these days, without it rock music may not have existed in its present form.

In this chapter...

✓ Three chords and 12 bars

✓ Playing blues rhythms

✓ Playing the shuffle

✓ Classic blues rhythm guitar

✓ Playing a simple blues lead

Three chords and 12 bars

THE BLUES EVOLVED *from African folk music that arrived with the slave trade in the United States during the 18th century.*

It developed in the black communities of the Mississippi Delta and Texas toward the end of the 19th century, and is closely tied to the early development of rock music – post-war Chicago Urban Blues stars like Muddy Waters were a huge influence on young, white rock groups. However, even now, much mainstream rock music remains firmly based in the blues tradition, especially in the area of soloing.

One of the great beauties of the blues is its essential simplicity. The classic blues structure comprises three chords, with root notes taken from the first (1), fourth (IV), and fifth (V) degrees of a key.

Track 50

These chords are played using variations on a 12-bar structure. The chord chart shown below is in the key of G major. This means that the chords used are G major (I chord), C major (IV chord), and D major (V chord). The basic 12-bar format is shown in the chord chart. There are many variations on this structure. For example, the 12th bar commonly returns to the I chord instead of the V. Listen to CD track 50 to hear a medium-tempo, blues backing track – one of two in this chapter that you can use to practice exercises.

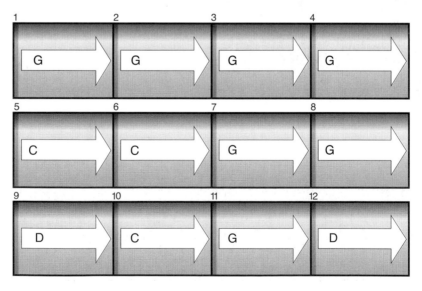

■ **Chord chart** *for 12-bar structure in G major.*

Playing blues rhythms

Track
51

BLUES CAN BE PLAYED *using different rhythms. You can begin by playing a straight 4/4 blues in the key of G (following the chord chart on page 238). Give each chord a value of a quarter note – that means you play the chord once each beat. For the exercise below, you can use an E-shaped bar chord played with pick downstrokes. Muting the strings is also effective for these rhythms.*

■ **A man who played** *for the moment: John Lee Hooker.*

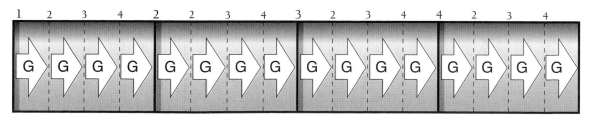

■ **A simple** *blues rhythm.*

Playing the shuffle

THE BACKING YOU PLAYED in the previous exercise is just about as straight a rhythm as you can get. To bring in some rhythmic interest, you can add a swing to this basic rhythm to create what's called a shuffle or boogie. You can get a feel for the timing by counting out the sequence below, emphasizing every fourth number (the ones highlighted).

Track

52

You can hear a second, full-length blues backing sequence on track 52 of the CD. This is a slow shuffle in C – the chords used are C major, F major, and G major.

■ **Count aloud** and emphasize the highlighted notes to get a feeling for the blues.

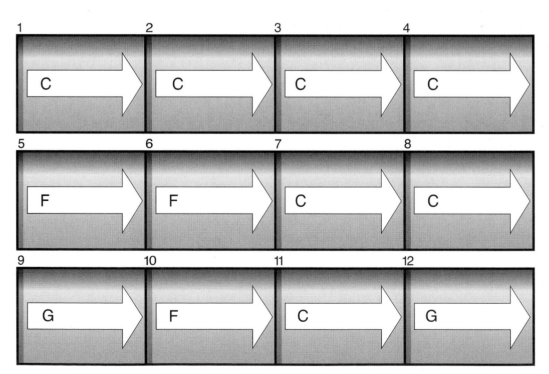

■ **Try this slow shuffle** in C.

This rhythm can be shown in several ways in written music, but all of them show groups of notes joined by a beam or curved line with the number 3 marked above. This marking indicates that each beat in the bar is divided into three equal measures.

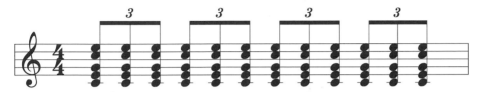

■ **The rhythm** *of the shuffle.*

Getting to know the timing of the shuffle, or boogie, rhythm can be a bit tricky at first. Here's an easy way to work it out.

1 Play a C-major chord (use the E-shaped bar on the 8th fret).

2 Play the chord in the same way as the 12-beat count above, again emphasizing every first and third chord in each beat: 1-2-3-2-2-3-3-2-3-4-2-3.

Track

53

3 When you are comfortable with this, leave out the second chord of each beat. Here is the same count with the second chord of each beat replaced with "and," which represents a rest: 1-and-3-2-and-3-3-and-3-4-and-3.

Now play the complete rhythm over the backing track, CD track 53, following the notes below.

■ **Play to** *the beat!*

Classic blues rhythm guitar

OF COURSE, IT'S NOT NECESSARY *for you to play full chords when* playing a rhythm guitar part.

One of the classic blues boogie sounds uses just two strings and is commonly played using the E-shaped bar. The intervals you need are root to perfect fifth (which is the bottom two strings of an E-shaped bar), a root to major sixth, and a root to minor seventh. Here are the three intervals shown in the key of C.

C

F

G

■ **Three blues** *boogie intervals.*

Track 54

You can play the same pattern of notes in the keys of F or G by moving the bar up to the 13th or 15th frets, respectively. Alternatively, you can slide down to the 1st or 3rd frets – this creates the same intervals an octave lower.

Play this full sequence over the shuffle blues backing as heard on track 54 of the CD.

Extending blues chords

The examples you've played so far have used major chords. A common variation uses the sixth and seventh chords – the seventh chord can be used throughout or can be mixed in with major chords as shown in this chord chart.

Minor chords and ninths are also frequently used in blues playing.

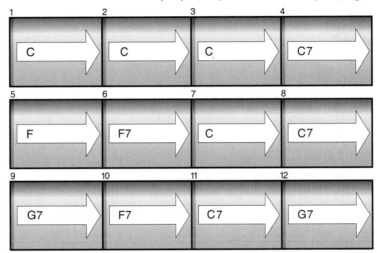

■ **More blues**
chord charts.

Playing a stabbing rhythm

Here is an alternative rhythmic idea for you to try out. Instead of playing on the beat, this example introduces a "stabbing" effect. You can use any chord type you like, but here we'll use ninth chords. You can play this over the shuffle backing, so the chords you need are C9, F9, and G9. You can find these chord shapes in the Chord Dictionary, on pages 377, 387, and 391.

Track
○
55

You can hear the example played in full on track 55.

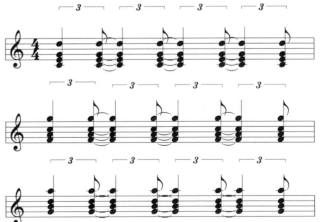

■ **Try playing** *this stabbing rhythm.*

Playing a simple blues lead

YOU HAVE ALREADY ENCOUNTERED *the major and minor scales in Chapter 15.*

Known as diatonic scales, these are the most widely used in most forms of music – in the Western world, at least. However, there are plenty of other scale types that are made up using different combinations of intervals. These are known as synthetic scales. The pentatonic scale is one of the most widely used synthetic scales. It also happens to be at the very heart of blues lead playing.

Pentatonic scales

■ **The Dobro** *resonator was developed as a response to demands for louder instruments: try playing a blues lead on one of these.*

Pentatonic scales are built using five different pitches from the root to the octave. The two most common forms of this type of scale are the major and minor pentatonic scales. The minor pentatonic scale is most strongly associated with blues music.

The minor pentatonic scale uses five notes from the natural minor scale, omitting the second and sixth notes. The set of intervals that make up the minor pentatonic are shown here, along with the finger positions for the minor pentatonic scales in the keys of G, C, and D. Remember that a good understanding of the minor pentatonic scale is a real must for any aspiring blues player.

Trivia...

Pentatonic scales are among the oldest known. Variations exist in the diverse ethnic musical cultures of Asia, Eastern Europe, and Native Americans.

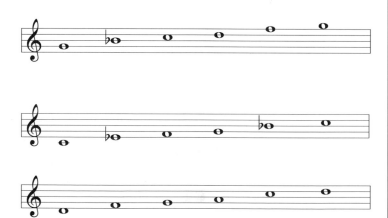

■ **Minor pentatonic** scales: G, C, and D.

Try out these two exercises. You can play them over the top of the blues backing in G (CD track 56). In the first example, you simply play up and down the scales, and in the second the notes of the scales are re-ordered for you.

Track 56

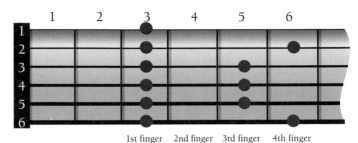

1st finger   2nd finger   3rd finger   4th finger

1st finger   2nd finger   3rd finger   4th finger

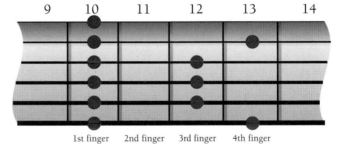

1st finger   2nd finger   3rd finger   4th finger

■ **Finger diagrams** *for the minor pentatonic scales: G, C, and D.*

Extending the minor pentatonic

Of course, there are no rules that dictate that you must only use the notes from the minor pentatonic scale in your blues playing. You can extend the pentatonic scale in any way you see fit. The most common additions are the diminished fifth and the major third. The major second and major sixth can also be used. The fingering for these new scales is shown here. Play through them and get used to the way they sound.

■ **E minor** *pentatonic with diminished fifth (red dot) and major third (black dot) additions. Every open string is played.*

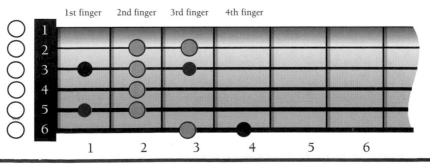

1st finger   2nd finger   3rd finger   4th finger

ALTERED TUNINGS

Standard tuning – that's E, A, D, G, B, and E bottom to top – is the most common tuning used. However, this is not the only way you can tune a guitar. Altered, or alternate, tunings can be used to create some really interesting effects.

Some of these tunings evolved from Delta blues players who played slide guitar and also from Hawaiian musicians. We'll take a look at slide or bottleneck playing in the next chapter, but for now let's concentrate on the tunings.

The most commonly used altered tunings result in a major or minor chord sounding when the open strings are strummed. Different chords can be played simply by sliding your finger (or a bottleneck) along the fingerboard. The four most commonly used open tunings are shown here:

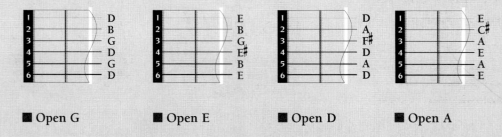

| ■ Open G | ■ Open E | ■ Open D | ■ Open A |

Try tuning your guitar to open G. To play along with the backing track (track 57) in G, play the open strings to sound G major, bar the 5th fret to sound C major, and bar the 7th fret to sound D major. The Rolling Stones' Keith Richards is famous for his use of open-G tuning – taking off the bottom string, he calls it "banjo tuning." Many of the Stones' best-known songs can only be played correctly using open-G tuning.

Track
57

Altered tunings can also provide you with a whole new vocabulary of unusual sounds – especially if you are prepared to learn a new set of chord shapes. The chords shown on the next page use open-D tuning. Joni Mitchell used this tuning on many of her best-known songs; in fact, she never bothered to learn how to use standard tuning!

You can also create some beautiful playing effects by using the bottom one or two strings as a pedal tone or drones while you fret chords on the top four strings. Listen to the work of folk guitarist Davey Graham to hear this kind of playing at its best.

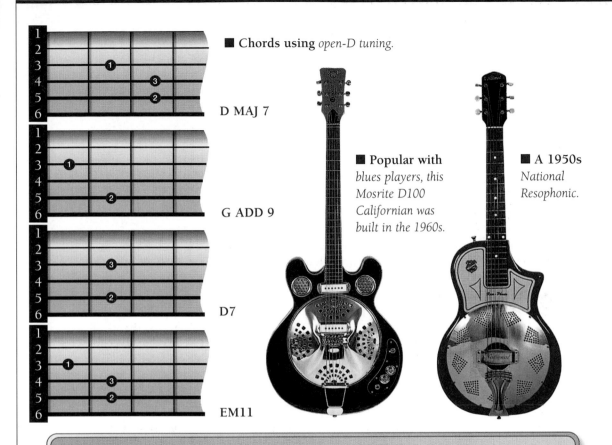

■ **Chords using** *open-D tuning.*

D MAJ 7

G ADD 9

D7

EM11

■ **Popular with** *blues players, this Mosrite D100 Californian was built in the 1960s.*

■ **A 1950s** *National Resophonic.*

A simple summary

✓ Originating in Africa, blues music's major developments took place in the black communities of the Mississippi Delta and Texas at the end of the 19th century.

✓ The most common blues structure is 12 bars long (the "12-bar blues") and usually contains three chords (the I, IV, and V chords).

✓ Major, sixth, seventh, and ninth chords are frequently used in blues.

✓ The five-note minor pentatonic scale is the scale most strongly associated with blues playing.

✓ There are numerous ways to tune a guitar that provide you with combinations of notes not easily fingered in standard tuning.

Chapter 18

Rock Lead Techniques

Mᴏʀᴇ ᴍᴜsɪᴄᴀʟ ᴀᴛʀᴏᴄɪᴛɪᴇs have been committed in the name of rock lead guitar than in any other of this instrument's varied guises. The main problem is that it's pretty easy to learn some neat-sounding tricks without understanding how to use them musically. You will learn some of the more important rock guitar playing techniques that can give your musicianship a distinctive quality, allowing you freedom of expression.

In this chapter...

✓ Hammering-on and pulling-off

✓ Finger tapping

✓ String bending

✓ Vibrato

✓ Sliding around

✓ Harmonics

Hammering-on and pulling-off

FUNDAMENTAL TO THE ROCK SOUND, *the hammering-on technique is used in every form of guitar music.*

This effect is produced by moving a left-hand finger to a higher fret on the same string while that string is still sounding.

In other words, a second, higher note is played without picking the note with your right hand. An opposite technique to hammering-on is pulling-off. This effect is achieved by playing a fretted note and releasing a left-hand finger to sound a lower note. Hammering and pulling techniques can be used for playing single notes or chords.

Hammering-on a single note

Try out the hammer-on by following these simple steps:

1 Put your first finger on the 5th fret of the 1st string. This note is A.

2 Strike the 1st string with your pick.

3 While the string vibrates, quickly put your third finger on the 7th fret of the 1st string. This note is B.

4 Let that note ring.

> ### Trivia...
> *In classical guitar tuition, the hammer-on is called a ligado; the pull-off is a descending ligado.*

■ **Fretting** *an A.*

■ **Hammering-on** *on the B-string.*

Pulling-off a single note

Now try the reverse of that technique – the pull-off.

1 Put your first finger on the 9th fret of the 1st string. This note is D♭.

2 Put your fourth finger on the 12th fret of the 1st string. This note is E.

3 Strike the 1st string with your pick.

4 While the string vibrates, remove your fourth finger from it, allowing the note D♭ to ring.

INTERNET

www.ultimateguitarpage.
com/technique

For more information on hammer-ons and pull-offs, as well as the lowdown on other techniques, too.

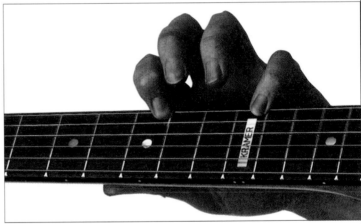

■ **Fretting** *an E.*

■ **Pulling-off** *to D♭.*

Hammering-on and pulling-off techniques

Track 58

Using a familiar backing track from the CD (track 58), you can practice the minor pentatonic scale you learned in Chapter 17, but this time you can hammer-on and pull-off some of the notes.

As a warm-up for the exercise, listen to the backing track (track 59 on the CD) without playing along. Then play along with it by simply strumming the chords. The chart is shown below. Now you're ready to add the special effects!

You'll start by playing the D-minor pentatonic scale over the D-minor chord. These are quarter notes, so they are played on each beat. Pick only the first and third notes of each bar; the second and fourth notes will be hammered-on. The diagram below (and those to follow) will make things clear: At the bottom of the page is a fretboard chart showing you an overhead view of the fingering on the fretboard; alongside you can see how the written music and tablature looks.

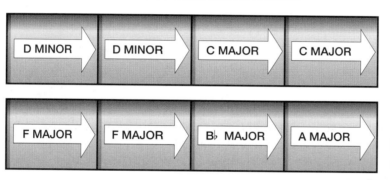

| D MINOR | D MINOR | C MAJOR | C MAJOR |

Track 59

| F MAJOR | F MAJOR | B♭ MAJOR | A MAJOR |

■ Play the exercise using this chord chart.

Hammering-on and pulling-off are shown in written music as two notes joined by a curve. You hammer-on when the letter h is shown and pull-off when the letter p is shown.

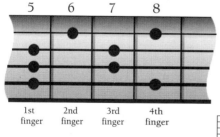

■ Fretboard chart

■ Practice hammering-on and pulling-off with this exercise.

Hammering-on and pulling-off: bars one and two

Once you have the first exercise down, you can speed things up, cramming all eight notes into the first bar. This means that each note is played on the half-beat. You should find it more natural to hammer-on at this speed.

In the second bar, you'll reverse the sequence of notes and use the pull-off technique. Once again, you only pick every other note. The finger positions are the same as in the fretboard chart at the bottom of the opposite page. Remember, to pull-off notes, both fretting fingers must be in the correct position.

■ **Speed it** *up now.*

■ **Remember** *only to pick every second note in this exercise.*

Using the major pentatonic scale: bars three and four

The scale you'll use over bars three and four (and on all the other bars on this track) is not quite the same as the minor pentatonic, although it still uses only five different notes. This is the major pentatonic scale mentioned in Chapter 17. This scale uses notes from the major scale but leaves out the fourth and seventh notes of that scale. The pattern of intervals from root to octave is:

Step • Step • Step+Half-Step • Step • Step+Half-Step • Step • Step

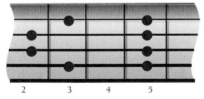

For example, from root to octave, the C-major pentatonic uses the notes C, D, E, G, A, and C. Play the sequence shown below.

■ **Fretboard chart** *showing fingering for the C-major pentatonic scale.*

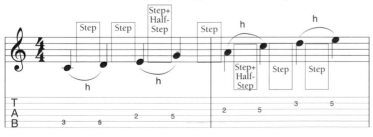

■ **Play the major** *pentatonic scale with this exercise.*

Using the major pentatonic scale: the other bars

Track
60

The other bars use the chords F major, Bb major, and A major. Play the appropriate major pentatonic scales in the same way as above by following the three fretboard diagrams.

Putting it together

Now that you've worked out the individual bars, you can play the sequence from beginning to end. Listen to track 60 on the CD to hear how it should sound.

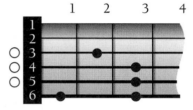

■ **Fretboard chart** *showing fingering for the F-major pentatonic scale.*

■ **Now play** *the whole sequence with the backing track.*

HAMMERING-ON CHORDS

Hammering-on and pulling-off techniques can be applied to chords as well as single notes. In this example, you can bar the 2nd, 3rd, and 4th strings with the first finger, and hammer-on a second bar with the third finger.

1 Create a first-finger bar across the 5th fret.

2 Play the 2nd, 3rd, and 4th strings with the pick. This is a C-major chord.

3 While the chord is still sounding, hammer-on a bar on the 7th fret using your third finger. This creates a chord of D major.

■ **Bar on** *the 5th fret.*

■ **Hammering** *the bar.*

Hammering-on and pulling-off bars is pretty simple using this method. But you can also hammer-on a variety of chord shapes on top of a first-finger bar. Here is an alternative that involves hammering-on a specific chord shape.

1 Create a first-finger bar on the 5th fret.

2 Play the 2nd, 3rd, and 4th strings with the pick. This is a C-major chord.

3 While the chord is still sounding, hammer-on the 6th fret of the 2nd string with your second finger, and hammer-on the 7th fret of the 4th string with your third finger. This creates an inversion of F major.

■ **Using the** *techniques you have learned, try hammering a chord shape.*

Here's a chord-hammering exercise that you can play over the backing track (61 on the CD). Look at the tablature beneath the music to see the fret positions you need to find.

Track

61

■ **Try this chord-hammering** *exercise with tablature.*

255

Finger tapping

FINGER TAPPING (or fret tapping, as some folks prefer) is an extension of the hammering-on and pulling-off techniques. Tapping technique uses a right-hand finger rather than a pick to "tap" a note on the fretboard, hold that note, and then pull-off onto another note. Although this technique has become a rock-guitar cliché, tapping remains popular for guitarists who prize speed – there's no faster way to play!

Tapping the simple one-finger way

Here's an example that shows you how to do a simple tapping technique.

1 Put your first finger on the 5th fret of the 2nd string.

2 Pluck the string close to the 10th fret with the first finger of your right hand. Let the note ring. This note is E.

3 While the note is still ringing, hammer-on at the 7th fret with the second finger of your left hand. Let the new note ring. This note is F♯.

4 While that note is still ringing, tap on the 10th fret by pressing the first finger of your right hand down onto the fretboard. Let the note ring. This note is A.

5 With your left hand still in position, pull-off the 10th fret by releasing the first finger of your right hand, giving the string a slight pluck as you pull your finger away. The pitch of the note returns to the note F♯.

■ **Tapping a** *single note.*

> ## Trivia...
>
> Top tappers include Eddie Van Halen, Steve Vai, and Joe Satriani. The man who started it all is widely thought to have been U.S. session man Harvey Mandel. He experimented with the idea on his Shangrenade album in the early 1970s. A related technique is used by jazz musician Stanley Jordan who plays the guitar on his lap – rather like a piano keyboard – and presses down on the strings with both hands. It's an impressive sight to behold – and it doesn't sound bad, either!

Tapping notes the trickier two-finger way

Here is a quite-tricky exercise that you may find difficult to play at first. You'll follow a left-hand hammer-on with a right-hand hammer-on. In effect, only the first note is played in the conventional way by the right hand, the remaining three are all hammered-on. The notes are then pulled-off again.

The five bars of music shown below can be played over the backing track (CD track 62 Play the following example over D minor. This example, which covers only the first bar, should enable you to figure out the remaining four bars, all of which work in the same way. Simple!

1 Put the first finger of your left hand on the 7th fret of the 3rd string.

2 Pluck the string with the first finger of your right hand at the 10th fret.

3 While the note is ringing, hammer-on at the 9th fret of the 3rd string with the third finger of the left hand.

4 While the note is still ringing, tap on the 10th fret of the 3rd string with the first finger of your right hand.

5 While that note can still be heard, tap on the 12th fret of the 3rd string with the second finger of your right hand.

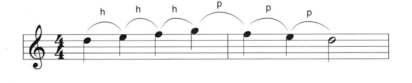

6 Pull off each finger in turn to play the sequence of notes in reverse.

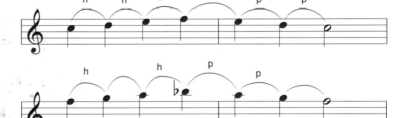

■ **Two-finger** *finger-tapping exercise.*

String bending

STRING BENDING IS A BASIC but effective technique used by electric guitarists in all types of music, especially in rock and blues styles. As you might guess from the name, this technique involves playing a fretted note and then bending the string with your left hand to alter the pitch.

The string-bending technique is affected by the thickness of the string on the guitar. In short, the lighter the gauge (that means the thinner the string), the easier it will be to execute the bend.

Perfecting your string-bending technique

The basic string-bending technique is simple, you just pull or push the fretting finger up or down. Try this exercise.

1 Fret the 5th fret of the 3rd string with the third finger of your right hand to sound the note C.

2 While the note is ringing, push the string firmly upwards until the pitch increases by a tone to the note D.

■ **Fretting** *a C.*

■ **Bending** *to a D.*

Using the pre-bending technique

You can also bend down to play a note lower in pitch than the one you started with, called the pre-bending technique. To do this, you have to bend the string to a new note *before* you strike it. You then release the tension and bring it back to its natural position. This is a much tougher proposition since you have to be able to assess the correct pitch of the first note before you actually hear it.

1 Put your third finger on the 5th fret of the 2nd string, and push the string upwards.

2 Hold the bend in position, and strike the string with your pick.

3 While the note is ringing, slowly push the string back to the regular 5th-fret position.

Bending multiple strings

You can also bend more than one string at the same time.

1 Put your second finger on the 7th fret of the 3rd string.

2 Put your third finger on the 7th fret of the 2nd string.

3 Strike the 2nd and 3rd strings together with your pick.

4 While the notes are still ringing, push both fingers down.

Track

63

■ **Fingers** *in position, ready to bend the strings.*   ■ **Fingers** *bending the strings.*

You can bend a string either by pushing upward or pulling downward. This is a matter of personal preference, although it's not a good idea to push the top string upward or pull the bottom string downward. In both cases, your fingers will invariably slip off the fretboard.

The three different types of bends can be heard on track 63 of the CD.

Vibrato

A MUSIC EFFECT RELATED TO *string bending is vibrato. Literally meaning "to shake," vibrato is the sound created by minute variations in pitch on either side of a note. It can be used to intensify the impact of single notes within a solo.*

There are several ways in which vibrato can be produced on the guitar. One way is to rock your finger back and forth along the length of the string. This is done not by moving the finger itself, but by moving your whole hand.

This movement is extremely slight, making the variation in pitch barely audible – more of gentle wobbling sound.

A fuller-bodied vibrato can be created by rocking your finger across rather than along the string – more of a gentle form of string bending.

■ **A vibrato effect** *is achieved by moving the finger rapidly side to side.*

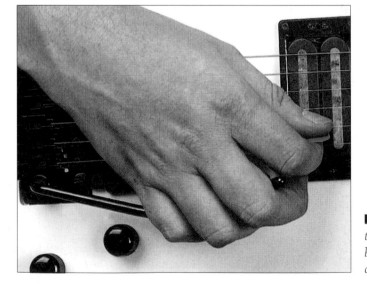

■ **Tremolo arms** *are used to produce bends that would be impossible to achieve using conventional means.*

Track
64

Sliding around

THE TERM "SLIDE" CAN HAVE *several different meanings for a guitarist. It can mean running one or more fingers of the left hand along the length of a string. It can also mean playing the guitar with a glass or metal tube fitted over one of the fingers of the left hand to achieve a similar effect. It can even be the name applied to that glass or metal tube.*

There are many different fingered slide effects, but two are more commonly used than others: sliding to a new fret and sliding to a struck note.

Here is an exercise for sliding to a new fret.

1 Put your first finger on the 7th fret of the 1st string.

2 Play the note.

3 While the note is ringing, move your hand firmly along the fretboard until your first finger is on the 12th fret.

Track
65

This next exercise is for sliding to a struck note:

When sliding to a struck note, you play the note on the 12th fret – this results in two picked notes.

On track 65 of the CD you can hear the straight slide followed by the same slide to a struck note.

■ **Many guitarists** *use a metal tube as a slide.*

Harmonics

WE HAVE BRIEFLY *touched on harmonics in Chapter 7 already (see page 123). Harmonics are bell-like tones produced by damping the strings with the left hand at specific frets before playing them.*

Natural harmonics

Harmonics occur over most of the frets on the fretboard, but the most clearly audible are located on the 5th, 7th, and 12th frets. Harmonics on the 12th fret are an octave higher than the open strings. Harmonics on the 5th fret create notes that are two octaves higher than the open strings. The 7th fret produces harmonics that are an octave plus a perfect 5th above the open strings.

SLIDE GUITAR

Slide, or "bottleneck," guitar began when early blues players found that they could imitate the expressiveness of the human voice by sliding the neck of a glass bottle along the strings. Slide playing can be integrated with regular guitar tuning and is also very effective with some of the altered tunings shown on page 246. Slides come in many shapes, sizes, and materials, although glass produces a cleaner sound than metal.

A

A Nickel *half-slide*
B Rickenbacker *lap-steel guide*
C Glass *slide*
D Metal tube *slide*

C **D**

Many slide players wear their bottleneck on the fourth finger of their left hand. This allows the other fingers to be used to fret notes or chords in the usual way. To play in tune, the slide must always be placed directly above the fret of the note required.

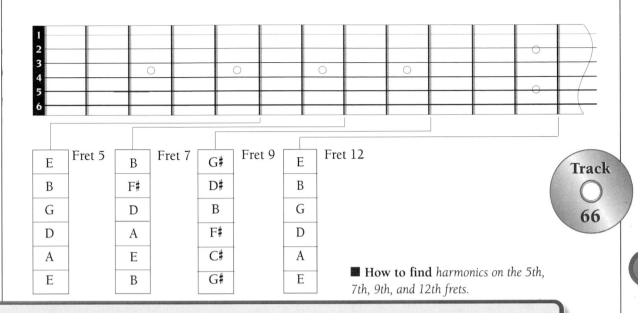

E	Fret 5
B	
G	
D	
A	
E	

B	Fret 7
F#	
D	
A	
E	
B	

G#	Fret 9
D#	
B	
F#	
C#	
G#	

E	Fret 12
B	
G	
D	
A	
E	

Track

66

■ **How to find** *harmonics on the 5th, 7th, 9th, and 12th frets.*

If the slide is not correctly positioned, the note will be either flat or sharp.

When you attempt to play slide guitar, don't lean the slide at an angle across the fretboard because if you are playing chords, they won't be in tune.

Also, if you press the slide too hard on the strings, you will get a variety of buzzing noises. You can overcome this by raising the action – the height of the strings – of the instrument (see page 396).

Follow this example using standard tuning (that is, EADGBE). You can hear it on CD track 66.

1 Hold the slide over the 2nd fret, and pick the 2nd, 3rd, and 4th strings with your right hand. This is an inverted A-major chord.

2 While the notes are ringing, slowly move the slide long the fretboard until it is directly above the 14th fret. This sounds the same chord, one octave higher.

■ **Here, the player** *wears the slide on the fourth finger.*

■ **You must position** *the slide correctly, or else your note will either be flat or sharp.*

Artificial harmonics

You can also produce artificial, or fretted, harmonics for any fretted note. To do this, you fret notes with your left hand and create the harmonic by simultaneously damping and plucking the string with your right hand.

1 Put the first finger of your left hand on the 2nd fret of the 2nd string.

2 Gently put the first finger of your right hand over the 14th fret, and at the same time pluck the note with your right thumb.

The harmonic is generated because the 14th fret is one octave higher than the 2nd fret. In this example, fretted harmonics could also be created on the 7th and 9th frets.

All together now!

Here is a solo sequence that you can play over the backing track (67 on the CD) integrating most of the techniques you've been shown throughout the chapter.

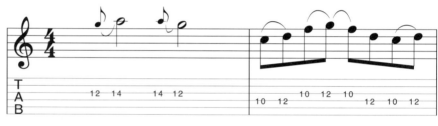

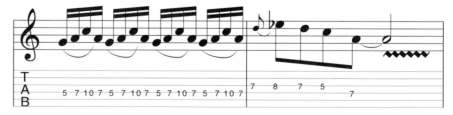

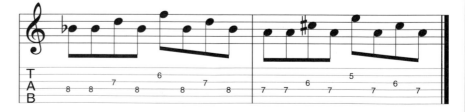

RECOGNIZING EFFECTS IN WRITTEN MUSIC

All of the playing effects you've learned in this chapter are indicated by special notations in written formal music, as shown in this diagram. You'll need to know some of these to play the solo provided in the next section.

BENDING UP

BENDING DOWN

VIBRATO

SLIDING TO A STUCK NOTE

SLIDING BETWEEN NOTES

A simple summary

✓ A hammer-on is produced by fretting a higher note while the note you have just played is still ringing.

✓ In addition to single notes, the hammer-on technique can also be applied to chords.

✓ Finger tapping is a further modification of the hammering-on and pulling-off techniques, and is highly effective when playing fast passages.

✓ String bending is one of the most common guitar techniques, especially in rock and blues.

✓ When playing slide guitar, the slide should be placed directly over a fret when sounding a note.

Chapter 19

Country Styles

COUNTRY MUSIC is one of the most popular of musical forms, and the guitar is at the heart of most of its greatest recordings. There is no all-encompassing style that can be termed "country," so here we'll concentrate on the traditional strumming styles associated with the Country-and-Western genre. Within C&W there are many variations on straight strumming, for example the "bass-strum" rhythm or "country swing."

In this chapter...

✓ Separating the bass notes

✓ Playing country swing

✓ Altering the time signature

✓ Clementine

✓ Sophisticated bass parts

✓ Country chord techniques

✓ She'll Be Coming Round the Mountain

GARTH BROOKS IS AT THE HEART OF COUNTRY MUSIC

Separating the bass notes

THE MOST BASIC COUNTRY RHYTHM *uses simple, open-string chords accompanied by separate bass notes – usually the root notes of the chords. You can hear how this works by following the diagram and exercise below. Play both the single notes and the chords using downstrokes of the pick.*

1 Form an open E-major chord.

2 Count out a beat in 4/4 time.

3 On the first beat of the bar, strike only the 6th string.

4 On the second beat of the bar, strum across the remaining five strings.

5 On the third beat, play only the 6th string again.

6 On the fourth beat, strum across the remaining five strings again.

7 Repeat the exercise until you can play it with a nice, flowing rhythm.

■ **Great guitar:**
the Gibson SJ 200.

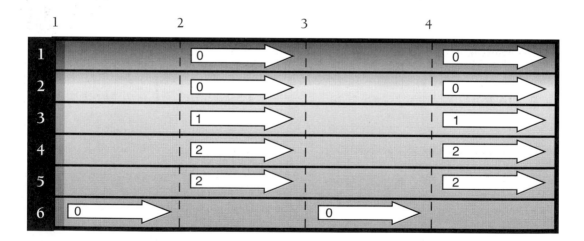

■ **This exercise** *will help you separate the bass notes.*

Now following those steps again, but with an open A-major chord, as shown in the diagram below. This time pick the open 5th string on the first and third beats, and strum across the top four strings on the second and fourth beats.

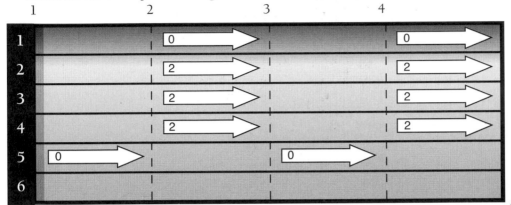

■ **This time use** *an open A-major chord.*

■ **The country player**
Chet Atkins is renowned for his finger picking; this is the 1990 Gibson Chet Atkins SST.

Track
68

Now put the two together. Work through the chord chart between E and A as shown. You can hear how this should sound on track 68 of the CD.

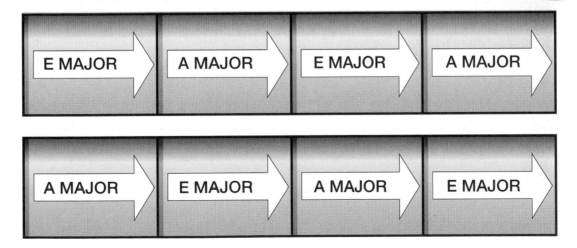

■ **Practice playing** *E and A major chords.*

Playing country swing

ON A LOT OF COUNTRY SONGS, *you'll hear the bass-strum rhythm played slightly differently – with a slight swinging feel to it. This is often known as country swing.*

The difference between simple bass-strum rhythm and country swing is that, in country swing the chords played on the second and fourth beats of the bar are subdivided. The quarter note is divided into a dotted eighth note (giving it a value of three-quarters of a beat) and a sixteenth note (giving it a value of a quarter of a beat). The first chord is still played as a downstroke, but the second, shorter chord follows as an upstroke.

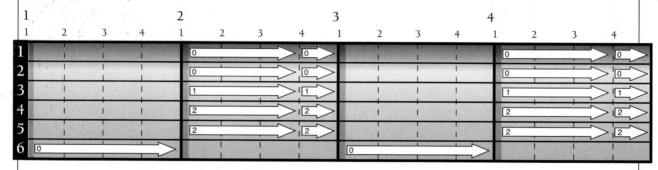

■ **This exercise** *will help you get to grips with the country swing rhythm.*

That's a rather wordy way of introducing a familiar rhythm. If we say that it has a "boom-chugga-boom" rhythm, you'll probably understand immediately.

This exercise is played with a country-swing rhythm. You can hear how it sounds on track 69 of the CD.

Track

69

Altering the time signature

UP TO THIS POINT, *all the exercises and examples you've played have been in 4/4 (four-four) time. This means that the notated music has the numbers 4 over 4 at the start of the staff and that there are four beats in every bar. Although 4/4 is the most common time signature by far, it's by no means the only one. Country music – especially the ballad – is often played in 3/4 time.*

This means that the numbers 3 over 4 are shown at the start of the staff, and that there are three beats in the bar.

If you count out from one to three in a repeating cycle (emphasizing the first beat), you'll get the idea of how this time signature swings along.

■ **Designed by** *Merle Travis and Paul Bigsby, this unique instrument suits the needs of requirements of country music.*

Clementine

NOW YOU'RE READY to put everything together by playing Clementine, a traditional American folk song, shown below. You can play this song in 3/4 time using a country-swing rhythm – it's nice and simple because it only uses two chords: A and E7.

Track

70

There's a bonus exercise built into the music diagram, too. You can see in the music below that there are two linked lines of staff – the bottom line contains the chord rhythms for you to work through, the top line contains the melody. You can listen to the piece on track 70 of the CD. Get the chords and the rhythm right to start with. After you've mastered those, why not have a crack at the melody itself?

If you are feeling really confident, you can also sing along while you are playing – the lyrics are included after the diagram on the facing page. You don't even need the backing track for this as country music often has very basic arrangements. When you're starting out, playing and singing at the same time can seem like an impossibility. But you'll be surprised at how quickly your left hand becomes accustomed to chord shapes, and how your right hand can automatically figure out pick patterns. With practice, both hands will work automatically, leaving you free to think about your singing.

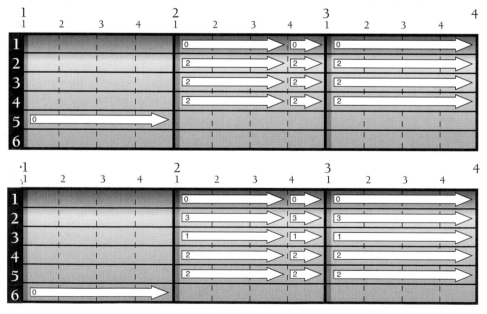

A CHORD (TOP) AND E7 CHORD (BOTTOM)

Clementine

In a cavern, in a canyon,
Excavating for a mine,
Dwelt a miner, forty-niner, and his
Daughter Clementine.

Light she was and like a fairy, and her
Shoes were number nine,
Herring boxes without topses, sandals
Were for Clementine.

Drove she ducklings to the water every
Morning just at nine,
Hit her foot against a splinter, fell into
The foaming brine.

Ruby lips above the water blowing
Bubbles soft and fine,
But alas I was no swimmer, so I lost my
Clementine.

In a churchyard near the canyon where
The myrtle doth entwine,
There grow roses, pretty roses, fertilized
By Clementine

Then the miner, forty-niner, soon began
To peak and pine
Thought he oughtta join his daughter,
Now he's with his Clementine.

In my dreams she still doth haunt me,
Robed in garment soaked with brine
Though in life I used to hug her, now
She's dead I draw the line.

How I missed her, how I missed her,
How I missed my Clementine,
Till I kissed her little sister and forgot
My Clementine.

Sophisticated bass parts

YOU CAN MAKE THE FUNDAMENTAL bass-strum rhythm more interesting by playing bass notes on the first and third beats with a bit of a twist. One approach is to alternate the root bass note with other notes from the chord, creating a "bouncing" bass line. A more demanding alternative is to integrate other notes from the same scale, linking chords together with a little flourish of bass notes.

Alternating bass notes

To play an alternating, or bouncing, bass line, use the same rhythm as shown previously in this chapter but instead of playing the root note on the third beat of the bar, choose a different note from the same chord.

The note that works best with most chords is the perfect fifth. This example uses an open A-major chord and 4/4 time, the basic country rhythm.

1 Strike the open 5th string (the root note, A) on the first beat of the bar.

2 On the second beat, strum across the top four strings.

3 On the third beat, strike the open 6th string (the perfect 5th, E).

4 On the fourth beat, strum across the top four strings.

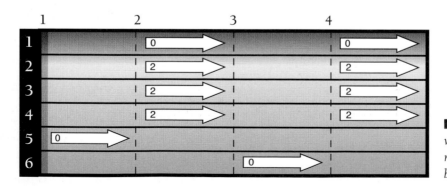

■ **This exercise** *will help you play more sophisticated bass notes.*

Track

71

Play through this next example, using the chords A major, D major, and E major. When playing the D-major chord, alternate between the open 4th string (D) and the open 5th string (A). For the E-major chord, alternate between the open 6th string (E) and the fretted 5th string (B). You can hear this sequence played on track 71 of the CD.

Adding a bass run

■ **Play the** *A major, D major, and E major chords.*

An even neater way of moving the bass notes around is to link the chords with a simple bass run, a sequence of notes taken from the same scale as the chord. Think of almost any Johnny Cash song, and you'll get the idea. Let's look at how that works using the example above. This time, you'll replace every other bar with a run of four notes that links the root of one chord to the root of another. The first two bars now look like this:

INTERNET

www.netradio.com/learn/country/index.html

Want to know more about the styles that are a part of this genre? Descriptions of styles include key recordings channels where you can listen.

■ **Link the chords** *with a bass run.*

Here's how you play the second bar step by step:

1 Play the open 5th string (A) on the first beat.

2 On the second beat, play the open 5th string (A).

3 On the third beat, play the 2nd fret of the 5th string (B).

4 On the fourth beat, play the 4th fret of the 5th string (C♯).

Using the the D chord, play the third bar.

If you recall the scales shown in Chapter 15, you'll notice here that in moving from A to D, you are using the first four notes of the A-major scale to get from A to D (A, B, C♯, and D).

You can also do bass runs that go down in pitch. For example, when moving from D to E, you can use the last four notes of a descending E-major scale in a similar way. Play the last two sets of exercises over the top of the backing track (track 72 of the CD).

Track

72

■ **This bass** *run uses a descending E-major scale.*

USING OUR FINGERS

Fingerpicking is a right-hand playing technique widely used in country music. There are various ways in which you can play the rhythms shown in this chapter without using a pick. One method is to use the classical right-hand   A THUMBPICK technique in which your thumb plucks the bass strings and your fingers play the individual treble strings. A common variation is for your thumb to pick alternating bass notes while your fingers lightly strum the treble strings. To produce a louder, or more even, sound, some country players use plastic fingerpicks and thumbpicks.

Country chord techniques

YOU HAVE ALREADY SEEN *how hammering-on works with single notes (in Chapter 17). It is also possible to hammer-on single notes from within a chord – a technique popular in Country-and-Western music. You can also integrate this hammering-on with the other rhythms you've learned so far in this chapter.*

Let's try this out with an open E-major chord.

1 Fret an open E-major chord.

2 Lift your second finger off the 2nd fret of the 5th string.

3 Strum the top five strings of the chord.

4 While the notes are ringing, quickly re-fret the 2nd fret of the 5th string with your second finger, creating a full E-major chord once more.

The following 6 diagrams shown below and on page 278 show a complete range of open-string chords for which notes can be hammered-on. In each case, the colored dot represents the note (or notes) to be hammered-on from the open-string position. Of course, the same principles can also be applied to all bar-chord shapes.

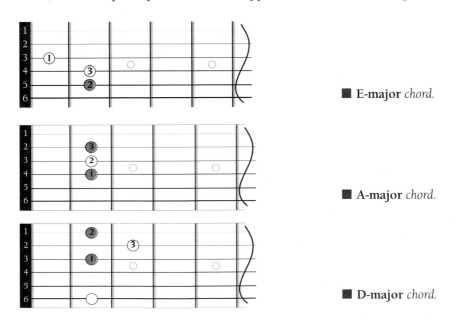

■ **E-major** *chord.*

■ **A-major** *chord.*

■ **D-major** *chord.*

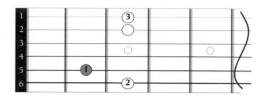

■ **G-major** *chord.*

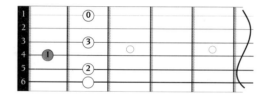

■ **C-major** *chord.*

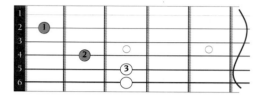

■ **B-major** *chord.*

She'll Be Coming Round the Mountain

To hear these chords in practice, listen to the backing track example, the traditional folk song "She'll Be Coming Round the Mountain," on track 73 of the CD. It contains the chords A major, E major, and D major. The fingering and hammering-on for the chords is shown above. The music shows the melody on the top staff and the guitar part beneath. This arrangement includes alternating bass notes.

Track

73

She'll be coming round the mountain when she comes
She'll be coming round the mountain when she comes
She'll be coming round the mountain, coming round the moutain,
Coming round the mountain when she comes!

Chorus

Singing yi-yi-yippee-yippee-yi
Singing yi-yi-yippee-yippee-i
Singing yi-yi-yippee, yi-yi-yippee
Yi-yi-yippee-yippee-yi!

She'll Be Coming Round the Mountain

A simple summary

✓ Simple, country-style rhythm playing requires little more than open-string chords accompanied by bass notes.

✓ Although 4/4 time is the most common time signature in country music, 3/4 time is also very popular, especially for ballads.

✓ The basic bass-strum rhythm can be made more interesting by alternating the root bass note with other notes from the chord.

✓ The hammer-on can be incorporated into chords as well as in single-note playing.

Chapter 20

Jazz and Latin Styles

JAZZ IS ARGUABLY the most demanding music for any guitarist to play. If you listen to any of its greatest exponents, you will soon realize that the jazz-guitar virtuoso has the technical skills of a classical player, a good understanding of technical theory, and an advanced vocabulary of chords and scales. And of course, the accomplished jazz player also has the requisite imagination necessary to improvise creatively. For the sake of convenience, we've included Latin American playing styles in with jazz. Although Latin styles are clearly musical genres in their own right, there is a fair bit of crossover with jazz, especially in a style such as the Brazilian bossa nova.

This chapter gives you a gentle introduction to a selection of jazz styles in addition to a couple of fairly simple exercises that will give you a good foundation for further development – if that's the way you want to go.

In this chapter...

✓ Approaches to jazz

✓ Jazz progression

✓ Latin American style

JAZZ MAN GEORGE BENSON

Approaches to jazz

THE BEST STARTING POINT *for the fledgling jazz guitarist is to listen carefully to the work of the experts.*

If you are a newcomer to jazz, refer to pages 402–418 for a recommended listening list. Remember that many of the greatest players (and even composers) started life imitating their heroes before finding their own sound and moving on to greater things.

INTERNET

www.jazzguitar.com

…is exactly what you might expect, a site dedicated to jazz guitar.

Jazz progression

THIS AND EACH OF *the following sections present one part of a complete piece composed for the guitar. The top line of the staff in the accompanying diagrams shows the solo, and the bottom line shows the chords. Because both the rhythm and lead parts are fairly complex, tablature is provided under each staff.*

VIP

This tablature shows you exactly which frets and strings you should use for every note.

Start off with the chords, taking it slowly at first. When you are familiar with the one, play it over the jazz backing track (74 on the CD). The lead part is the most challenging solo you'll find in this book, but it's well worth persevering! Don't be too concerned if you can't master it right away – think of it as a goal to work toward.

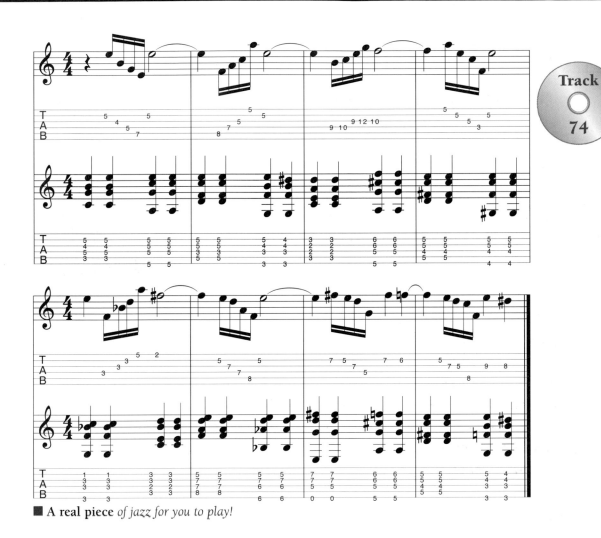

Track 74

■ **A real piece** *of jazz for you to play!*

Latin American style

THE USE OF THE TERM "LATIN AMERICAN" to describe a musical
form is convenient but not entirely appropriate as it is too broad – South and
Central America contain numerous musical cultures, many of them not strongly
related to one another. Similarly, the musics of particular regions within, say,
Central America, are also very different. However, a common factor evident in
much Latin American music is a strong rhythmic content – not so surprising
since much of it is used for dancing.

One of the most popular musical exports from Brazil is the bossa nova. Meaning "new style" in Spanish, the bossa nova evolved in the 1950s as a cross between North American "cool jazz" and the traditional Brazilian samba style. Central to the bossa nova sound is the use of a nylon-string acoustic guitar that is often used to create a harmonic and rhythmic framework for the vocalist.

Track

75

The following example provides a flavor of the bossa nova rhythm. The key element in the sound is the careful syncopation between the bassline, played with the thumb, and the chords played off the beat by the fingers.

Trivia...

One of the finest exponents of the bossa nova is João Gilberto, whose gentle, syncopated guitar work underpins an equally gentle, almost whispered vocal.

■ **João Gilberto** *is a master of the bossa nova style.*

A simple summary

✓ Good technical skills, an understanding of musical theory, and knowledge of chords and scales is required to play jazz effectively.

✓ The term "Latin American" when used to define a musical genre is too broad because it lumps together unrelated styles.

✓ The bossa nova evolved from a merging of North American cool jazz and Brazilian samba.

Chapter 21

Classical Techniques

B Y NOW YOU SHOULD have a reasonable understanding of basic fingering techniques (playing without a pick), even if your fingers are not yet nimble enough to work their way through an entire piece without a few glitches. In this chapter, we'll begin with a few basic finger exercises and then look at some classical guitar pieces selected from the work of Fernando Sor and Ferdinando Carulli, two of the guitar's best-known 19th-century composers, and a piece by Johann Sebastian Bach. As with most traditional classical guitar music, these pieces should be played on a nylon-strung instrument.

In this chapter...

✓ Classical techniques

✓ Open-string free-stroke exercises

✓ Different voices

✓ Playing your first recital

CLASSICAL MASTER JOHN WILLIAMS

Classical techniques

CLASSICAL GUITAR TECHNIQUE *uses the PIMA right-hand fingering system you first encountered on page 168.*

In standard classical technique, two playing strokes are normally used: the free stroke and the rest stroke. In a free stroke, the finger strikes the string in a pulling motion and comes to rest above the adjacent string. The rest stroke is played in the same way, but here the finger comes to rest against the adjacent string.

Open-string free-stroke exercises

TO GET YOU USED TO *playing free strokes, here are two simple exercises. You don't need to worry about fretting notes on the fingerboard – open strings are adequate for this exercise.*

INTERNET

www.guitarist.com/
cg/cg.htm

The classical guitar homepage.

Track

76

The first exercise uses only your thumb. This is indicated by the letter P above the notes on the music. Note that only the bottom three open strings are played.

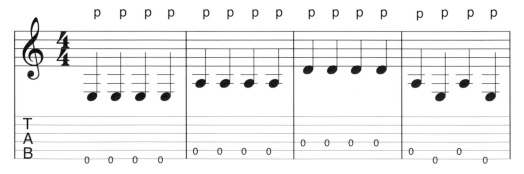

■ **Play this** *exercise on the bottom three open strings.*

Track

77

The second exercise repeats the first one but adds your three right-hand fingers, which play the top three strings. Start practicing the exercise with the IMA fingers only. When you're happy with these, include the bass notes (those played by the thumb), and play the complete exercise as shown below. You can hear both pieces played on tracks 76 and 77 of the CD.

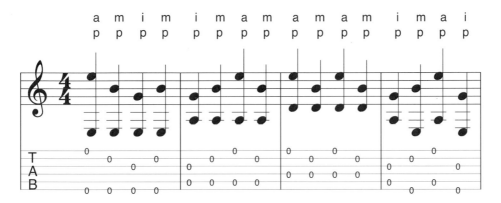

■ **Add your** *three right-hand fingers when you play this exercise.*

Different voices

IF YOU ADD UP THE VALUE *of the notes in bar one of the music on page 290, you will see that it contains four quarter notes and one whole note, which gives a value of eight beats; similarly, the second bar contains four quarter notes and two half notes – again giving a total of eight beats. But as the time signature is 4/4, there should only be four beats in each bar.*

This can occur in written music to allow for situations where two or more notes of different time values are played at the same time.

■ **Made by Greg Williams** *in 1987, the Smallman is a 20th-century classic.*

Track
78

In this example, in the first bar, the whole note middle C sustains for four beats (the whole bar); the first quarter note (C) starts at the same time as the whole note – the other three quarter notes are played on each beat of the bar whilst the whole note is still being sustained. In the second bar, half notes are played on the first and third beats at the same time as the quarter notes are being played on the beat.

■ **This exercise** *will help you play two notes at once.*

Where this occurs, the two notes are shown with stems pointing in opposite directions. Each of these notes is referred to as a separate voice or part. ßHere are two examples of playing with multiple voices. The first was written by Dionisio Aguado and the second by Mauro Giuliani, both pioneering composers of guitar music in the 19th century, long before the guitar was considered a credible classical instrument.

In both cases, the lower voice (with the downward-pointing stem) is played by the thumb (P), and the upper voice is played by the three fingers (IMA). You can hear both examples played on track 79 of the CD.

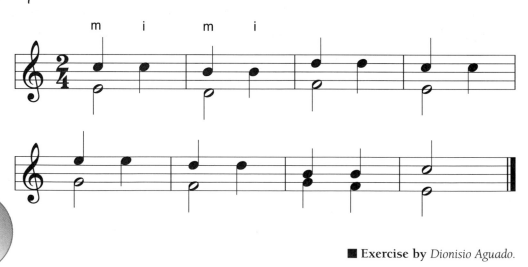

Track
79

■ **Exercise by** *Dionisio Aguado.*

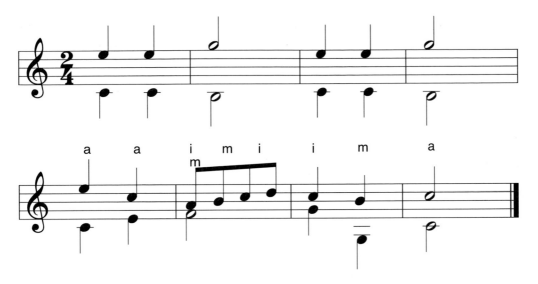

■ **Exercise by** *Mauro Giuliani.*

Playing your first recital

*Okay, that title may be a slight overstatement, but here for your playing pleasure
we proudly present four short classical pieces. You have the technical knowledge to
play all of these pieces, although you'll need to practice each one very carefully if
you want to play them properly. But then again, this is the final playing chapter,
so it seems only right that these should be the toughest exercises you encounter in
the book. You can hear all four pieces played on CD tracks 80–82.*

Study in G by Fernando Sor

Prelude in D by Ferdinando Carulli

Track 81

Minuet in A by Johann Sebastian Bach

Track
82

Waltz in A by Ferdinando Carulli

A simple summary

✓ Traditional classical guitar music is nearly always played on a nylon-strung acoustic guitar.

✓ Classical guitar technique uses the PIMA system for naming the fingers on the right hand.

✓ Classical technique uses two types of right-hand finger stroke: the free stroke and the rest stroke.

PART FIVE

SOUNDS, STUDIO, AND STAGE

Mastering the guitar for your own amusement in the confines of your bedroom is all well and good, but taking your work to an *audience* is a very different matter. Here you will learn the crucial issues you need to know about if you want others to pay to listen to you.

The first two chapters show you how to get the best out of your amplifier and familiarizes you with some of the better-known effects devices. You'll hear how different amplifier settings and effects pedals can change the sound of even the most basic chords. We'll provide you with useful tips for working in a *recording* studio and for recording demo tapes at home and give you pointers on how to make a name for yourself in your area as well as in the recording industry. By now you should be a pretty competent guitarist – easily good enough to form or join a band. So what are you waiting for? Finish the book, and then go and do it.

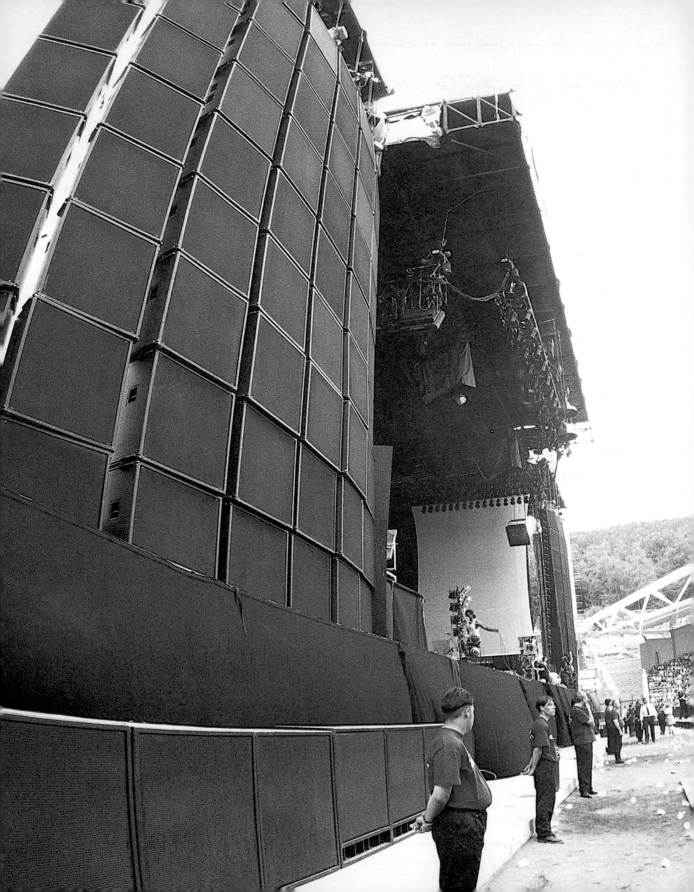

Chapter 22

Amplification

I F YOU HAVE AN ELECTRIC GUITAR you'll also need a combination of an amplifier and a speaker to produce a useful sound. The first amplifiers boosted the volume of the guitar so it could be heard alongside louder acoustic instruments. But guitarists soon began to move toward certain types of amplifiers that exhibited characteristic sounds. Today, the choice of amplifier can be as significant as your choice of guitar in the impact it has on your sound.

In this chapter...

✓ What's in an amplifier?

✓ Some sample sounds

✓ Speakers

✓ Pickups and sound

✓ Direct injection (DI)

✓ Using a speaker simulator

THESE SHOULD MAKE YOUR PLAYING SOUND A LITTLE LOUDER...

THE HISTORY OF THE AMPLIFIER

The earliest amplifiers were built in the 1930s, using basically the same valve technology found in the record players and radios of the day. Their output was pretty meager – usually between 5 and 20 watts. But as electric guitars became more popular, demand grew for louder amplifiers. In 1949, Leo Fender launched the 50-watt, single-speaker Fender Super amp, which was one of the most popular models in the 1950s. Later models, such as the Fender Twin Reverb and the British Vox AC30, added a second speaker. Those amps became popular with blues and early rock musicians not only because of the warmth of their tone, but because of their sound when the valves were overdriven – not a deliberate design feature, but an effect that nonetheless helped define the classic rock-guitar sound.

As rock music became popular and was played in larger auditoriums, even more power was required. That was when British engineer Jim Marshall stepped forward with a 100-watt amplifier connected to a stack of four 12-inch speakers, still known as "four-by-twelves" to this day. The "Marshall stack" became the norm throughout the heavy-rock era. By that time, though, valve technology was deemed to be way out of date – radios were made using cheaper solid-state, transistor circuitry. Guitar manufacturers quickly joined in, but the majority of guitarists hated the change: When valves were overdriven, they sounded warm and lovely and great; transistors produced hideous, howling feedback.

Nevertheless, guitarists of differing breeds have found a place in their hearts for both types of amp. Most serious performance amplifiers feature valves; less expensive models or practice amps – ideal for beginners – are usually solid-state.

What's in an amplifier?

EVERY AMPLIFIER *has at least one input socket. To make a sound, the output of your guitar has to be connected to the input of the amplifier using a guitar cord – a cable with quarter-inch jack plugs at either end. For any sound to come out, the output of the amplifier has to be connected to a suitable speaker.*

■ **The vintage** *4 x 10 Fender Bassman combo.*

Although amplifiers *come in different forms, with different specific features, there are a number of functions common to nearly all types: The pre-amplifier controls the input channel level and tone controls; the power amplifier controls the overall output – the master volume.*

✓ Input channel volume – The volume of the guitar's output signal is first determined by the input channel volume control. This pre-amp stage boosts the output signal and passes it through to the tone controls.

✓ Tone controls – The tone controls work in the same way as the bass and treble controls on your stereo. Most decent amps feature at least a bass, midrange, and treble control. The tonally altered signal is then passed on to the power amplifier.

✓ Master volume – The power amplifier governs the overall volume of the guitar's output signal. This is controlled by the master volume control.

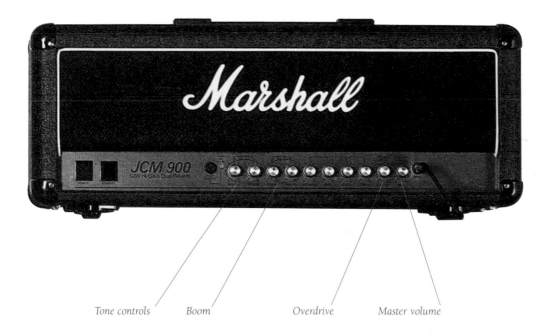

Tone controls   *Boom*   *Overdrive*   *Master volume*

■ **Most amps** *feature similar controls to the one pictured here.*

FOUR THINGS NOT TO DO WITH AN AMPLIFIER AND SPEAKER

Now that you know some amplification basics, here are a few words of warning to preserve your health and safeguard your expensive equipment.

✓ If your amp is an open-backed model, don't poke your hands above and behind the speaker while it's switched on – you may get a very nasty shock.

✓ Amps and speakers make beautiful drink tables – that's what many musicians seem to think, anyway. But beware: Spillage can seep down into the circuitry, which generally reacts badly to such treatment.

✓ Don't kick the speaker grate, no matter how mad you get. It's there to protect the speaker, which, in spite of the immense noise it can generate, is a rather delicate flower that can tear very easily.

✓ Don't be rough with or drop your amp while you're moving it around. Amps may appear to be pretty sturdy beasts, but the electronic circuitry – especially on valve models – can be easily upset.

Valves or solid-state?

If truth be told, we guitarists can be a conservative bunch. By and large, we tend to favor the sound of the classic valve amplifiers which we prize for their warmth, smooth tone, and pleasant overdrive. Most solid-state amplifiers are capable of dealing with a wider range of frequencies than valve amplifiers but have a "brittle" quality to their sound. On the whole, they just don't sound as good.

■ **Valve amps tend to be** *the most highly prized by guitarists.*

Some sample sounds

JUST AS WITH LEARNING TO PLAY THE GUITAR, getting the best out of an amp requires practice.

Spend some time getting to know the way your amplifier works. For example, experiment with different EQ settings, or try overdriving the pre-amplifier to varying degrees by boosting the input channel volume.

To give you an idea of the kinds of sound you might be able to get from your amp, here are five basic amplifier settings. There are four controls to select: input volume, bass, treble, and master volume. Of course, the precise way they sound will depend on the specific model of amp and the guitar you use, but you'll get the idea of how a "clean" sound can be altered by manipulating the controls.

Clean sound

Setting each of the four controls to a central position should produce a classic "clean" sound with little or no distortion. This kind of sound is ideal for simple rhythm-guitar work. If you alter the level of the master volume control, it will boost or cut the overall volume without changing the basic sound.

Track

84

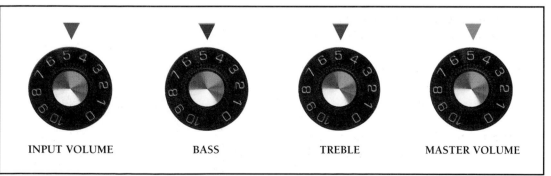

INPUT VOLUME   BASS   TREBLE   MASTER VOLUME

CLASSIC, CLEAN SETTING

Treble sound

Track

85

If you increase the treble control, the guitar will produce a brighter, trebly sound. By boosting the treble, you are also increasing the overall volume of the sound, and so you may want to reduce the master volume control setting to compensate. This is a nice, clean, country-ish setting.

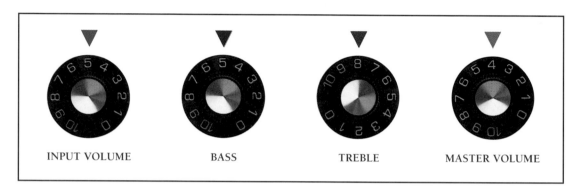

INPUT VOLUME   BASS   TREBLE   MASTER VOLUME

COUNTRY-STYLE SETTING

Gentle distortion

Track

86

Increasing the input volume causes the pre-amp stage to begin distorting. By boosting the input volume, you are also increasing the overall volume, and so you may want to reduce the master volume to compensate. The bass is increased to produce a better all-round sound. This is a good, thrashy rock-guitar setting.

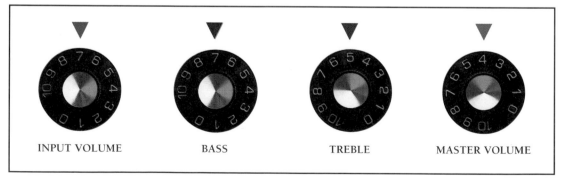

INPUT VOLUME   BASS   TREBLE   MASTER VOLUME

ROCK-GUITAR SETTING

Maximum distortion

Track
○
87

With the input volume on full, the pre-amplifier distorts as much as it can. The additional increase in treble produces a cutting, lead-guitar sound. The bass sound is not so important in maximum distortion where you are looking to increase the raspy sound produced by increasing the treble.

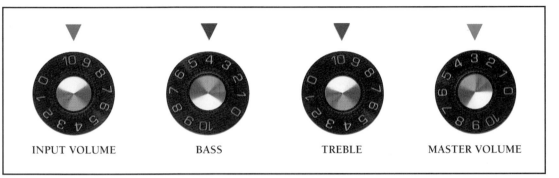

LEAD-GUITAR SETTING

Muffled distortion

Track
○
88

Reducing the treble produces a muffled sound. This results in a loss of volume which is balanced by boosting the master volume. This is also a lead-guitar effect, and it will work best with a valve amplifier. Here you are only interested in the relative effect of the treble on the sound, so the bass is not increased.

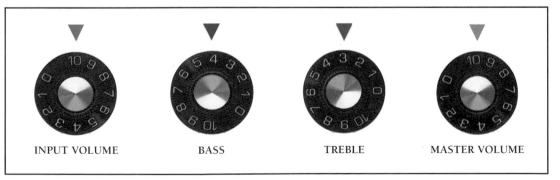

ANOTHER GOOD LEAD-GUITAR SETTING

Knobs on your guitar

Most electric guitars are equipped with, at the very least, a volume and a basic tone control. Strangely, though, many players rarely touch these controls, leaving them permanently on "full" and choosing to make tonal and volume changes only on the amplifier.

The problem with using the guitar controls is that it can be difficult to get precise settings, but it's always worth experimenting. For example, cutting treble is a good way of overcoming feedback problems. The volume control is sometimes used to create "swell" effects – for example, playing a note with the volume turned off and then quickly fading the volume up while the note is still ringing.

Speakers

■ **For a different** *type of sound, try adjusting the controls on your guitar.*

A SPEAKER IS BASICALLY a microphone in reverse. It consists of four basic elements: a cardboard cone, a diaphragm, a magnet, and a voice coil. The voice coil is positioned between the poles of the magnet. When the coil receives the signal from the output of an amplifier, it generates a magnetic field that causes the diaphragm (and hence the cone) to vibrate. This movement disturbs the surrounding airwaves, and creates an audible noise.

Like microphones, speakers are rated in terms of their impedance value. This is measured in units of electrical resistance – ohms. Most speakers designed for use with guitar amplifiers are rated as 8 ohms or 15–16 ohms.

If you're connecting your own speaker cabinets, pay careful attention to these values – they're critical to the sound and volume. Most (although by no means all) guitar amps are designed to use 8-ohm speakers. If you connect a 15–16-ohm speaker, the higher electrical resistance will reduce the overall output volume and alter tonal characteristics.

Pickups and sound

ONE FINAL AND IMPORTANT *aspect that will affect your sound is your choice of pickup position. As we have already noted, there are two types of pickup in common use – the single-coil and the double-coil (or humbucker) – each of which can create very different types of sounds.*

Because a guitar string vibrates in different ways at different points along its length, the sound will change dramatically depending on where the pickup is positioned. This is why most electric guitars have at least two pickups that you can choose using a selector switch.

The pickup closest to the bridge creates the brightest sound – it's often called the bridge, back, or lead pickup. The pickup closer to the start of the fingerboard – called the rhythm pickup – creates a mellower sound. Listen to track 89 on the CD to hear the difference between the same musical example played first on the bridge pickup and then on the rhythm pickup.

Track

89

■ **Remember that** *your pickup position will affect the sound quality.*

Direct injection (DI)

NO, WE HAVEN'T MYSTERIOUSLY *moved on to discuss automobile engines. Direct injection, or DI, refers to plugging an instrument directly into an input channel on a mixing board. So, you may think, you don't always need an amplifier. Or do you? The answer is a very big yes.*

The clean signal that comes out of your guitar will sound horrid when plugged straight into a mixing board. It'll be lifeless and clinical and . . . uh, just don't do it, okay?

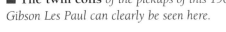

■ **The twin coils** *of the pickups of this 1960 Gibson Les Paul can clearly be seen here.*

Using a speaker simulator

THERE IS AN ALTERNATIVE *to direct injection that is becoming increasingly popular with guitarists – the use of a speaker simulator. This is a unit that's connected between the speaker output of the amplifier and the mixing board. Essentially, what you get is the sound of the amplifier but at a controllable volume.*

For example, powerful valve amplifiers need to be played at high volumes to achieve their characteristic overdrive. In an enclosed environment, this may result in deafening volume and unwanted feedback. By recording via a speaker simulator, you not only bypass these problems, but you can also accurately monitor the sound being recorded. For live use, it gives the sound engineer greater control than can be achieved by miking up a speaker cabinet.

■ **Speaker simulators** *are placed between the amp and the mixing board to give a better tone of sound.*

Purists, of course, reject this entirely. But speaker simulators are worth investigating, especially where loud noise becomes problematic.

By the way, never plug the speaker output from an amplifier directly into a mixing board without it first passing through a speaker simulator or other device that "soaks" the amplifier's output – you'll blow the input channel on the mixing board (and goodness knows what else).

■ **The classic amp:** *the Marshall.*

■ **The Gibson** *ES-175 plus amp.*

INTERNET

**www.sound.au.com/
project27.htm**

*There is no amp that satisfies
everyone's requirements, and
this site tells you how to
build your own 100-watt
amp that you can modify to
suit your own needs. Of
course, great care is required
when undertaking any
project of this kind.*

A simple summary

✓ If you use an electric guitar,
you'll need an amp and speaker
(and a guitar cord) to hear it in
all its glory. But you knew all
that, of course!

✓ Some amps have built-in
speakers – these are called
combos. An amp without
speakers is called a head.

✓ Amplifiers create their sound
using valves (or tubes),
transistors (solid-state circuitry),
or a combination of two.

✓ You can create a distorted sound
on a valve amplifier by
overdriving the pre-amplifier.

Chapter 23

Altering Your Sound

THE KINDS OF SOUNDS that can be made with even modest guitar setups have gone through the roof in recent years. Early electro-pioneers in the 1940s were just grateful for the chance to be heard alongside the other instruments in the band. The engineers of the day were only concerned with amplifying the signal while trying to retain the acoustic sound of the instrument. During the early 1950s players realized they could create vastly different sounds using their amps. For the guitar, this was the birth of the electric era. It would only be a matter of time before other, more radical ways of modifying a guitar sound would be sought.

In this chapter...

✓ Effects units

✓ Reverberation

✓ Delay effects

✓ Tonal effects

✓ Using effects

WOOF!

VIBRATO?

Effects units

BY THE TIME A GUITAR SIGNAL bursts out of the loudspeaker, it has already been significantly altered by the characteristics of the amplifier itself. In this chapter of the book, however, we're more interested in those mysterious add-ons that really mess up those traditional sounds. Whether they are simple, hand-sized foot pedals or painfully expensive digital black boxes, these effects units enable the guitarist to produce a vastly greater range of sounds than could be achieved with just an amplifier and guitar. Indeed, it's no exaggeration to say that many of the most familiar guitar sounds can only be achieved with some sort of effects unit.

Effects units come in all shapes and sizes, but the kinds of sounds they create can be placed into three broad categories:

✓ Reverberation
✓ Delay
✓ Tone alteration

Most of the effects used by guitarists are cheaper, less sophisticated versions of those used in studio recording.

■ **The function of** *a compressor is to adjust the guitar's volume to required level during recording.*

■ **Effects units** *give the guitarist a much-increased range of sounds.*

Reverberation

WHEN YOU ADD *reverberation to a dry guitar signal, this "reverb" creates the ambient effect of the sound spreading out.*

The original, simulated-reverb units of the 1950s used a spring that was vibrated by the guitar signal. Generally, these units made vaguely amusing clunky noises – although they were far preferable to the deeply unpleasant electronic analog units that appeared in the following decades. Nowadays, digital reverb is the norm, with even the most basic units allowing the luxury of creating the effect of sound bouncing around in rooms of different sizes, or simulating the time it takes for the signal to decay and fade away.

Track

90

Listen to track 90 of the CD to hear the following variety of common reverb effects:

1 Small room, low decay

2 Large room, medium decay

3 Large room, long decay

4 Auditorium, long decay

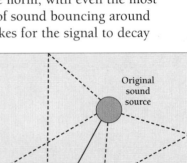

Original sound source

Listener

■ **How reverberation** *works.*
→ *Direct sound (original source)*
----→ *Early reflections (first bounce from surfaces)*
——→ *Late reflections (subsequent bounces)*

■ **There is not** *much natural reverb in The Cavern (of The Beatles' fame).*

Delay effects

DELAY IS ALSO A NATURAL EFFECT – *think of an echo, for example, which is the sound of a reflection from a distant surface. Many of the most popular effects are variations on the idea of processing a repeated signal. In the old days, delay effects were created by passing a loop of quarter-inch tape across a series of record and playback heads – a system based on a tape recorder. Once again, though, digital technology has moved things to amazing new heights.*

Different types of delay effects can be created depending on the length of the delay and the way in which the delayed signals are processed.

A delay of between 7 and 12 milliseconds is called phasing; between 12 and 20 milliseconds is called flanging; chorus and automatic double-tracking (ADT) effects are possible between 20 and 35 milliseconds; anything over 35 milliseconds constitutes an echo.

A good digital delay unit can produce all of these effects, although foot pedals are usually built to create specific types of delay effect.

Phasing and flanging

A visual interpretation of a sound wave shows a line that passes through peaks and troughs.

Track

O

91

When two identical signals are played back slightly out of alignment so that the peaks on one signal coincide with the troughs on another, a gentle sweeping sound called phasing results. If the delay is greater, the sweep becomes more dramatic, creating the effect of flanging. Electronic simulations of flanging usually add a slight variation in pitch and speed of sweep.

Listen to track 91 to hear the following phasing and flanging effects:

1 Phasing with low speed and sweep
2 Phasing with high speed and sweep
3 Flanging with low speed and sweep
4 Flanging with high speed and sweep

ADT and chorus

Automatic double-tracking (ADT) creates the effect of "doubling up" a performance so that it sounds like two musicians playing the same piece at the same time. It is often used to beef up vocals or a wimpy guitar sound. *Chorus* works within the same delay times as ADT, but creates a richer effect by modulating the repeated signal.

Listen to track 92 to hear the following examples of ADT and chorus in action:

1 ADT
2 Chorus with low modulation
3 Chorus with high modulation

Track

92

DEFINITION

An extension of ADT, chorus is an electronic effect that simulates more than one instrument playing the same part.

Trivia...

The full-bodied, lush, and sustained sound that chorus creates is especially effective when playing chords.

■ **Foot pedals are used** *to produce many effects, such as reverb.*

Echo

An echo occurs when a delayed signal can be heard as a distinct sound in its own right. Electronic delay units not only let you adjust the length of the delay, but also the number of times the signal is repeated until it fades away – this is usually called feedback. A single, fast repeat played back at the same volume as the original signal is known as slap-back echo; longer delays allow for the creation of a variety of interesting musical effects.

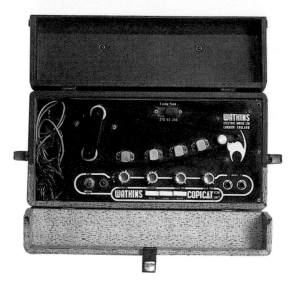

■ **The Watkins Copicat** *is valued by many players for its unique echo sounds.*

Listen to track 93 of the CD to hear the following echo effects being played:

1 Single slap-back echo
2 Medium echo with low feedback
3 Long echo with high feedback

Track

93

■ **Not all** *special effects require special equipment.*

Pitch shift

A digital pitch shifter – as the name suggests – alters the pitch of an incoming signal. This is also a delay effect, even though to be effective the delay needs to be as transparent as possible. The principle is simple, even if the technology behind it is wonderfully clever: The original signal is delayed by the shortest possible time it takes to convert a sound into a *digital sample* and then replay it at a different speed.

The most common use for a pitch shifter is in generating automatic harmony lines that are mixed equally with the original signal. Most units have a range of one octave above and one octave below the original signal, with half-step stops in between. Some of the more costly units are capable of generating multiple harmonies of up to four or five parts.

Listen to track 94 of the CD to hear the following pitch-shifting effects:

Track 94

1 Pitch shift, one octave up
2 Pitch shift, one octave down
3 Pitch shift, major third up
4 Pitch shift, perfect fifth down

INTERNET

www.geofex.com

Home of the Guitar Effects FAQ, the Tube Amp FAQ, the Tube Amp Debugging Page, and "The Technology of" effects series.

A PITCH SHIFT PEDAL

Tonal effects

YOU CAN ALTER THE TONE *of a sound either by altering the EQ (equivalent to bass and treble controls on a home amplifier) or by creating distortion effects. You've already seen how amplifiers can be used to create distortion, and you can get a wider range of such effects by using external units.*

Track

95

Fuzz

The first distortion foot pedals to be used were fuzz boxes in the 1960s. Over the years, many variations have appeared.

Listen to track 95 of the CD to hear examples of the following three fuzz effects:

1 Classic fuzz box
2 Heavy-metal distortion
3 Simulated valve overdrive

■ **The Hyper Metal** *footpedal enables you to add a controlable level of distortion to the original sound.*

■ **This Hyper Fuzz** *pedal reproduces the sounds of the 1960s fuzz boxes.*

■ **With this pedal,** *you can switch between two types of sound, each used to create distinct effects.*

Wah-wah pedals

There are a number of effects that manipulate the EQ of the guitar signal. The most famous is the wah-wah pedal, a foot pedal that alters the tone as you move your foot. It can either be used in one position as a tone control in its own right, or rocked back and forth while playing.

Track
96

Listen to track 96 of the CD to hear the following examples of the wah-wah pedal at work:

1 Clean wah-wah signal
2 Distorted wah-wah signal
3 Distorted wah-wah signal held in position

■ **Subscribers to the** *wah-wah sound include Jimi Hendrix and Eric Clapton.*

Volume pedals

Not really an effect in its own right, a volume pedal is essentially a loudness control you can operate with your foot. You can use it when switching between playing lead and rhythm guitar so that you don't have to find the extra hand to tweak the volume knob on the guitar or amplifier while you are still playing. Volume pedals can also be used effectively in conjunction with delay effects.

Trivia...

Jimi Hendrix was the undisputed master of the wah-wah effect. Listen to his playing on the Electric Ladyland *album for the proof.*

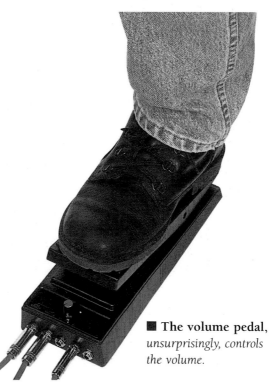

■ **The volume pedal,** *unsurprisingly, controls the volume.*

Using effects

THE PRINCIPLE ON WHICH *all effects units operate is simple – they are inserted in between the guitar and amplifier.*

To do this you need a second guitar cord. The output from the guitar is plugged into the effect's "In" socket; a second cord is connected between the effect's "Out" socket and the amplifier.

The majority of foot pedals are powered by a standard 9-volt battery. If you regularly play live, never leave home without spare batteries in your guitar case.

Alternatively, you can consider the option of using a power adapter – most pedals can be powered in this way – and do away with the need for a battery. In theory, it's possible to insert any number of pedals between the guitar and amplifier by using a daisy-chain of cords.

In each case, the output from one effect is sent directly to the input of the next effect in the chain. If you are planning to link several effects in this way, it's a good idea to get some 6-inch patch cables instead of relying on full-length guitar cords. If you only use long cables, your setup will soon become a tangled mess – which can not only be a bit of a pain, but also quite dangerous!

Multiple-effects modules

The great thing about foot pedals is that they are inexpensive and easy to use. But what happens in a live context if, say, you have four foot pedals connected and you want to alter the controls on all of them between, or even during, songs? In a lot of cases, this simply isn't practical (or even possible). The answer is to buy a multiple-effects module. These are high-quality digital units capable of producing all of the traditional foot-pedal effects simultaneously. And they're programmable, meaning that dozens of complex settings can be stored and recalled at the click of a foot-switch.

■ **The unit shown** *here can chain up to 13 different effects.*

A final word

Beware of the seductive lure of trying to mask bad playing with electronic effects. Your chord work may sound nice and crunchy when your distortion unit is turned up to 11; but when you switch it back to clean, you may just find that half the notes are not accurately fretted. This is especially important when you first start playing, when you're at the stage where bad habits are hard to shake off.

■ **This unit produces** *a phasing effect, popular with the psychedelic bands of the 60s.*

A simple summary

✓ In the pre-effects early 1950s, guitarists started to experiment with different sounds by varying the settings on their amplifiers.

✓ The introduction of effects units enabled musicians to achieve a range of sounds not readily available in the simple guitar-and-amplifier setups of the old days.

✓ Some of the most familiar and sought-after "classic" guitar sounds are best achieved with the creative use of effects units.

✓ Effects broadly fall into one of three categories: reverberation, delay, and tone alteration.

✓ When you first start playing, don't be seduced by the multiplicity of effect units available to mask bad technique. Practice, practice, practice.

Chapter 24

Recording Yourself and Your Guitar

QUESTION: How many guitarists does it take to change a light bulb? Answer: None; they just steal someone else's light.

There comes a time when most musicians want to bare their souls to the outside world, and guitarists seem more prone to this affliction than other instrumentalists. Some like to exhibit themselves before a live audience; others choose to express themselves through their recordings. Whichever way you go, you'll need to learn different skills and disciplines.

In this chapter...

✓ Laying it down

✓ Home or studio recording?

✓ Professional studios

✓ Working with studios

✓ Learning your way around a studio

✓ Studio effects

Laying it down

RECORDING YOUR OWN MUSIC is great fun and immensely satisfying (when it all goes right, that is). It can also be a bit scary at first – you know, all of that amazing technology, the rows of little LED lights that flicker away like Christmas trees every time you cough.

What does it all do? Don't worry, we can help you out here! By the end of this chapter, you may not be ready to set up as a professional sound engineer, but at least when the producer says, "What d'ya think about the EQ on the gated snare, man? Bit more top, maybe?", you won't have to stare blankly and feel stupid.

Home or studio recording?

SO, WHERE TO BEGIN? Basically, there are two options open to you. You can either record in a professional studio or do it at home. Which one you choose will depend largely on the type of music you make, how you prefer to work, and how much money you want to spend. If your band excels on stage, you could also think about having one of your gigs recorded, but it's pretty tough getting a good sound without digging deeply into your pockets.

For bands that use a real drummer, it's usually easier to rent a studio. Almost any studio offering its services professionally will be better equipped than a decent home studio, not only in terms of technology and expertise, but in the way that surfaces like walls and floors are treated acoustically.

It really is hard getting a decent drum sound in a small apartment – not to mention the risk of alienating family, pets, and neighbors.

INTERNET

www.soundwave.com

For an all-round look at this vast industry, this web site features information of interest to recording studios, producers, musicians, equipment manufacturers and dealers.

A BIT OF HISTORY

Before the first tape recorders appeared in the 1930s, the only way of capturing a sound that could be played time and time again was to "cut a disc." Although this was a pretty amazing achievement, the music couldn't be altered after it had been recorded.

With numerous refinements, the earliest tape machines were based on a principle that became the norm for 60 years. A spool of plastic ribbon or tape coated with a magnetic oxide surface was passed over electromagnetic heads on a recording machine. The sound was permanently captured on the tape until it was erased.

The stereophonic sound we all now take for granted evolved in the late 1940s. By adding a second loudspeaker and amplifier, different levels of sound could be processed through each speaker to create the illusion that sounds were positioned in a different part of the stereo vista.

During that same period, modern studio techniques involving multichannel tape recorders were developed. These allowed a basic rhythm track to be recorded on one part of the tape and other sounds to be overdubbed afterwards on an immediately adjacent part of the tape. By the 1970s, studio tape recorders were routinely capable of recording 16 or 24 individual tracks. Imagine how different today's music would sound had such innovations never been invented!

Conventional tape recorders were superceded in the early 1990s when digital technology (in the form of digital tape recorders) offered higher quality alternatives and made noise-free recordings a reality. The greatest developments were made in the area of hard-disk recording with music software such as ProTools and Cubase, allowing high-quality, multitrack recordings to be made on affordable desktop computers. The facilities built into even the cheapest home recording systems would have seemed unfeasible to most professional studio engineers working in the 1970s. And this rapid development shows no sign of slowing down. Great!

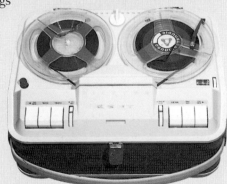

■ **This would have** *been state-of-the-art when introduced to the marketplace (circa 1950s).*

Professional studios

THE TERM "PROFESSIONAL" covers a multitude of sins. Unlike doctors, architects, and lawyers, anyone can announce themselves to the world as a professional sound engineer. What this job title means in practice depends on the level at which you are working.

The cheapest studios, aimed at impoverished or semiprofessional musicians, are usually owner-run affairs, with one person doing all the different jobs. The higher up the ladder you go, you'll find that different types of tasks are assigned to individuals with a fair degree of specialized expertise.

The tape operator

The tape operator, or "tape op," is the lowest in the studio pecking order. Although the job title may suggest main-man status, the tape operator is more likely to be the studio gopher who does everything that the engineer or musicians don't want to do.

Don't be too abusive to him, though, as it's from this menial but worthy position that many of the world's best-known engineers and producers have emerged.

The engineer

It's the job of the engineer to get the sound of the musicians onto tape in the best possible way. A good engineer knows microphone techniques inside out, including which type of equipment is best suited to the various instruments or voices. Most engineers harbor ambitions to become producers. Many will have graduated from tape-op status, although some specialist studios favor engineers who have learned about sound recording on a university course.

THE MIXING BOARD

The producer

In an ideal world, the producer exists to help recording artists achieve the results they are looking for. He or she knows what has to be done, where it has to be done, and who should do it. Some producers take an extremely hands-on approach, supervising or even taking over the engineering tasks. At the other end of the spectrum, some producers are simply given responsibility for creating the sound of the final mixes.

Sound programmers

Dance music and new technology have changed many aspects of studio life since the mid-1980s. The complexity of modern computer-based MIDI sequencers and hard-disk recording systems has spawned a new generation of producers who are best described as sound programmers. These producers may be called upon to build a completely new track with only a vocal part to work with. Similarly, such is the speed at which fashions change within the dance-music world that some of the most successful current producers are essentially club DJs who may know little or nothing about recording techniques, but have a finger firmly on the pulse of what turns club audiences on.

Trivia...

In some cases, a producer's role is so pivotal that he or she becomes a quasi member of the band. Paul McCartney is known to have been more than a little irritated at the level of public credit given to producer George Martin after the seminal Sgt. Pepper *album hit the stores. And yet, through his classical training and intimate understanding of The Beatles' ideas and creative processes, Martin was able to introduce interesting elements that greatly enhanced their music.*

■ **Powerhouse:** *The Power Station Recording Studios, New York.*

■ **George Martin** *(second right): the man behind* Sgt. Pepper.

Before you start

After making a democratic band decision to go into the studio (of course, all bands are democratic bodies … yeah, right!), you will need to make some fundamental decisions about how to proceed.

Typically this will involve how much money you want to spend and how much work you want to get done — and you should treat this process as "work" to get the best results. These two factors are intimately connected.

Studios usually charge daily or hourly rates, so look at the table below to estimate what you may be able to achieve during different types of recording sessions. Many factors can radically affect your costs, including the competency of the band and whether your drummer could find his way to the studio on time (you'll know he's at the door because the knocking keeps speeding up).

Estimating your studio time

Direct to two-track – no overdubs
✓ 3 hours to get the basic sound and mix
✓ 1 hour per song
Very intense; take regular breaks.

Multitrack (16 channels) – no overdubs
✓ 2 hours for basic setup
✓ 1 hour per song
✓ 2 hours per mix
While recording, you only hear a rough mix; you can alter the levels and sound of each instrument during the final mixing of a song.

Multitrack (24 channels) – with overdubs
✓ 2 hours for basic setup
✓ 4 hours per song
✓ 4 hours per mix
Record the rhythm section together; add solo instruments and vocals afterwards on separate tracks.

■ **Renting instruments** *may be a significant extra cost.*

Working with studios

ONCE YOU KNOW *approximately how much you're going to try to get done, then comes the task of choosing the environment in which you want to lay down your little masterpieces. Here is a checklist of points you should think about before you decide.*

Choosing a studio

1 Audition the studio. Ask to hear examples of their recordings – if they are not proud of what they produce, ask yourself why.

2 Check the environment. Studio work is stressful – it's always easier in pleasant surroundings.

3 Check the condition of the equipment. If it looks neglected or well worn, it might not sound that great; and if it breaks down, it can waste your time and money.

4 Audition the owner (often also the engineer/producer). Does he or she inspire you with confidence?

5 Take a demo tape – however low the quality – and play it for the producer. Does he or she seem sympathetic to your music? If he or she only knows about drum 'n' bass, will he or she understand what it takes to make Old Tom's Bluegrass Boys sound great?

6 Ask what you will be getting for your money. Do the costs quoted include such things as personnel, multitrack tape, mixdown tape, copies of mixes, or instrument rental?

■ **It can all** *seem a bit daunting at first, but don't be put off!*

Using a studio

Rehearse! Rehearse! Rehearse! Studio rent is expensive. The better prepared you are, the more efficiently you can use that time. Unless you have loads of cash at your disposal, save the experiments for rehearsals – a simple, yet often expensively neglected point.

VIP Adopt a "No Hangers-on" policy. Studio recording is stressful, so keep the body count down to a bare minimum – ideally just the musicians (and the drummer!).

■ **It is essential** *to have spare strings at any recording session.*

Ensure that your own gear is in good shape. Always take along several sets of strings, as well as spare cords, picks, and batteries. Get there on time. Whenever you arrive late for the session, you'll usually be charged for the time. Arrive half an hour early and get some of those dull but useful things, such as setting up drum kits or tuning instruments, out of the way.

Think ahead. If you are recording a handful of songs, save time by getting all the drum or rhythm tracks out of the way at the same time.

■ **Tuning before** *the session can save you precious minutes.*

■ **Take extra picks** *along in case of loss or breakage.*

If you're not happy with a take, do it again. If you don't, it will come back to haunt you every time you listen to the final recording. When mixing, give the engineer/producer the final say when the inevitable disputes arise. Understandably, each musician will be focusing closely on their own performance rather than the overall sound.

Consider taking time out between the recording and the mixing. If you've spent all day recording one song, you'll probably wake up in the middle of the night with the same sound swirling around in your head. A break of a few days will enable you to approach the final mix with fresh ears.

■ **The mixing** *consoles are the domain of the producer and engineer.*

Learning your way around a studio

FEAR CAN EASILY GRIP *you when you first enter a recording studio, but having a basic understanding of the various components found in most studios will help put you at ease. It may also inspire you to explore and develop further creative ideas.*

The mixing board

For recording on to a multitrack machine (whether analog or digital tape, or computer hard disk), the microphones or instruments are plugged into a *mixing board*. Here, the sounds can be individually altered by using facilities built into the board, such as volume or EQ (tone control), or by patching in external effects such as reverb or delay. These signals (waves of information) are then routed into the various channels of the multitrack recorder.

In the mixdown, each channel of the multitrack is plugged into one of the board's input channels. Each sound on the multitrack can then be altered as before or positioned within the stereo spectrum. The channels are played together to produce a balanced sound – this is the stereo mixdown.

■ **To the uninitiated,** *the mixing board is a baffling array of controls.*

Some computer-based recording systems now offer on-screen mixing. While less flexible than a physical unit, these systems are nevertheless very effective tools that don't take up much space.

What's on each channel?

At the heart of every mixing board is a series of identical input channels. These are the typical features you'll find on boards of all sizes and complexity:

Gain – Every piece of electrical equipment has a different output level. The gain control levels out these different impedances with the input of the board. Most feature a "mic/line" switch and a variable control to fine tune.

Equalization (EQ) – The equalization controls enable you to adjust the tone, much like expanded versions of the bass and treble on a home sound system. The range of audible signal is split into separate bandwidths – within each one, the specific frequencies can be cut or boosted according to taste.

■ **Computer-based** *software mixer.*

■ **Making sweet music:** *The studio is where it all goes down.*

Auxiliaries – The auxiliary controls enable you to patch in external effects such as digital reverb or delay. Each auxiliary control has "send" and "return" connections that are linked to the input and output of the external effect. Turning the board's auxiliary control alters the amount of signal sent through and returned to the external effects unit.

Pan – The pan controls where the signal will be positioned between the two speakers of a stereo system. For example, if you turn the control to either extreme, all of the signal will come from only one of the speakers.

Volume fader – The volume fader is a slider that governs the overall volume of the signal on that channel. The higher it is pushed, the higher the volume.

■ **This Solid State** *Logic Console is a state-of the-art mixing board, with compressor, computer keyboard, and 48 channel modules, amongst other features.*

Effects can be faded in using sliders or switched on or off using buttons

Multi-effects and pan controls

Each channel has separate volume, effects, and pan control

The channel sliders can be controlled manually by the engineer or, on more advanced set-ups, by computer

Volume

Studio effects

MANY COMMONLY HEARD STUDIO EFFECTS are merely high-quality versions of effects used by guitarists. Most effects are produced in shiny black boxes that fit neatly into the industry-standard 19-inch rack. These boxes are described in terms of their width in "U's" (meaning units); the racks themselves are sized according to how many "U's" they can hold. Things are much neater in the world of computer recording – even if their parameters work in much the same way – where effects take the form of "plug-in" programs.

Reverberation (reverb) and delay are perhaps the most important effects – you've already seen how they work in Chapter 23. Nowadays, these are often combined into digital multi-effects. Here are some other essential studio effects that you should know about.

Compressor/Limiter – Instruments such as the guitar can produce a very wide dynamic range, which can result in a big difference between the softest and loudest sounds. In a mixdown, this means that the signal can sometimes be too loud and at other times may disappear altogether. To stop this from happening, you can use a compressor to automatically boost or bring down the volume – so you don't have to continually "ride" the volume fader yourself. A limiter is a cruder version of a compressor.

■ **Eddie Van Halen** *is renowned for using a wide variety of effects in his playing, including heavy compression and distortion.*

Noise gate – Sometimes a signal contains a lot of unwanted *background noise*. You may find that your amplifier lets out a gentle, low-volume buzz when the guitar is not being played. In a typical mix, similar things can be happening on other channels – the singer coughing and breathing or the drummer dropping his sticks – all of which can "muddy" the overall sound. You can stop this from happening by using a noise gate. The reverse of a limiter, the noise gate dictates the volume at which the signal can be heard. Until the signal reaches that point, the output is suppressed.

DEFINITION

Background noise *can include anything from unwanted sounds to high levels of tape hiss or electrical buzzing.*

Enhancer – Enhancers, or exciters, make your mixes sound more lively, professional, and generally better, and they can also breathe new life into old tapes. The workings of an enhancer are difficult to explain without getting very technical, so suffice to say that a number of fundamentally different systems are used. For example, by using what is called harmonic regeneration, a dry signal played through an enhancer is given depth, clarity, and sparkle. Valve circuitry is sometimes also used to give warmth to the overall sound.

■ **A noise gate** *would be used in this situation to reduce the treble.*

A simple summary

✓ During the 1940s, the first multitrack tape recorders were developed, which allowed the overdubbing of different instruments and sounds over a basic rhythm or drum track.

✓ The choice of location when recording your own music, whether at home or in the studio, largely depends on the type of music you want to record and the funds at your disposal.

✓ To achieve an authentic live sound using real drums, you have to be prepared to rent a studio and the expertise of a competent sound engineer.

✓ Renting studio time and equipment, and hiring personnel, can be costly. So don't use paid-for studio time for basic rehearsals or cutting-edge experiments. Prepare thoroughly before you set foot in the studio.

✓ Check your equipment beforehand, and arrive early at the studio to set everything up before you start paying for the services of an engineer or producer.

✓ Take a break of a few days between the recording and the mixing process. The interval will enable you to approach the material with fresh ears.

■ **Even recording** *a simple drum sound can be a complex process.*

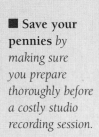

■ **Save your pennies** *by making sure you prepare thoroughly before a costly studio recording session.*

Chapter 25

Home Recording

WHY NOT TRY RECORDING at home? There are many examples of musicians working in this way and you can get really good results. First you need to acquire basic recording equipment and then learn how to use it. Although mastering sound engineering may take a bit of work, you'll be surprised how quickly you get acceptable results.

In this chapter...

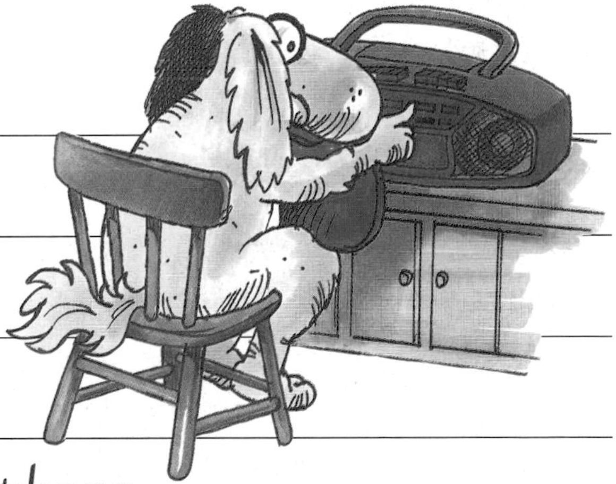

- ✓ What do you need?
- ✓ Recorders
- ✓ Hard-disk recording
- ✓ Recording acoustically
- ✓ Recording with a microphone
- ✓ Recording your guitar
- ✓ MIDI and the guitarist

THE PORTASTUDIO MAKES HOME RECORDING SIMPLE

What do you need?

DECIDING PRECISELY WHAT *studio equipment you need depends on numerous factors, not the least of which is how much money you want to spend. Like everything relating to technology, the cost of studio equipment is changing all the time.*

Thirty years ago, a well-equipped home studio could cost as much as a small apartment; 15 years ago, the price of a new car. Nowadays you can get a pretty sophisticated setup – especially if you're computer-literate – for under $1,000. Another important factor is your home environment. Do you want to set up a permanent small studio in a spare room, or do you want something small and portable that you can hide away in a closet when you've finished your masterpiece? Whatever route you pursue, a home recording system contains the same basic elements that you'll find in a professional studio.

The difference in sound quality between professional studios and home recording formats is getting less noticeable. An increasingly popular option is to use high-quality digital home studios to do basic composing and recording, and then finish off the tracks in a professional studio, taking advantage of a wider range of facilities.

Starting with the basics

First of all, you need some kind of recording machine like a tape recorder or its equivalent (we'll look at some of the different recording formats in a moment). You will also need some method of combining input and output signals, such as a small mixing board. For cool electronic effects try a digital multiple-effects unit that can provide you with reverb and delay. If you want to record acoustically – say vocals or drums – you'll need at least one microphone. If you look in any music technology magazine, you'll find good-quality, low-cost versions of pretty much everything you'll find in a professional studio.

Recorders

ALTHOUGH YOU CAN CERTAINLY hook up a
mixing board to a plain-old stereo cassette deck to produce a
live stereo recording, we'll assume for now that you want at
least a basic multitracking capability – that is, the ability to
record on one channel of the tape machine and play it back
while recording something else on a second channel.

The cheapest and easiest approach is to use an all-in-one system
that combines recorder and mixer. This allows you simply to plug
in and play. Original units used four-track cassettes. Nowadays you
can buy eight-track digital equivalents that record on to video
cassette, mini disc, or hard-disk formats. These systems are ideal if
you have limited space at home. And they sound great – easily good
enough to produce releasable results.

> ### Trivia...
> *Teac introduced the first*
> *combined cassette recorder*
> *and mixer in 1979 – the*
> *famous Tascam Portastudio.*
> *About the same size as a fax*
> *machine, the sound quality*
> *was not great – but the idea*
> *caught on big time.*

■ **This handy 4-track** *Portastudio unit records your masterpieces onto cassette.*

The digital multitrack

If you are looking for a dedicated digital multitrack recorder – just the basic machine with no other built-in facilities – the ADAT system is the most commonly used.

The ADAT allows eight digital tracks to be recorded either individually or together on SuperVHS video tape. A similar, though incompatible system, developed by Tascam, is aimed more at professional users. One of the great advantages of these recorders is that you can link any number of them together – you can even control them from a computer sequencer if you're so inclined.

■ The latest in *ADAT technology: Tascam's 8-track digital tape recorder, which uses Hi-8 video tapes.*

Magnetic tape versus digital

The traditional method of storing sound is on magnetic tape (analog). The modern alternative is to convert sound to a digital signal. The main advantage is that digital systems don't suffer from the background noise or tape hiss that beset the good old-fashioned reel-to-reel and cassette recorders.

The majority of musicians buying a new recording system automatically go for the clarity of digital, even if many still prefer the analog sound, which is undeniably warmer and less clinical. Oddly, as recording systems have become cleaner, some artists have sought to add a rougher element to their music. Listen to excellent groups like Portishead, Blur, or the Beta Band deliberately "sabotaging" the pure digital sound with all manner of grungy effects!

Hard-disk recording

CONTEMPORARY RECORDING *involves no tape at all. Sounds are recorded on to a computer hard disk and stored in the same way as any other computer file.*

There are two approaches you can take to hard-disk recording. The first is to use a dedicated hard-disk recorder. This is rather like a tapeless tape recorder – you plug in your source signal, press the record button, and the signal is converted to a digital file and saved on to the unit's hard disk. The second is to use a computer.

INTERNET

www.homerecording.
about.com

Everything you ever wanted to know about home recording....

■ **The particular sound** *favored by Blur, among others, is produced by a corruption of the digital recording process.*

343

The nuts and bolts

The biggest development area in home recording is using hardware and software that works on a personal computer – either PC or Apple Macintosh. The **hardware** required is a slot-in sound card through which you can record and play back your sound. The **software** takes the form of an on-screen digital recorder and mixer, which often incorporates MIDI sequencing. If you use MIDI equipment, you'll also need a MIDI interface unit that allows MIDI signals to be sent to and from the computer. The great advantage of recording in this way is that you can edit sounds on screen or "cut and paste" entire sections of a song. Also, if you already have a good computer that you use for nonmusical applications, setting up a system can be really inexpensive.

DEFINITION

*When discussing computer systems, **hardware** refers to the physical parts, such as the computer, monitor, keyboard, and sound cards. **Software** refers to the programs that run on the computer. Without software a computer can't do anything – it's a useless piece of technology.*

■ **Due to improved** *technology for home computers, home recording has become simpler (and more common).*

No pain, no gain!

Be warned that, if you are a computer novice or a technophobe, you'll have a steep learning curve to ascend before you even get down to the business of making music.

And furthermore, no matter how good your computer is, you can guarantee that it will crash at the most inopportune moments, causing you grief, wasting your time, and generally making you wish that you'd taken up stamp collecting instead.

■ **Slot this card** (*or something similar*) *into your computer to hear your tunes.*

HOME ACOUSTICS

In most top-end professional recording studios, a significant proportion of the budget goes toward producing an acoustically ideal environment. When you record at home, no matter how good your equipment, you won't be able to match such acoustic perfection.

Every characteristic of a room in some way affects the sound you hear. The major problem you face is dealing with reflective surfaces, such as walls and ceilings, from which the sounds will bounce back and forth. The aim is to get a room sounding as "dry" as possible – you can do this by covering walls, floors, and ceilings with an absorbent fabric such as that used in heavy drapes.

A more practical problem is likely to be that of noise. There's no getting away from it: Home recording can be an antisocial pursuit, and if you live in a small apartment there's really nothing you can do to prevent your neighbors from hearing you at some stage. Sorry, but you've just gotta keep that noise down!

■ **While you may** *enjoy thrash metal, your neighbor may not be so enamored of it….*

Recording acoustically

EVEN IN THIS ERA OF DIGITAL EVERYTHING, *the art of sound recording still revolves around the effective use of a microphone. There are two basic types of microphones: dynamic mikes and condenser mikes.*

Dynamic microphones comprise a coil joined to a diaphragm that is set around a magnetic cap. When a sound hits the diaphragm, the coil moves, thus creating a voltage output. Condenser microphones have a diaphragm coated with a thin layer of metal and a separate metal backing plate. A polarizing voltage is contained between the two pieces of metal, and it fluctuates according to pressure altered by movements in the diaphragm. Condenser microphones have a built-in pre-amplifier that boosts the level of the output.

■ **The basis of any** *recording is the microphone; the most common mike used for guitar is the Shure SM57 (second from left).*

Microphone pickup patterns

Every microphone has a pickup pattern that indicates the area around the microphone that can "hear" a sound. Some microphones are designed to pick up signals equally from any direction – these are known as omnidirectional. Microphones designed to pick up sound predominantly from one direction are called directional. Most directional microphones feature a cardioid pickup pattern – you can see why it's so named by referring to the diagram below. The strongest signal is picked up from the front and little is picked up from the rear.

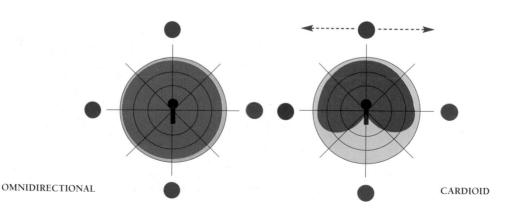

OMNIDIRECTIONAL

CARDIOID

Recording with a microphone

SOUND ENGINEERS CAN GET *very passionate about microphones and frequently disagree over which models sound best, how they should be positioned, and which types are best suited to various instruments.*

Basically, there aren't any fixed rules on microphone use. You can record different types of sound depending on how far the microphone is from the sound source – your guitar. The farther away the microphone, the more you'll hear the sound of the room acoustics. Some commonly used techniques for recording the guitar are described in the following sections. Actually, they're good principles for other instruments as well, even the human voice.

Close miking

Putting a microphone up to 18 inches away from the guitar (or speaker cabinet) produces the most detailed sound and is called close miking. The recording that results from using this method can sound odd, as the signal will contain little or no natural room reverberation. Digital effects are often used to add a bit of life to the sound.

■ **The result of** *close miking is often not very natural-sounding; this can be adjusted by clever effects.*

Distance miking

Putting a microphone about three feet or more away from the sound source is called distance miking. This method creates a natural balance between the sound of the instrument and the acoustic characteristics of the surrounding room. A more extreme version of this is ambient miking, in which the microphone is at least eight feet away from the sound source so that the signal will be mostly ambient room reflections.

■ **Wonder what** *effect this produced?*

Experimenting with mikes

If you sit facing close to a speaker and focus on the signal coming out, the simple act of turning your head by a couple of inches can make it sound very different. So it is with microphone placement: If you don't like the results you're getting, experiment with different positions. Just bear in mind that moving a microphone farther away from the sound source not only reduces the volume but also reduces the bass level.

Recording your guitar

THE BEST WAY TO RECORD *an acoustic guitar is to position a microphone near the soundhole – this is where the volume is loudest.*

If you move the microphone along the strings toward the bridge, the tone will become more bassy; moving it in the other direction will boost the treble. As with a lot of microphone recording, the results can be unpredictable, so experimentation is usually needed before you get things right.

Recording an electric guitar is – in theory, at least – a good deal more straightforward. The simplest approach is to position a directional microphone at the same height as the center of the speaker, and at a distance of up to six inches.

In more complex setups, it's not unusual for a number of different microphones to be used – in the close, distant, and ambient positions – and then balancing the different signals on the mixing board.

■ **Place the mike** *near the sound hole to get the best acoustic recording.*

MIDI and the guitarist

ONE OF THE MOST IMPORTANT *technical advances of the past 20 years has been the development and evolution of MIDI (Musical Instrument Digital Interface). To keep it simple, this is a kind of computer language that allows computers, synthesizers, drum machines, sequencers, and other digital units to communicate with one another.*

MIDI basics

The main use of MIDI is as a mode for recording performances on a computer sequencer. The principles are relatively simple: you plug the MIDI OUT from, say, an electric keyboard to the MIDI IN on a sequencer. Then press the record button and play the keyboard part. The information about that performance – the pitch of the note, its duration, and its volume – are stored on the sequencer. The sound itself is not recorded. To play back the recorded part, a MIDI OUT signal is sent to an external sound module that can be set to any kind of sound. So any piece of MIDI music can be played back using the different sounds of any MIDI module. Also, once stored, MIDI data can be edited, so that playing errors can be corrected.

That's all very interesting, you may say, but what does it have to do with guitars? Well, MIDI is so central to much modern music that many creative guitarists now feel compelled to pick up rudimentary MIDI and keyboard skills so they can program sequencers and be able to sample or create rhythm patterns on drum machines.

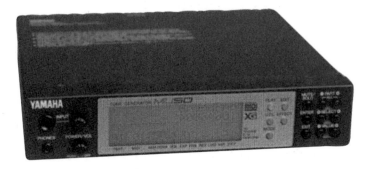

■ **This tone generator** *includes a drum machine and a full orchestra of sounds driven by MIDI.*

349

MIDI guitars

Of course, we should also mention the MIDI guitar. By attaching a special pickup to your guitar, the signals from each string can be converted into MIDI information, meaning that the guitar can be used to record a MIDI performance. Somehow, as much as companies like Roland have tried, MIDI guitars have never really caught on.

THE MIDI PICKUP

■ **This custom-built floor unit** *consists of. an electronic switching system made by Rocktron/Bradshaw with a volume pedal. The switching system uses MIDI to control amplification and effect preserving. It features 25 groups of "song" presets. Each bank contains five individual presets.*

■ **Guitar synthesizers** *can be used, via MIDI, to drive an array of other MIDI devices, like drum machines or tone boxes, to produce an orchestra of effects.*

Using MIDI

Probably the most practical application of MIDI to guitarists is to program effects units or amplifier settings so they can be called up from a MIDI floor unit. This is very handy for live work.

■ **An example of** *how a guitarist might use MIDI; the units are "daisy-chained" using the Midi thru connections.*

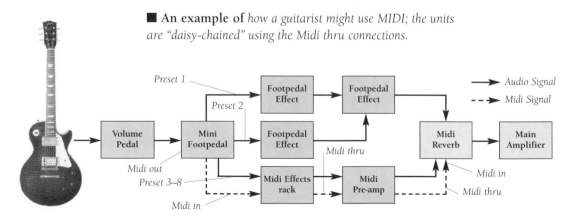

GUITARS AND SAMPLING

As technology gets less expensive and more user-friendly, an increasing number of guitarists are experimenting with the techniques of digital sampling and hard-disk editing. At its simplest (and dullest), it could mean that the part you play in the chorus of a song can simply be sampled so that exactly the same part can be heard in every chorus of the song. More interesting uses can revolve around creating sample loops to repeat the same part over and over again, or to play back samples at a different pitch – that is, "stretching" the sound.

A simple summary

✓ Home recording systems, once the province of the well-heeled, are getting less expensive and better all the time.

✓ With care, you can easily produce releasable results on even the most modest home-studio setup.

✓ If you already own a decent computer – and know how it works – it can form the heart of your multitrack recording system.

✓ The acoustics of the room in which you record will affect the quality of the sound you produce.

✓ Some microphones pick up the strongest signals from the front; other models pick up signals equally from all around.

✓ Guitars are usually recorded with a microphone that is less than six inches from the soundhole (or the speaker in the case of amplified guitars).

✓ MIDI (Musical Instrument Digital Interface) can be used to communicate between computers, sequencers, keyboards, drum machines, and samplers. It can also be used to control amplifier and effects parameters.

Chapter 26

Making a Name for Yourself

HERE WE'LL TAKE a look at some of the more obvious ways of getting yourself known to a wider public – through performing live or releasing your music. To be perfectly honest, this is one area of the book for which results *can't* be guaranteed. But hey, making a large fortune is not the only motivating force. Some of us just want to peddle our own unique art or just simply have a bit of a laugh – and both of those aims are eminently noble.

In this chapter...

✓ Taking to the stage

✓ Assembling your starter's kit

✓ The guitarist on stage

✓ Marketing your product

✓ Releasing your own music

✓ Using the Internet

Taking to the stage

■ **Prince certainly** *has stage presence!*

FOR MANY MUSICIANS, *performing live is the most meaningful way of communicating with an audience. But for the newbie, setting foot on stage for the first time can be, frankly, as scary as hell!*

It also presents a brand-new learning curve – being a good performer is not the same thing as being a good musician or being adept in the ways of the recording studio. Indeed, the stage novice has to face the same issues that affect other types of performers, like confidence, projection of image, and overcoming stage fright. On a more mundane level, there are also new technical skills to be learned (or at least to be aware of). These will vary depending on the type of venue you find yourself in.

DEFINITION

*In the term **PA system**, PA is an abbreviation for public address.*

The PA system

The type of equipment you need to perform in public – aside from your regular gear – will depend largely on the size of the venue. For all but the smallest club or bar, the central requirement is a PA *system*. This may be little more than an amplifier, a speaker, and a single microphone for vocals, costing a total of just a few hundred dollars. At the opposite end of the spectrum, a major-venue PA system will look more like several digital recording s tudios linked together!

Whatever the venue, an ideal PA system will allow the levels of all instruments and vocalists to be controlled from a single mixing board. This is usually operated by a sound engineer at the back of the room.

■ **Do you think** *that Kiss ever had stage fright?*

Assembling your starter's kit

LET'S MAKE A MODEST START. For performing in a small club or bar, it's common for each of the musicians to provide their own amplification, which they control from the stage.

Drums and brass instruments in small venues may be more than loud enough without needing to be miked. An additional amp and microphone will be required for vocals. To be honest, with no mixing board and no external engineer controlling the overall sound, the balance among the instruments will be – shall we say – hit-or-miss. Okay, it'll almost certainly sound pretty bad, but at least you're up there doing your thing, right?

Strive for self-sufficiency

A modest PA system with even the most basic mixing board will improve matters no end. All it takes is a simple six-channel mixing board, a reasonably powerful stereo amplifier (500 watts per channel should be ideal for small venues), speaker stacks, and a few microphones. You'll be surprised how cheaply you can pick this kind of thing up second-hand. As well as making you self-sufficient, owning your own PA system will make a big difference when you rehearse.

■ **Humble beginnings:** *Many a famous band has gigged in small venues to start with.*

Hire a sound engineer

Even better than having your own PA system is having your own sound engineer as well. Look around the periphery of your own band – you can bet there'll be some nerdy guy or gal hanging around who can't play an instrument but wishes he or she was in the band. He might be ideal (if there are two of them, you have a lighting person as well!).

A good, sympathetic sound engineer who knows your material is a valuable member of the band, even if he remains invisible to the audience.

■ **Having someone** *who knows the ropes is so important.*

Monitoring your progress

When playing small venues, you can get along without a sound engineer to control levels dynamically from a mixing board. And being able to monitor your sound – hear yourself play – is not essential. When you move to larger venues, however, monitoring your sound is crucial, particularly if you are working without a sound engineer. Without a monitoring system, you won't be able to hear yourself play.

The bigger the venue, the better system you'll need. A basic professional PA system invariably incorporates monitoring facilities. These enable musicians to hear a mix of the sound via a small floor speaker positioned in front of them on the stage. At really big venues, the monitoring system comprises an independent PA system that provides individual mixes tailored to the needs of each band member. At the real luxury end of the market, musicians can hear their own mixes through earpieces rather than bulky stage monitors.

The guitarist on stage

ON STAGE, THE ELECTRIC GUITAR is treated in much the same way as in a recording studio: the amplifier is close-miked or DI'd (where the amplifier is input directly into a mixing board) according to taste. Playing live is somewhat more problematic for acoustic guitars. These suffer from players moving away from the microphone as well as the intrusion of external sounds from the rest of the band. As if that weren't bad enough, the mike can start feeding back on itself. The easiest way to get around this is to use an electroacoustic guitar. Simple.

Trivia...

It's usually the sound of the other instruments that prevent you from hearing your own performance when playing on stage. The Beatles had a more fundamental problem – a screaming audience. After conquering the U.S. in 1964, the band claimed that they never again were able to hear what they were doing in concert – unsurprisingly, they retired from live music two years later.

The use of radio or wireless transmitters on stage is becoming more and more popular – especially since the *Spinal Tap*-style radio interference problems of the early models have now been eliminated. Instead of plugging the guitar into an amplifier, a transmitter worn on the guitarist's belt or guitar strap is plugged into the guitar. The signal from the guitar is picked up by a VHF receiver plugged into the amp. This allows the player to move around the stage without having to worry about tripping over guitar cords.

■ **Use an electroacoustic**
for minimal sound problems.

RADIO TRANSMITTER SYSTEM

Guitar + electricity = noise

Ah, what a great equation that is. However, you should also be aware that two of those elements – electricity and noise – have potentially dangerous side effects.

So much research has now been done on the long-term effects of loud noise on human hearing that there really can be no doubt that prolonged exposure to extremely loud music – the kind of volumes that you get from an average gig – can cause permanent damage.

This usually occurs in a slowly degenerative way, although you'll know when you really have a problem when your ears ring for days after a gig. If this happens, consult a physician for further advice.

As central as electricity is to our everyday lives, electricity can kill. Although thankfully rare, numerous musicians have suffered electric shocks while performing or recording – some of them fatal. These tragedies are almost always a result of faulty grounding of electrical equipment – which means that the shocks could probably have been avoided by regular servicing of equipment. Listen for tell-tale signs that something is faulty, such as excessive amplifier buzz that changes when your hand comes into contact with the strings or with other metal parts of the guitar.

The golden rule is this: No matter how smart you are, if you don't know exactly what you're doing, leave the tampering to qualified electricians.

■ **Beware: exposure**
to loud sounds can cause permanent damage to your hearing.

Marketing your product

BEING A GOOD LIVE BAND is one thing. Having some good-quality recordings of your own music is another. But at some stage, most musicians will feel an urge to commit their work to posterity – in other words, to release an album or single.

DIY or LSEDIFY?

■ **You could find** *yourself flying first-class with all the other rock stars.*

The are two ways in which you can get your own music out on to the streets: You can Do It Yourself or Let Someone Else Do It For You. The latter means getting yourself a record deal. Once you've done that, you can have a few hits, tour the world, and eventually retire a multimillionaire – simple as that. But seriously folks, if that's the route you want to choose, your best bet is to start off by finding a decent manager.

Taking the independent route

Anyone who works in the mainstream music business will tell you that, nowadays, rarely does anyone get signed up to a major label by sending out endless streams of demo tapes or CDs. In most cases, they'll barely get a listen unless they are presented by a manager who can jam his boot in the door. That said, quite a few really good bands have graduated from cult success on a smaller, independent label. It is here that specialized types of music can thrive more easily. Independent labels have the advantage of knowing their own markets particularly well, even if their potential for making a massive fortune is somewhat lower. The best way to make these labels sit up and take notice of you is to develop a reputation on your own terms – a good starting point is to put out something independently yourself.

If you're good and if you're strongly motivated (and that second "if" is the biggest second "if" of them all), then some record company executive will find a place for you eventually.

Good luck – you'll need it on this one!

■ **An uncontroversial** *manager is often the best option, as Elvis discovered….*

359

Releasing your own music

THE BIG ADVANTAGE OF RELEASING *your own music is that you can present yourself exactly the way you want to. Nobody else can tell you to compromise anything – well, they can, but you don't have to listen to them. The downside, of course, is that you get to pay for the privilege.*

There are five principal formats for prerecorded music – CD, vinyl, cassette, mini disc, and the computer file MP3.

Although vinyl is still popular in specialized dance markets, the CD is far and away the most important format and is very cost effective to produce in small quantities. The CD is popular with music stores because it takes up comparatively little space, and its size and weight make it inexpensive to send through the mail. Cassettes and mini discs are now mainly used by the domestic home-taping markets. The MP3 format is a slightly different kettle of fish in that it doesn't involve mass production – songs saved as MP3 files can be downloaded from a web site. We'll take a look at that shortly – it's a fast-developing area.

■ **Although not as** *common as the CD, mini discs are still a viable format on which to release music.*

Manufacturing your product

Whatever format you choose, the manufacturing process consists of a number of stages generally performed by different groups of people or companies. But it's generally cheaper and easier to find a brokering company that specializes in doing the complete job. These people usually advertise in the back pages of music and technology magazines. Remember to get quotes from a number of different sources – you'll be surprised at the variation in price you might find even over the smallest of your chosen format.

At its simplest, the whole process can involve little more than handing over a master tape, some artwork, and a pile of cash – and then waiting for the delivery van to roll up outside your door a few weeks later.

■ **CDs are** *the most popular format in which music is sold these days.*

Making a CD

In spite of the amazing technology involved, producing a CD is pretty simple. What's more, it can be produced from music recorded on any format: CD, cassette, reel-to-reel tape, mini disc, or DAT. Working from your original, the stereo recording is digitally re-mastered and *PQN codes* are added. From here, a glass master is produced – this is the template from which all your final CDs will be pressed.

■ **A cassette tape** *has a limited life; transferring it to a CD will save it for posterity.*

You will usually be given the option of attending the re-mastering in person (in some cases, you might have to pay extra for this privilege). The mastering room offers you the chance to make last-minute audio changes, such as altering volumes and EQ between tracks, tidying up fade-outs, or adding compression. A good mastering engineer can also act as a useful spare set of ears, using his or her experience to recommend possible courses of action.

DEFINITION

PQN codes *provide the CD with the information needed for it to function correctly. This encoding process includes adding track numbers, index points, start times, and duration times.*

■ **CDs are produced** *from glass masters, which are essentially templates.*

Artwork production

Love 'em or hate 'em, the hideous plastic jewel case is the most common method of packaging CDs. There are two forms in which you can present your artwork for the CD inserts: Camera-ready or film. If you have access to a computer with suitable desktop publishing software, you can save a wad of money by doing your own designs. Then find a bureau with the facility to produce film for the printer. Otherwise, you can simply present your finished design on paper ready for the camera to do its job. Creating camera-ready art can be a more expensive process.

■ **Designs for CD covers** *can either be presented as camera-ready artwork or film.*

Vinyl

The mastering process for vinyl is traditionally known as "the cut." Your master tape is played back through a mixing console linked to a lathe that cuts a groove into a blank lacquer disc.

After the lacquer has been produced, it is sent off for plating. The lacquer is coated with a thin layer of silver and electroplated in a nickel solution. When this coating is stripped away, it holds a negative impression of the original lacquer. This impression is used to make the "mother" mold from which the final stamper is produced. The stamper holds a negative impression of the original lacquer, which is then used to press the vinyl. The pressing process uses molten vinyl compressed hydraulically between the stampers. This creates the finished record.

Selling your product

Selling your soul is more like it! This can be the depressing bit. The CD manufacturer has turned up on your doorstep with boxes and boxes of your masterpiece. What are you going to do with them now? You'll probably be able to sell some copies directly to friends and family or at gigs. But to reach a wider audience you'll need to get a *distributor* involved. Without one, you won't have the slightest chance of getting your music into the stores, and that's where nearly all music is bought. A good distributor has links to a whole array of music stores, as well as to distribution networks in other countries. Most distributors work on a sale-or-return basis, which means that if he can't sell your CDs they'll be returned to you. Distributors often specialize in particular types of music, so it's always a good idea to find out who distributes similar artists or groups to you.

Some distributors also double up as mail-order outlets. If you can get on their mailing lists, you can create interest through association with like-minded or more successful artists on the list.

■ **A distributor** *takes the hard work out of distribution.*

■ **What to do** *now with all your CDs?*

Promoting yourself

This is critically important – that's why the biggest labels devote millions of dollars to marketing a new album by a major artist. If you don't promote yourself, how will anyone know you exist? Promotion is also an aspect that many worthy artists find demeaning in the extreme. To be frank, it's impossible to do a really effective job without devoting a whole lot of time and money to the process – and that's time and money you could devote to making more music. Here are a few ideas for promotion on the cheap, but it still requires a lot of time and good organization.

1 Create a press pack. At the very least this should include a copy of the music and a basic press release. Photographs and other promotional gimmicks can be useful, but only if they're done professionally.

2 Compile and continually update a list of music-business figures, such as journalists and radio DJs, who might be interested in your work. Keep them informed and up-to-date about all your activities.

3 Follow up your press mailings. Journalists and DJs get hundreds of new releases sent to them every week. Even if they really like your music, they're probably not going to have time to call you in person. Don't be afraid to hassle them in order to get some kind of response.

■ **A press pack** *that includes a photograph is usually the best way to promote your band.*

Using the Internet

THE WORLD WIDE WEB *is one of the greatest phenomena of the past decade. Unsurprisingly, independent musicians have jumped at the opportunity to create a permanent presence on a distribution medium that can be accessed all over the world.*

So if you're serious about reaching an audience, you simply must get your own web page. Furthermore, you can include samples of your music that listeners can download and, hopefully, then purchase the complete version. More and more music will be bought and sold over the Internet over the coming decade.

MP3s: The way ahead

One of the hottest topics in the music business recently has been the development of the MP3 system. This is an amazing file format that allows music to be compressed and downloaded very quickly from a web site to a home computer. Thankfully, you no longer need a vast expanse of web space at your disposal to hold an album's worth of your music. The absence of traditional manufacturing and distribution costs is drawing more and more independent musicians toward MP3 as a means of reaching their market.

INTERNET

www.mp3.com.

Find out more about MP3.

■ **Create a funky** *web page for your band as more and more people surf the Net.*

Copyright issues

If you record a song that someone else has written, you are legally obliged to pay a small fee called the mechanical copyright to the publisher of the music. This cost is calculated on the number of copies you produce. So when you decide to make a CD using other peoples' songs, remember that it could make your costs around 5 percent more expensive.

■ **If your song** *hits the playlists, you will be entitled to a fee!*

INTERNET

www.ascap.com and www.bmi.com

To find out more about copyright organizations visit these sites.

On the other hand, if a piece of music you have composed is played on TV, radio, in a film, or anywhere in public, you are entitled to a performance fee. The only way of collecting these royalties is to register with a copyright protection or performing rights organization.

A simple summary

✔ A good stage performer is not the same beast as a good musician. You have to face issues such as confidence, projection of image, and stage fright.

✔ To play live, you'll need access to a PA (public address) system. If you can purchase your own, all the better.

✔ Decent PA systems have independent monitoring features that enable each musician to hear a special mix of the overall sound.

✔ Close-miking techniques are used for picking up guitar signals and passing them through the PA system.

✔ If you want your music to hit the streets, you can try to get a record deal, or you can manufacture it and release it yourself.

✔ To sell your music through music stores, you need to find a distributor for your product.

Chord dictionary

THE LARGER YOUR CHORD VOCABULARY, *the more sophisticated a palette you'll have to work with as a guitarist and perhaps even songwriter or composer. The next 25 pages provide you with a reference guide for playing 19 different chord types in all 12 keys. In each case, an alternative voicing is provided, making a total of 456 finger positions. This is not to say, of course, that there are only 19 types of chords – these are simply the ones that will be most useful to the greatest number of people.*

Using the chord dictionary

Each chord shown in this appendix follows the same simple format. First come the diagrams of the chords themselves. The diagram on the left is the most commonly used chord shape, and the diagram on the right is a different voicing of the same chord, which means that although they sound slightly different, they have the same musical effect.

Each chord diagram represents an overhead view of the guitar's fretboard, so the strings run 1st to 6th from top to bottom. The small numbers beneath the diagram represent the fret position. The circles on the diagram indicate which finger you should use, from 1 to 4. An empty circle on a chord diagram indicates that the note is an optional one, while an "X" means that the string should not be played; you must make sure that you deaden it so that it is not played accidentally.

Beneath the chords is the abbreviated name or symbol by which the chord is known – for instance, C, next to which is its full name appears – for instance, C major.

You will also see the chord's "spelling." This refers to the position of notes in the major scale that make up that chord: C, E, and G are the 1st, 3rd, and 5th notes of the C-major scale.

Empty strings, those without a circle or an "X," are still part of the chord and are played open.

These are bar lines, and show you that one finger should hold down more than one string.

Fret

Nut

1st string   E
2nd string   B
3rd string   G
4th string   D
5th string   A
6th string   E

1   2   3   4   3   4   5   6

C (C major)
Spelling: 1st (C) 3rd (E) 5th (G)

The numbered circles give the chord fingering. The number inside the circle shows you which finger you should use.

Empty circles represent optional notes that you can add to the chord if you like, although you may need to alter the fingering.

Fret numbers indicate the position on the fingerboard the chord is played.

This is about as deep as I'm going to go into music theory. As you've already seen, some notes — the black keys on a piano — can have two different names. These are the enharmonic notes. If you really want to know why this happens, get a book on music theory — in fact, I've written a pretty good one myself! But to keep things neat, I'll refer to them here as B♭, C♯, E♭, F♯, and A♭ rather than A♯, D♭, D♯, G♭, and G♯.

The notes you see on the chord diagrams are named correctly. For example, the chord F 7-9 has a flattened ninth. In the key of F, the ninth note is flattened from a G to G♭. Hence, G♭ is the correct label, even though it is more common to refer to the note as F♯.

369

A chords

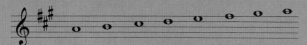

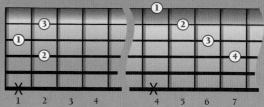

Amaj7/AΔ7 (A major seventh)
Spelling: 1st (A) 3rd (C♯) 5th (E) 7th (G♯)

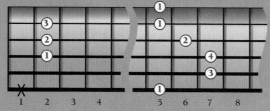

A (A major)
Spelling: 1st (A) 3rd (C♯) 5th (E)

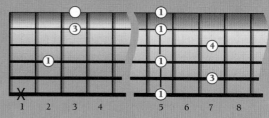

A sus 4/A sus (A suspended fourth)
Spelling: 1st (A) 4th (D) 5th (E) Note no 3rd

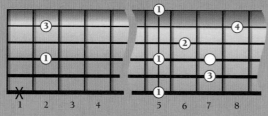

Am (A minor)
Spelling: 1st (A) ♭3rd (C) 5th (E)

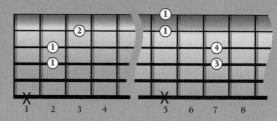

A7 sus 4/A7+4 (A seventh suspended fourth)
Spelling: 1st (A) 4th (D) 5th (E) ♭7th (G) Note no 3rd

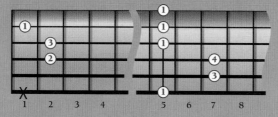

A7 (A seventh)
Spelling: 1st (A) 3rd (C♯) 5th (E) ♭7th (G)

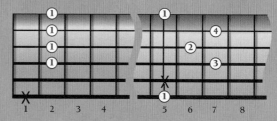

A6 (A sixth)
Spelling: 1st (A) 3rd (C♯) 5th (E) 6th (F♯)

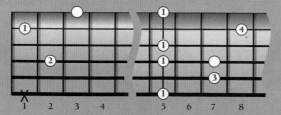

Am7 (A minor seventh)
Spelling: 1st (A) ♭3rd (C) 5th (E) ♭7th (G)

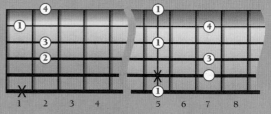

Am6 (A minor sixth)
Spelling: 1st (A) ♭3rd (C) 5th (E) 6th (F♯)

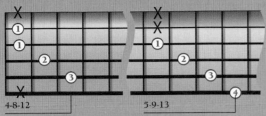

A aug/A+ (A augmented)
Spelling: 1st (A) 3rd (C♯) ♯5th (F)

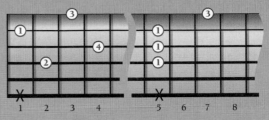

Am9 (A minor ninth)
Spelling: 1st (A) ♭3rd (C) 5th (E) ♭7th (G) 9th (B)

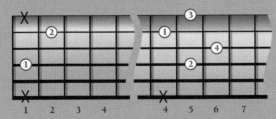

A dim/A° (A diminished)
Spelling: 1st (A) ♭3rd (C) ♭5th (E♭) ♭♭7th (G♭)

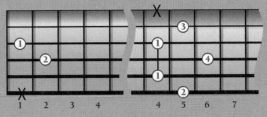

Amaj9/A△9 (A major ninth)
Spelling: 1st (A) 3rd (C♯) 5th (E) 7th (G♯) 9th (B)

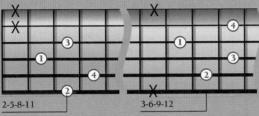

A7–5 (A diminished fifth)
Spelling: 1st (A) 3rd (C♯) ♭5th (E♭) ♭7th (G)

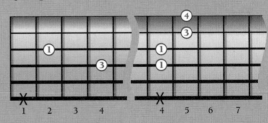

A6/9 (A six nine/A major sixth added ninth)
Spelling: 1st (A) 3rd (C♯) 5th (E) 6th (F♯) 9th (B)

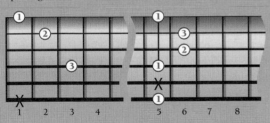

A7+5 (A seventh augmented fifth)
Spelling: 1st (A) 3rd (C♯) ♯5th (F) ♭7th (G)

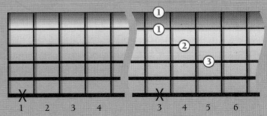

A11 (A eleventh)
Spelling: 1st (A) 3rd (C♯) 5th (E) ♭7th (G) 9th (B) 11th (D)

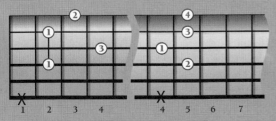

A9 (A ninth)
Spelling: 1st (A) 3rd (C♯) 5th (E) ♭7th (G) 9th (B)

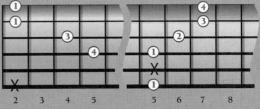

A13 (A thirteenth)
Spelling: 1st (A) 3rd (C♯) 5th (E) ♭7th (G) 9th (B) 13th (F♯)

A#/B♭ chords

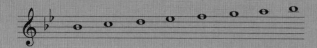

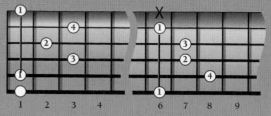

B♭ maj7/B♭∆7 (B flat major seventh)
Spelling: 1st (B♭) 3rd (D) 5th (F) 7th (A)

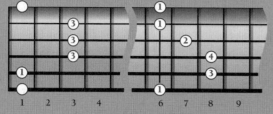

B♭ (B flat major)
Spelling: 1st (B♭) 3rd (D) 5th (F)

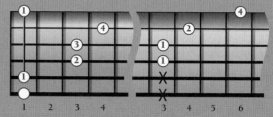

B♭ sus 4/B♭ sus (B flat suspended fourth)
Spelling: 1st (B♭) 4th (E♭) 5th (F) Note no 3rd

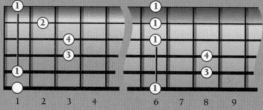

B♭ (B flat minor)
Spelling: 1st (B♭) ♭3rd (D♭) 5th (F)

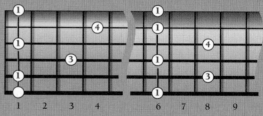

B♭ 7 sus 4/B♭ 7+4 (B flat seventh suspended fourth)
Spelling: 1st (B♭) 4th (E♭) 5th (F) ♭7th (A♭) Note no 3rd

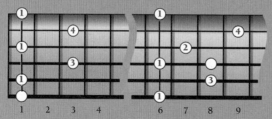

B♭ 7 (B flat seventh)
Spelling: 1st (B♭) 3rd (D) 5th (F) ♭7th (A♭)

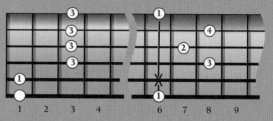

B♭ 6 (B flat sixth)
Spelling: 1st (B♭) 3rd (D) 5th (F) 6th (G)

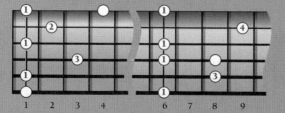

B♭ m7 (B flat minor seventh)
Spelling: 1st (B♭) ♭3rd (D♭) 5th (F) ♭7th (A♭)

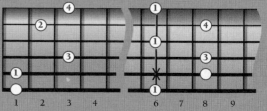

B♭ m6 (B flat minor sixth)
Spelling: 1st (B♭) ♭3rd (D♭) 5th (F) 6th (G)

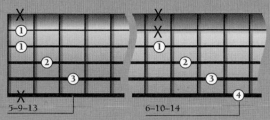

5–9–13   6–10–14

B♭ aug/B♭+ (B flat augmented)
Spelling: 1st (B♭) 3rd (D) #5th (F#)

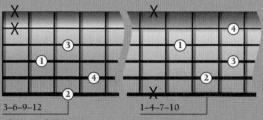

3–6–9–12   1–4–7–10

B♭ dim/B♭° (B flat diminished)
Spelling: 1st (B♭) ♭3rd (D♭) ♭5th (E) ♭♭7th (G)

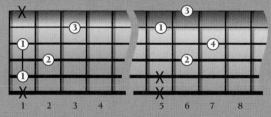

1 2 3 4   5 6 7 8

B♭ 7–5 (B flat diminished fifth)
Spelling: 1st (B♭) 3rd (D) ♭5th (E) ♭7th (A♭)

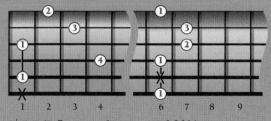

1 2 3 4   6 7 8 9

B♭ 7+5 (B flat seventh augmented fifth)
Spelling: 1st (B♭) 3rd (D) #5th (F#) ♭7th (A♭)

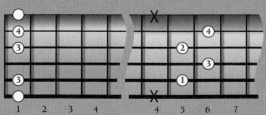

1 2 3 4   4 5 6 7

B♭ 9 (B flat ninth)
Spelling: 1st (B♭) 3rd (D) 5th (F) ♭7th (A♭) 9th (C)

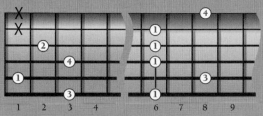

1 2 3 4   6 7 8 9

B♭ m9 (B flat minor ninth)
Spelling: 1st (B♭) ♭3rd (D♭) 5th (F) ♭7th (A♭) 9th (C)

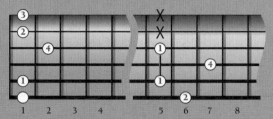

1 2 3 4   5 6 7 8

B♭ maj9/B♭ Δ9 (B flat major ninth)
Spelling: 1st (B♭) 3rd (D) 5th (F) 7th (A) 9th (C)

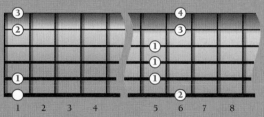

1 2 3 4   5 6 7 8

B♭ 6/9 (B flat six nine/B flat major sixth added ninth)
Spelling: 1st (B♭) 3rd (D) 5th (F) 7th (A) 9th (C)

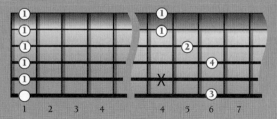

1 2 3 4   4 5 6 7

B♭ 11 (B flat eleventh)
Spelling: 1st (B♭) 3rd (D) 5th (F) ♭7th (A♭)
9th (C) 11th (E♭)

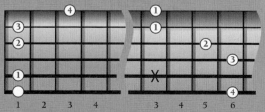

1 2 3 4   3 4 5 6

B♭ 13 (B flat thirteenth)
Spelling: 1st (B♭) 3rd (D) 5th (F) ♭7th (A♭) 9th (C)
13th (G)

B chords

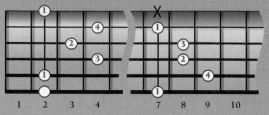

Bmaj7/B△7 (B major seventh)
Spelling: 1st (B) 3rd (D♯) 5th (F♯) 7th (A♯)

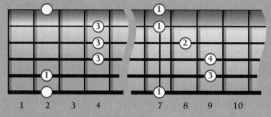

B (B major)
Spelling: 1st (B) 3rd (D♯) 5th (F♯)

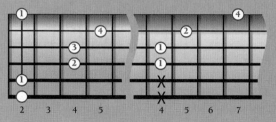

B sus 4/B sus (B suspended fourth)
Spelling: 1st (B) 4th (E) 5th (F♯) Note: no 3rd

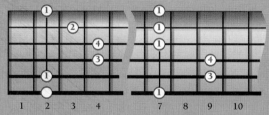

Bm (B minor)
Spelling: 1st (B) ♭3rd (D) 5th (F♯)

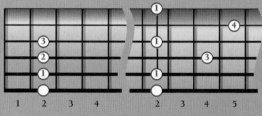

B7 sus 4/B7+4 (B seventh suspended fourth)
Spelling: 1st (B) 4th (E) 5th (F♯) ♭7th (A) Note no 3rd

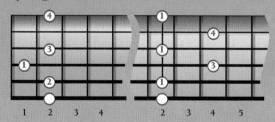

B7 (B seventh)
Spelling: 1st (B) 3rd (D♯) 5th (F♯) ♭7th (A)

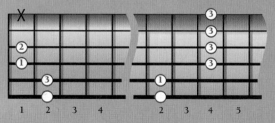

B6 (B sixth)
Spelling: 1st (B) 3rd (D♯) 5th (F♯) 6th (G♯)

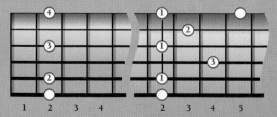

Bm7 (B minor seventh)
Spelling: 1st (B) ♭3rd (D) 5th (F♯) ♭7th (A)

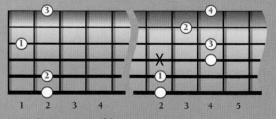

Bm6 (B minor sixth)
Spelling: 1st (B) ♭3rd (D) 5th (F♯) 6th (G♯)

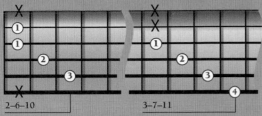

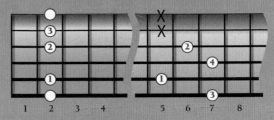

B aug/B+ (B augmented)
Spelling: 1st (B) 3rd (D#) #5th (G)

Bm9 (B minor ninth)
Spelling: 1st (B) ♭3rd (D) 5th (F#) ♭7th (A) 9th (C#)

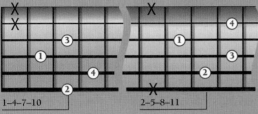

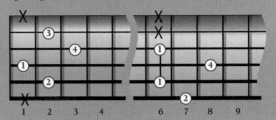

B dim/B° (B diminished)
Spelling: 1st (B) ♭3rd (D) ♭5th (F) ♭♭7th (A♭)

Bmaj9/B△9 (B major ninth)
Spelling: 1st (B) 3rd (D#) 5th (F#) 7th (A#) 9th (C#)

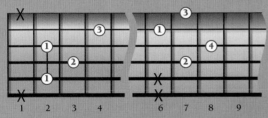

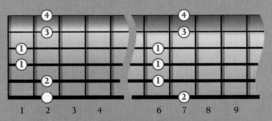

B7–5 (B seventh diminished fifth)
Spelling: 1st (B) 3rd (D#) ♭5th (F) ♭7th (A)

B6/9 (B six nine/B major sixth added ninth)
Spelling: 1st (B) 3rd (D#) 5th (F#) 6th (G#) 9th (C#)

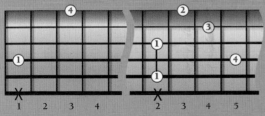

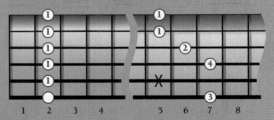

B7+5 (B seventh augmented fifth)
Spelling: 1st (B) 3rd (D#) #5th (G) ♭7th (A)

B11 (B eleventh)
Spelling: 1st (B) 3rd (D#) 5th (F#) ♭7th (A) 9th (C#)
11th (E)

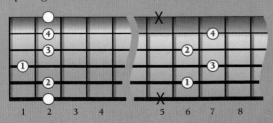

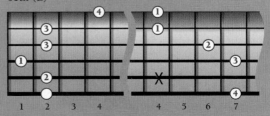

B9 (B ninth)
Spelling: 1st (B) 3rd (D#) 5th (F#) ♭7th (A) 9th (C#)

B13 (B thirteenth)
Spelling: 1st (B) 3rd (D#) 5th (F#) ♭7th (A) 9th (C#)
13th (G#)

C chords

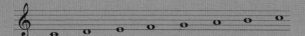

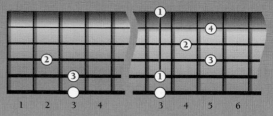

Cmaj7/CΔ7 (C major seventh)
Spelling: 1st (C) 3rd (E) 5th (G) 7th (B)

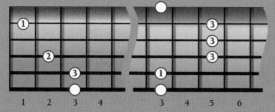

C (C major)
Spelling: 1st (C) 3rd (E) 5th (G)

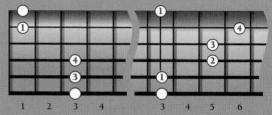

C sus 4/C sus (C suspended fourth)
Spelling: 1st (C) 4th (F) 5th (G) Note: no 3rd

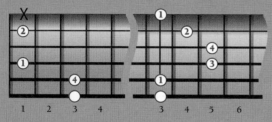

Cm (C minor)
Spelling: 1st (C) ♭3rd (E♭) 5th (G)

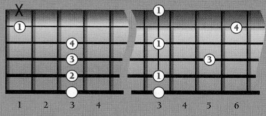

C7 sus 4/C7+4 (C seventh suspended fourth)
Spelling: 1st (C) 4th (F) 5th (G) ♭7th (B♭) Note no3rd

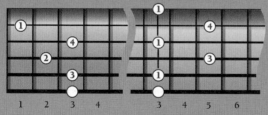

C7 (C seventh)
Spelling: 1st (C) 3rd (E) 5th (G) ♭7th (B♭)

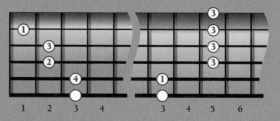

C6 (C sixth)
Spelling: 1st (C) 3rd (E) 5th (G) 6th (A)

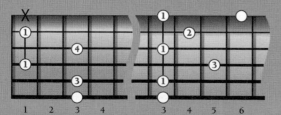

Cm7 (C minor seventh)
Spelling: 1st (C) ♭3rd (E♭) 5th (G) ♭7th (B♭)

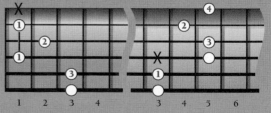

Cm6 (C minor sixth)
Spelling: 1st (C) ♭3rd (E♭) 5th (G) 6th (A)

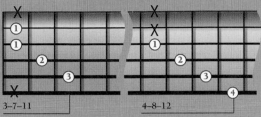

C aug/C+ (C augmented)
Spelling: 1st (C) 3rd (E) ♯5th (G♯)

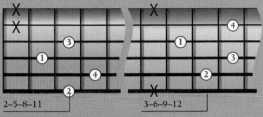

C dim/C° (C diminished)
Spelling: 1st (C) ♭3rd (E♭) ♭5th (Gb) ♭♭7th (A)

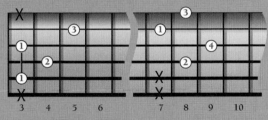

C7–5 (C diminished fifth)
Spelling: 1st (C) 3rd (E) ♭5th (G♭) ♭7th (Bb)

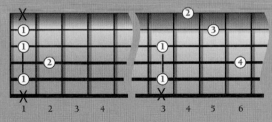

C7+5 (C seventh augmented fifth)
Spelling: 1st (C) 3rd (E) ♯5th (G♯) ♭7th (B♭)

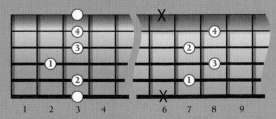

C9 (C ninth)
Spelling: 1st (C) 3rd (E) 5th (G) ♭7th (B♭) 9th (D)

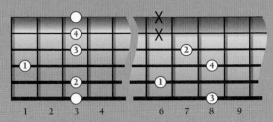

Cm9 (C minor ninth)
Spelling: 1st (C) ♭3rd (E♭) 5th (G) ♭7th (B♭) 9th (D)

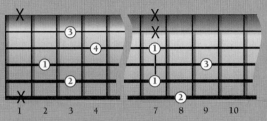

Cmaj9/C∆9 (C major ninth)
Spelling: 1st (C) 3rd (E) 5th (G) 7th (B) 9th (D)

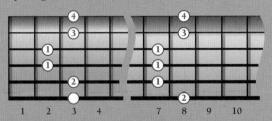

C6/9 (C six nine/C major sixth added ninth)
Spelling: 1st (C) 3rd (E) 5th (G) 6th (A) 9th (D)

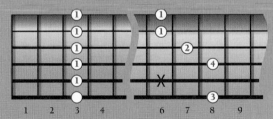

C11 (C eleventh)
Spelling: 1st (C) 3rd (E) 5th (G) ♭7th (B♭) 9th (D)
11th (F)

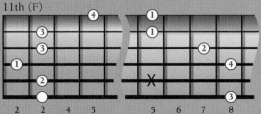

C13 (C thirteenth)
Spelling: 1st (C) 3rd (E) 5th (G) ♭7th (B♭) 9th (D)
13th (A)

C#/Db chords

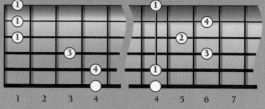

C#maj7/C#Δ7 (C sharp major seventh)
Spelling: 1st (C#) 3rd (F) 5th (G#) 7th (C)

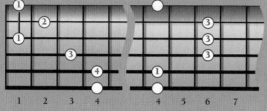

C# (C sharp major)
Spelling: 1st (C#) 3rd (F) 5th (G#)

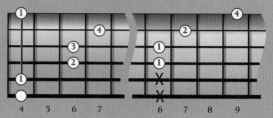

C# sus 4/C# sus (C sharp suspended fourth)
Spelling: 1st (C#) 4th (F#) 5th (G#) Note: no 3rd

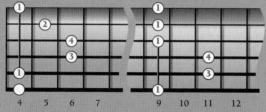

C# m (C sharp minor)
Spelling: 1st (C#) b3rd (E) 5th (G#)

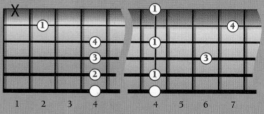

C#7 sus 4/C#7+4 (C sharp seventh suspended fourth)
Spelling: 1st (C#) 4th (F#) 5th (G#) b7th (B) Note no 3rd

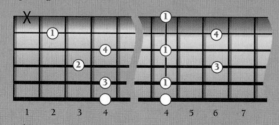

C#7 (C sharp seventh)
Spelling: 1st (C#) 3rd (F) 5th (G#) b7th (B)

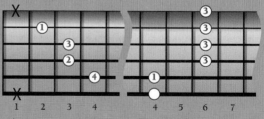

C#6 (C sharp sixth)
Spelling: 1st (C#) 3rd (F) 5th (G#) 6th (A#)

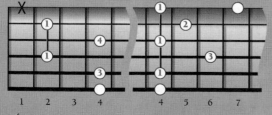

C#m7 (C sharp minor seventh)
Spelling: 1st (C#) b3rd (E) 5th (G#) b7th (B)

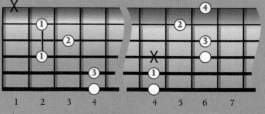

C#m6 (C sharp minor sixth)
Spelling: 1st (C#) b3rd (E) 5th (G#) 6th (A#)

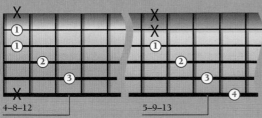

C♯ aug/C♯+ (C sharp augmented)
Spelling: 1st (C♯) 3rd (F) ♯5th (A)

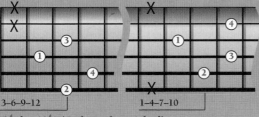

C♯ dim/C♯° (C sharp diminished)
Spelling: 1st (C♯) ♭3rd (E) ♭5th (G) ♭♭7th (B♭)

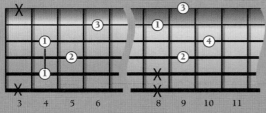

C♯7–5 (C sharp diminished fifth)
Spelling: 1st (C♯) 3rd (F) ♭5th (G) ♭7th (B)

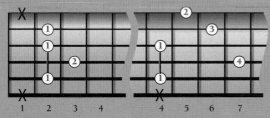

C♯7+5 (C sharp seventh augmented fifth)
Spelling: 1st (C♯) 3rd (F) ♯5th (A) ♭7th (B)

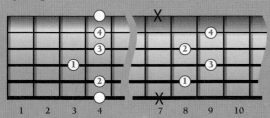

C♯9 (C sharp ninth)
Spelling: 1st (C♯) 3rd (F) 5th (G♯) ♭7th (B) 9th (D♯)

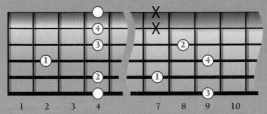

C♯m9 (C sharp minor ninth)
Spelling: 1st (C♯) ♭3rd (E) 5th (G♯) ♭7th (B) 9th (D♯)

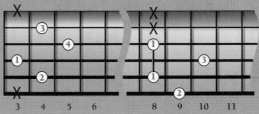

C♯maj9/C♯Δ9 (C sharp major ninth)
Spelling: 1st (C♯) 3rd (F) 5th (G♯) 7th (C) 9th (D♯)

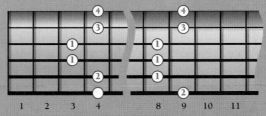

C♯6/9 (C sharp six nine/C sharp major sixth added ninth)
Spelling: 1st (C♯) 3rd (F) 5th (G♯) 6th (A♯) 9th (D♯)

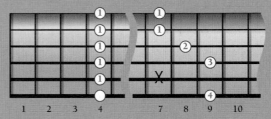

C♯11 (C sharp eleventh)
Spelling: 1st (C♯) 3rd (F) 5th (G♯) ♭7th (B) 9th (D♯)
11th (F♯)

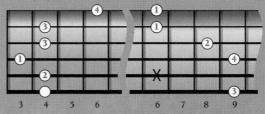

C♯13 (C sharp thirteenth)
Spelling: 1st (C♯) 3rd (F) 5th (G♯) ♭7th (B) 9th (D♯)
13th (A♯)

D chords

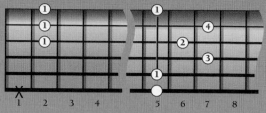

Dmaj7/D∆7 (D major seventh)
Spelling: 1st (D) 3rd (F♯) 5th (A) 7th (C♯)

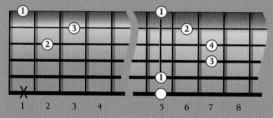

D (D major)
Spelling: 1st (D) 3rd (F♯) 5th (A)

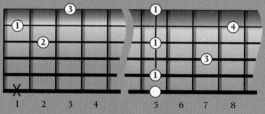

D sus 4/D sus (D suspended fourth)
Spelling: 1st (D) 4th (G) 5th (A) Note: no 3rd

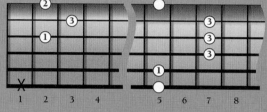

Dm (D minor)
Spelling: 1st (D) ♭3rd (F) 5th (A)

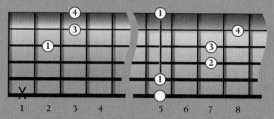

D7 sus 4/D7+4 (D seventh suspended fourth)
Spelling: 1st (D) 4th (G) 5th (A) ♭7th (C) Note: no 3rd

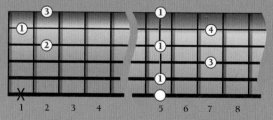

D7 (D seventh)
Spelling: 1st (D) 3rd (F♯) 5th (A) ♭7th (C)

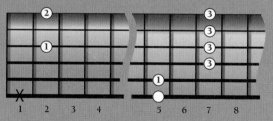

D6 (D sixth)
Spelling: 1st (D) 3rd (F♯) 5th (A) 6th (B)

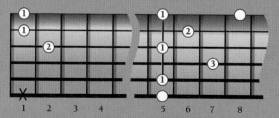

Dm7 (D minor seventh)
Spelling: 1st (D) ♭3rd (F) 5th (A) ♭7th (C)

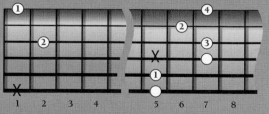

Dm6 (D minor sixth)
Spelling: 1st (D) ♭3rd (F) 5th (A) 6th (B)

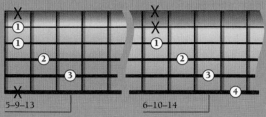

D aug/D+ (D augmented)
Spelling: 1st (D) 3rd (F♯) ♯5th (A♯)

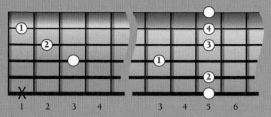

Dm9 (D minor ninth)
Spelling: 1st (D) ♭3rd (F) 5th (A) ♭7th (C) 9th (E)

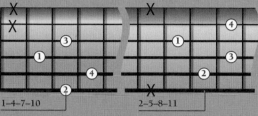

D dim/D° (D diminished)
Spelling: 1st (D) ♭3rd (F) ♭5th (A♭) ♭♭7th (B)

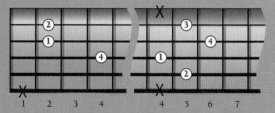

Dmaj9/DΔ9 (D major ninth)
Spelling: 1st (D) 3rd (F♯) 5th (A) 7th (C♯) 9th (E)

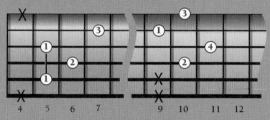

D7–5 (D diminished fifth)
Spelling: 1st (D) 3rd (F♯) ♭5th (A♭) ♭7th (C)

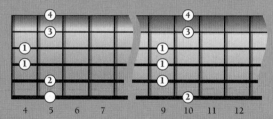

D6/9 (D six nine/D major sixth added ninth)
Spelling: 1st (D) 3rd (F♯) 5th (A) 6th (B) 9th (E)

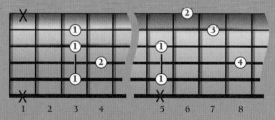

D7+5 (D seventh augmented fifth)
Spelling: 1st (D) 3rd (F♯) ♯5th (A♯) ♭7th (C)

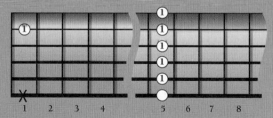

D11 (D eleventh)
Spelling: 1st (D) 3rd (F♯) 5th (A) ♭7th (A) 9th (E) 11th (G)

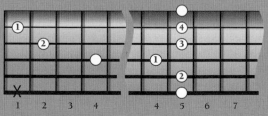

D9 (D ninth)
Spelling: 1st (D) 3rd (F♯) 5th (A) ♭7th (C) 9th (E)

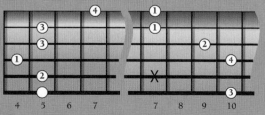

D13 (D thirteenth)
Spelling: 1st (D) 3rd (F♯) 5th (A) ♭7th (C) 9th (E) 13th (B)

D#/E♭ chords

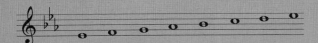

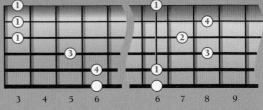

E♭maj7/E♭△7 (E flat major seventh)
Spelling: 1st (E♭) 3rd (G) 5th (B♭) 7th (D)

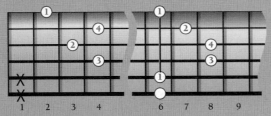

E♭ (E flat major)
Spelling: 1st (E♭) 3rd (G) 5th (B♭)

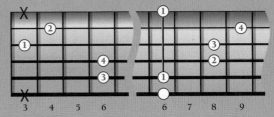

E♭ sus 4/E♭ sus (E flat suspended fourth)
Spelling: 1st (E♭) 4th (A♭) 5th (B♭) Note: no 3rd

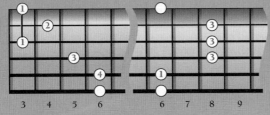

E♭m (E flat minor)
Spelling: 1st (E♭) ♭3rd (G♭) 5th (B♭)

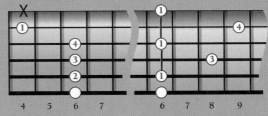

E♭7 sus 4/E♭7+4 (E flat seventh suspended fourth)
Spelling: 1st (E♭) 4th (A♭) 5th (B♭) ♭7th (D♭) Note: no 3rd

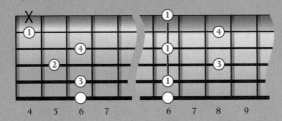

E♭7 (E flat seventh)
Spelling: 1st (E♭) 3rd (G) 5th (B♭) ♭7th (D♭)

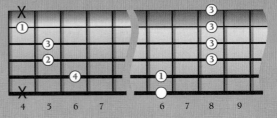

E♭6 (E flat sixth)
Spelling: 1st (E♭) 3rd (G) 5th (B♭) 6th (C)

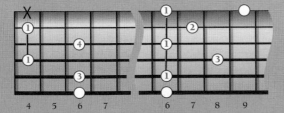

E♭m7 (E flat minor seventh)
Spelling: 1st (E♭) ♭3rd (G♭) 5th (B♭) ♭7th (D♭)

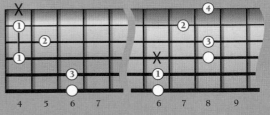

E♭m6 (E flat minor sixth)
Spelling: 1st (E♭) ♭3rd (G♭) 5th (B♭) 6th (C)

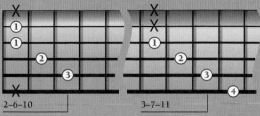

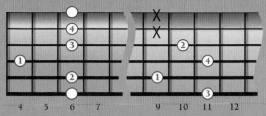

Eᵇ aug/Eᵇ+ (E flat augmented)
Spelling: 1st (Eᵇ) 3rd (G) ♯5th (B)

Eᵇm9 (E flat minor ninth)
Spelling: 1st (Eᵇ) ♭3rd (Gᵇ) 5th (Bᵇ) ♭7th (Dᵇ) 9th (F)

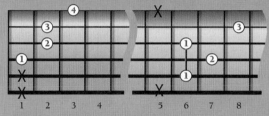

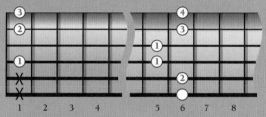

Eᵇ dim/Eᵇ° (E flat diminished)
Spelling: 1st (Eᵇ) ♭3rd (Gᵇ) ♭5th (A) ♭♭7th (C)

Eᵇmaj9/Eᵇ△9 (E flat major ninth)
Spelling: 1st (Eᵇ) 3rd (G) 5th (Bᵇ) 7th (D) 9th (F)

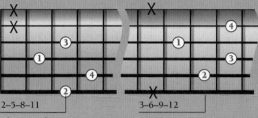

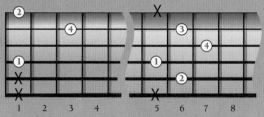

Eᵇ7–5 (E flat diminished fifth)
Spelling: 1st (Eᵇ) 3rd (G) ♭5th (A) ♭7th (Dᵇ)

Eᵇ6/9 (Eᵇ six nine/E flat major sixth added ninth)
Spelling: 1st (Eᵇ) 3rd (G) 5th (Bᵇ) 6th (C) 9th (F)

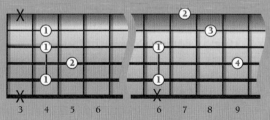

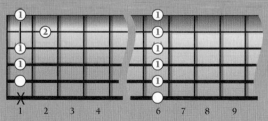

Eᵇ7+5 (E flat seventh augmented fifth)
Spelling: 1st (Eᵇ) 3rd (G) ♯5th (B) ♭7th (Dᵇ)

Eᵇ11 (E flat eleventh)
Spelling: 1st (Eᵇ) 3rd (G) 5th (Bᵇ) ♭7th (Dᵇ) 9th (F)
11th (Aᵇ)

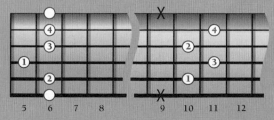

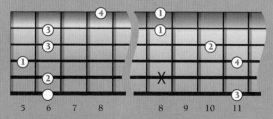

Eᵇ9 (E flat ninth)
Spelling: 1st (Eᵇ) 3rd (G) 5th (Bᵇ) ♭7th (Dᵇ) 9th (F)

Eᵇ13 (E flat thirteenth)
Spelling: 1st (Eᵇ) 3rd (G) 5th (Bᵇ) ♭7th (Dᵇ) 9th (F)
13th (C)

E chords

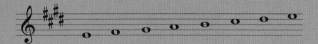

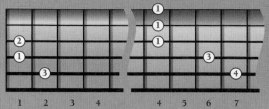

Emaj7/E△7 (E major seventh)
Spelling: 1st (E) 3rd (G♯) 5th (B) 7th (D♯)

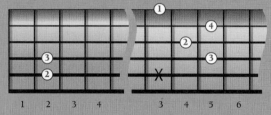

E (E major)
Spelling: 1st (E) 3rd (G♯) 5th (B)

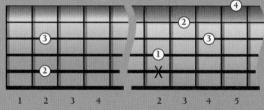

E sus 4/E sus (E suspended fourth)
Spelling: 1st (E) 4th (A) 5th (B) Note: no 3rd

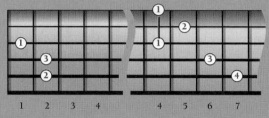

Em (E minor)
Spelling: 1st (E) ♭3rd (G) 5th (B)

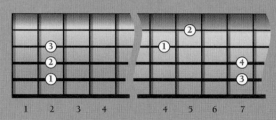

E7 sus 4/E7+4 (E seventh suspended fourth)
Spelling: 1st (E) 4th (A) 5th (B) ♭7th (D) Note: no 3rd

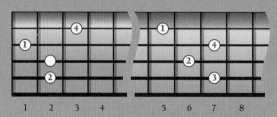

E7 (E seventh)
Spelling: 1st (E) 3rd (G♯) 5th (B) ♭7th (D)

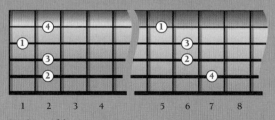

E6 (E sixth)
Spelling: 1st (E) 3rd (G♯) 5th (B) 6th (C♯)

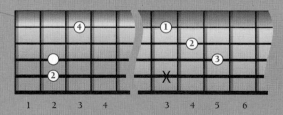

Em7 (E minor seventh)
Spelling: 1st (E) ♭3rd (G) 5th (B) ♭7th (D)

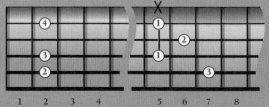

Em6 (E minor sixth)
Spelling: 1st (E) ♭3rd (G) 5th (B) 6th (C♯)

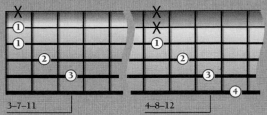

3–7–11   4–8–12

E aug/E+ (E augmented)
Spelling: 1st (E) 3rd (G♯) ♯5th (C)

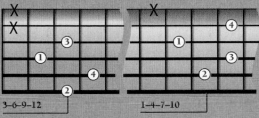

3–6–9–12   1–4–7–10

E dim/E° (E diminished)
Spelling: 1st (E) ♭3rd (G) ♭5th (B♭) ♭♭7th (D♭)

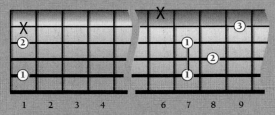

1 2 3 4   6 7 8 9

E7–5 (E seventh diminished fifth)
Spelling: 1st (E) 3rd (G♯) ♭5th (B♭) ♭7th (D)

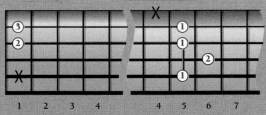

1 2 3 4   4 5 6 7

E7+5 (E seventh augmented fifth)
Spelling: 1st (E) 3rd (G♯) ♯5th (C) ♭7th (D)

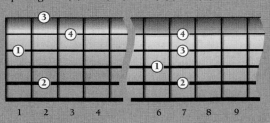

1 2 3 4   6 7 8 9

E9 (E ninth)
Spelling: 1st (E) 3rd (G♯) 5th (B) ♭7th (D) 9th (F♯)

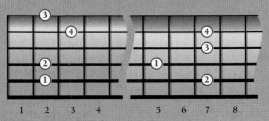

1 2 3 4   5 6 7 8

Em9 (E minor ninth)
Spelling: 1st (E) ♭3rd (G) 5th (B) ♭7th (D) 9th (F♯)

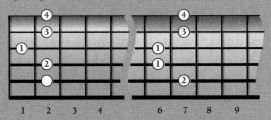

1 2 3 4   4 5 6 7

Emaj9/E∆9 (E major ninth)
Spelling: 1st (E) 3rd (G♯) 5th (B) 7th (D♯) 9th (F♯)

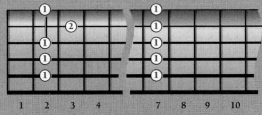

1 2 3 4   6 7 8 9

E6/9 (E six nine/E major sixth added ninth)
Spelling: 1st (E) 3rd (G♯) 5th (B) 6th (C♯) 9th (F♯)

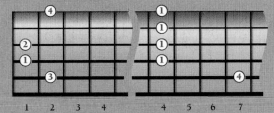

1 2 3 4   7 8 9 10

E11 (E eleventh)
Spelling: 1st (E) 3rd (G♯) 5th (B) ♭7th (D) 9th (F♯) 11th (A)

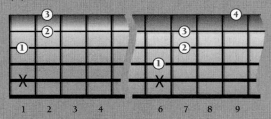

1 2 3 4   6 7 8 9

E13 (E thirteenth)
Spelling: 1st (E) 3rd (G♯) 5th (B) ♭7th (D) 9th (F♯) 13th (C♯)

F chords

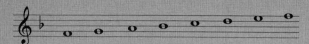

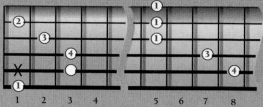

Fmaj7/FΔ7 (F major seventh)
Spelling: 1st (F) 3rd (A) 5th (C) 7th (E)

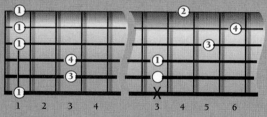

F (F major)
Spelling: 1st (F) 3rd (A) 5th (C)

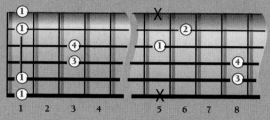

F sus 4/F sus (F suspended fourth)
Spelling: 1st (F) 4th (B♭) 5th (C) Note: no 3rd

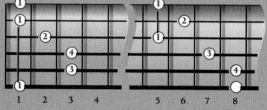

Fm (F minor)
Spelling: 1st (F) ♭3rd (A♭) 5th (C)

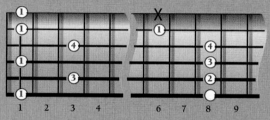

F7 sus 4/F7+4 (F seventh suspended fourth)
Spelling: 1st (F) 4th (B♭) 5th (C) ♭7th (E♭) Note: no 3rd

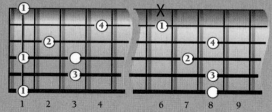

F7 (F seventh)
Spelling: 1st (F) 3rd (A) 5th (C) ♭7th (E♭)

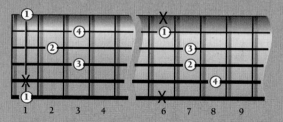

F6 (F sixth)
Spelling: 1st (F) 3rd (A) 5th (C) 6th (D)

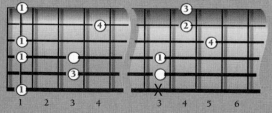

Fm7 (F minor seventh)
Spelling: 1st (F) ♭3rd (A♭) 5th (C) ♭7th (E♭)

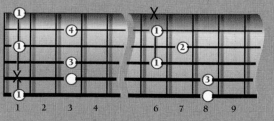

Fm6 (F minor sixth)
Spelling: 1st (F) ♭3rd (A♭) 5th (C) 6th (D)

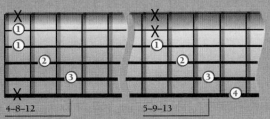

4–8–12 · 5–9–13

F aug/F+ (F augmented)
Spelling: 1st (F) 3rd (A) ♯5th (C♯)

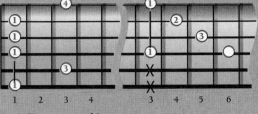

1 2 3 4 · 3 4 5 6

Fm9 (F minor ninth)
Spelling: 1st (F) ♭3rd (A♭) 5th (C) ♭7th (E♭) 9th (G)

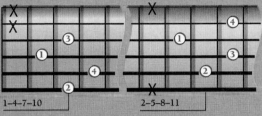

1–4–7–10 · 2–5–8–11

F dim/F° (F diminished)
Spelling: 1st (F) ♭3rd (A♭) ♭5th (B) ♭♭7th (D)

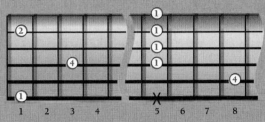

1 2 3 4 · 5 6 7 8

Fmaj9/F∆9 (F major ninth)
Spelling: 1st (F) 3rd (A) 5th (C) 7th (E) 9th (G)

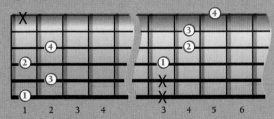

1 2 3 4 · 3 4 5 6

F7–5 (F diminished fifth)
Spelling: 1st (F) 3rd (A) ♭5th (B) ♭7th (E♭)

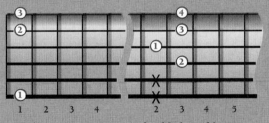

1 2 3 4 · 2 3 4 5

F6/9 (F six nine/F major sixth added ninth)
Spelling: 1st (F) 3rd (A) 5th (C) 6th (D) 9th (G)

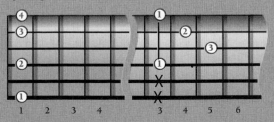

1 2 3 4 · 5 6 7 8

F7+5 (F seventh augmented fifth)
Spelling: 1st (F) 3rd (A) ♯5th (C♯) ♭7th (E♭)

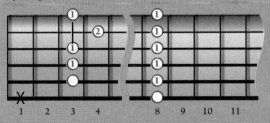

1 2 3 4 · 8 9 10 11

F11 (F eleventh)
Spelling: 1st (F) 3rd (A) 5th (C) ♭7th (E♭) 9th (G) 11th (B♭)

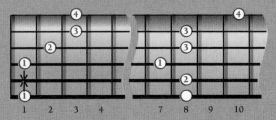

1 2 3 4 · 7 8 9 10

F9 (F ninth)
Spelling: 1st (F) 3rd (A) 5th (C) ♭7th (E♭) 9th (G)

F13 (F thirteenth)
Spelling: 1st (F) 3rd (A) 5th (C) ♭7th (E♭) 9th (G) 13th (D)

F#/Gb chords

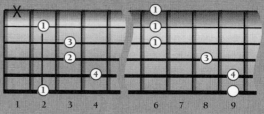

F#maj7/F#Δ7 (F sharp major seventh)
Spelling: 1st (F#) 3rd (A#) 5th (C#) 7th (F)

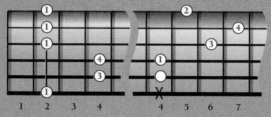

F# (F sharp major)
Spelling: 1st (F#) 3rd (A#) 5th (C#)

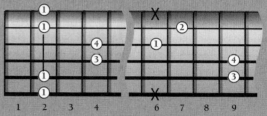

F# sus 4/F# sus (F sharp suspended fourth)
Spelling: 1st (F#) 4th (B) 5th (C#) Note: no 3rd

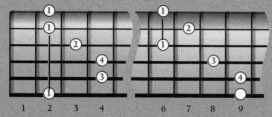

F#m (F sharp minor)
Spelling: 1st (F#) b3rd (A) 5th (C#)

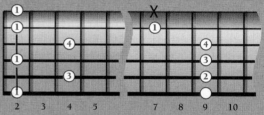

F#7 sus 4/F#7+4 (F sharp seventh suspended fourth)
Spelling: 1st (F#) 4th (B) 5th (C#) b7th (E) Note no 3rd

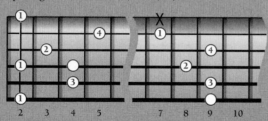

F#7 (F sharp seventh)
Spelling: 1st (F#) 3rd (A#) 5th (C#) b7th (E)

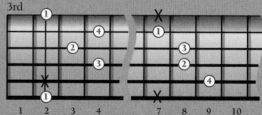

F#6 (F sharp sixth)
Spelling: 1st (F#) 3rd (A#) 5th (C#) 6th (D#)

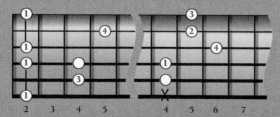

F#m7 (F sharp minor seventh)
Spelling: 1st (F#) b3rd (A) 5th (C#) b7th (E)

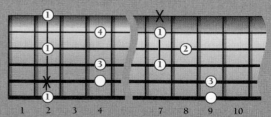

F#m6 (F sharp minor sixth)
Spelling: 1st (F#) b3rd (A) 5th (C#) 6th (D#)

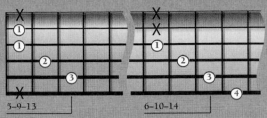

5–9–13   6–10–14

F♯ aug/F♯+ (F sharp augmented)
Spelling: 1st (F♯) 3rd (F♯) ♯5th (D)

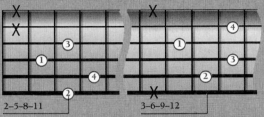

2–5–8–11   3–6–9–12

F♯ dim/F♯° (F sharp diminished)
Spelling: 1st (F♯) ♭3rd (A) ♭5th (C) ♭♭7th (E♭)

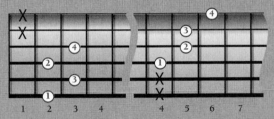

1 2 3 4   4 5 6 7

F♯7–5 (F sharp diminished fifth)
Spelling: 1st (F♯) 3rd (A♯) ♭5th (C) ♭7th (E)

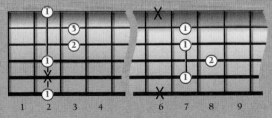

1 2 3 4   6 7 8 9

F♯7+5 (F sharp seventh augmented fifth)
Spelling: 1st (F♯) 3rd (A♯) ♯5th (D) ♭7th (E)

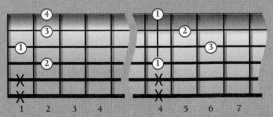

1 2 3 4   4 5 6 7

F♯9 (F sharp ninth)
Spelling: 1st (F♯) 3rd (A♯) 5th (C♯) ♭7th (E) 9th (G♯)

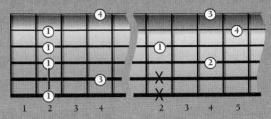

1 2 3 4   2 3 4 5

F♯m9 (F sharp minor ninth)
Spelling: 1st (F♯) ♭3rd (A) 5th (C♯) ♭7th (E) 9th (G♯)

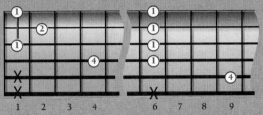

1 2 3 4   6 7 8 9

F♯maj9/F♯Δ9 (F sharp major ninth)
Spelling: 1st (F♯) 3rd (A♯) 5th (C♯) 7th (F) 9th (G♯)

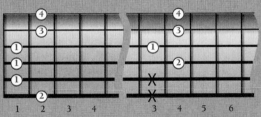

1 2 3 4   3 4 5 6

F♯6/9 (F sharp six nine/F sharp major sixth added ninth)
Spelling: 1st (F♯) 3rd (A♯) 5th (C♯) 6th (D♯) 9th (G♯)

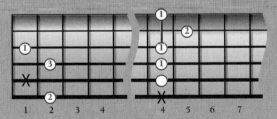

1 2 3 4   4 5 6 7

F♯11 (F sharp eleventh)
Spelling: 1st (F♯) 3rd (A♯) 5th (C♯) ♭7th (E) 9th (G♯) 11th (B)

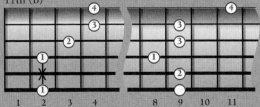

1 2 3 4   8 9 10 11

F♯13 (F sharp thirteenth)
Spelling: 1st (F♯) 3rd (A♯) 5th (C♯) ♭7th (E) 9th (G♯) 13th (D♯)

G chords

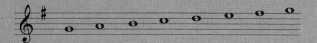

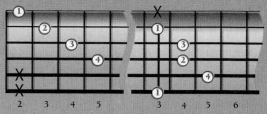

Gmaj7/G7 (G major seventh)
Spelling: 1st (G) 3rd (B) 5th (D) 7th (F♯)

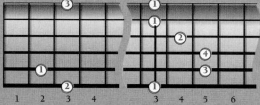

G (G major)
Spelling: 1st (G) 3rd (B) 5th (D)

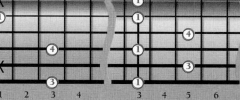

G sus 4/G sus (G suspended fourth)
Spelling: 1st (G) 4th (C) 5th (D) Note: no 3rd

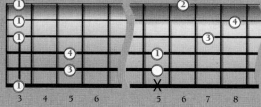

Gm (G minor)
Spelling: 1st (G) ♭3rd (B♭) 5th (D)

G7 sus 4/G7+4 (G seventh suspended fourth)
Spelling: 1st (G) 4th (C) 5th (D) ♭7th (F) Note no 3rd

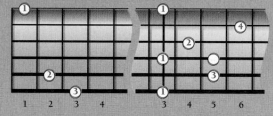

G7 (G seventh)
Spelling: 1st (G) 3rd (B) 5th (D) ♭7th (F)

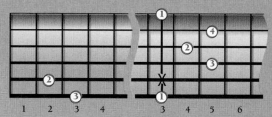

G6 (G sixth)
Spelling: 1st (G) 3rd (B) 5th (D) 6th (E)

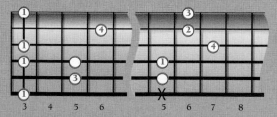

Gm7 (G minor seventh)
Spelling: 1st (G) ♭3rd (B♭) 5th (D) ♭7th (F)

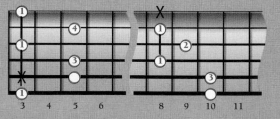

Gm6 (G minor sixth)
Spelling: 1st (G) ♭3rd (B♭) 5th (D) 6th (E)

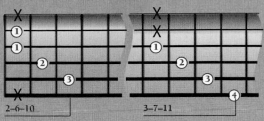

G aug/G+ (G augmented)
Spelling: 1st (G) 3rd (B) ♯5th (D♯)

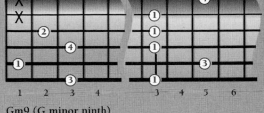

Gm9 (G minor ninth)
Spelling: 1st (G) ♭3rd (B♭) 5th (D) ♭7th (F) 9th (A)

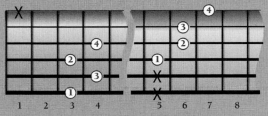

G dim/G° (G diminished)
Spelling: 1st (G) ♭3rd (B♭) ♭5th (D♭) ♭♭7th (E)

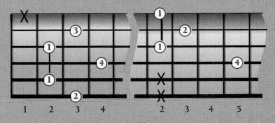

Gmaj9/GΔ9 (G major ninth)
Spelling: 1st (G) 3rd (B) 5th (D) 7th (F♯) 9th (A)

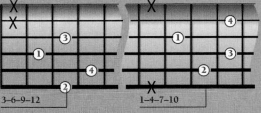

G7–5 (G seventh diminished fifth)
Spelling: 1st (G) 3rd (B) ♭5th (D♭) ♭7th (F)

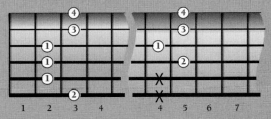

G6/9 (G six nine/G major sixth added ninth)
Spelling: 1st (G) 3rd (B) 5th (D) 6th (E) 9th (A)

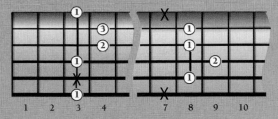

G7+5 (G seventh augmented fifth)
Spelling: 1st (G) 3rd (B) ♯5th (D♯) ♭7th (F)

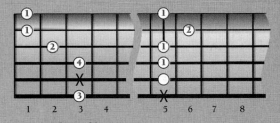

G11 (G eleventh)
Spelling: 1st (G) 3rd (B) 5th (D) ♭7th (F) 9th (A)
11th (C)

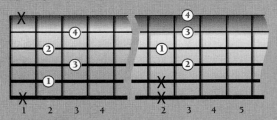

G9 (G ninth)
Spelling: 1st (G) 3rd (B) 5th (D) ♭7th (F) 9th (A)

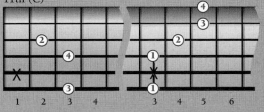

G13 (G thirteenth)
Spelling: 1st (G) 3rd (B) 5th (D) ♭7th (F) 9th (A)
13th (E)

G#/A♭ chords

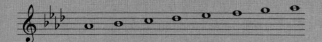

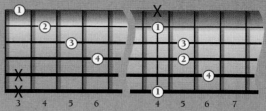

A♭maj7/A♭Δ7 (A flat major seventh)
Spelling: 1st (A♭) 3rd (C) 5th (E♭) 7th (G)

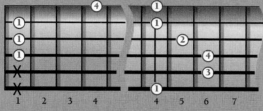

A♭ (A flat major)
Spelling: 1st (A♭) 3rd (C) 5th (E♭)

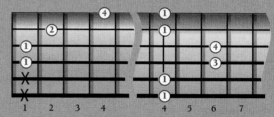

A♭ sus 4/A♭ sus (A flat suspended fourth)
Spelling: 1st (A♭) 4th (D♭) 5th (E♭) Note: no 3rd

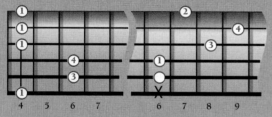

A♭m (A flat minor)
Spelling: 1st (A♭) ♭3rd (B) 5th (E♭)

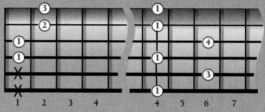

A♭7 sus 4/A♭7+4 (A flat seventh suspended fourth)
Spelling: 1st (A♭) 4th (D♭) 5th (E♭) ♭7th (G♭) Note no 3rd

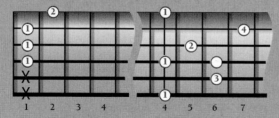

A♭7 (A flat seventh)
Spelling: 1st (A♭) 3rd (C) 5th (E♭) ♭7th (G♭)

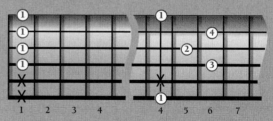

A♭6 (A flat sixth)
Spelling: 1st (A♭) 3rd (C) 5th (E♭) 6th (F)

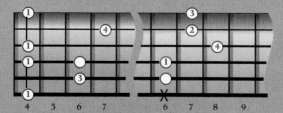

A♭m7 (A flat minor seventh)
Spelling: 1st (A♭) ♭3rd (B) 5th (E♭) ♭7th (G♭)

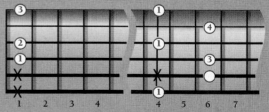

A♭m6 (A flat minor sixth)
Spelling: 1st (A♭) ♭3rd (B) 5th (E♭) 6th (F)

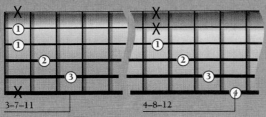

3–7–11   4–8–12

A♭ aug/A♭+ (A flat augmented)
Spelling: 1st (A♭) 3rd (C) ♯5th (E)

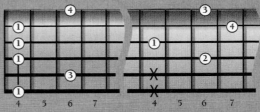

4 5 6 7   4 5 6 7

A♭m9 (A flat minor ninth)
Spelling: 1st (A♭) ♭3rd (B) 5th (E♭) ♭7th (G♭) 9th (B♭)

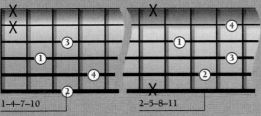

1–4–7–10   2–5–8–11

A♭ dim/A♭° (A flat diminished)
Spelling: 1st (A♭) ♭3rd (B) ♭5th (D) ♭♭3th (F)

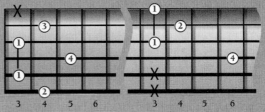

3 4 5 6   3 4 5 6

A♭ maj9/A♭Δ9 (A flat major ninth)
Spelling: 1st (A♭) 3rd (C) 5th (E♭) 7th (G) 9th (B♭)

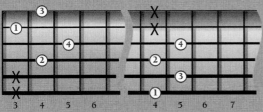

3 4 5 6   4 5 6 7

A♭7–5 (A flat seventh diminished fifth)
Spelling: 1st (A♭) 3rd (C) ♭5th (D) ♭7th (G♭)

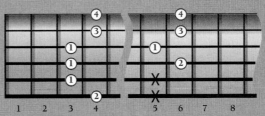

1 2 3 4   5 6 7 8

A♭6/9 (A♭ six nine/A flat major sixth added ninth)
Spelling: 1st (A♭) 3rd (C) 5th (E♭) 6th (F) 9th (B♭)

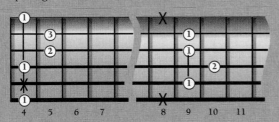

4 5 6 7   8 9 10 11

A♭7+5 (A flat seventh augmented fifth)
Spelling: 1st (A♭) 3rd (C) ♯5th (E) ♭7th (G♭)

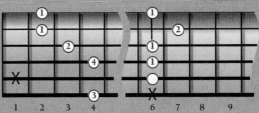

1 2 3 4   6 7 8 9

A♭11 (A flat eleventh)
Spelling: 1st (A♭) 3rd (C) 5th (E♭) ♭7th (G♭) 9th (B♭)
11th (D♭)

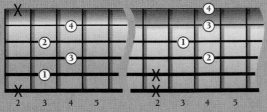

2 3 4 5   2 3 4 5

A♭9 (A flat ninth)
Spelling: 1st (A♭) 3rd (C) 5th (E♭) ♭7th (G♭) 9th (B♭)

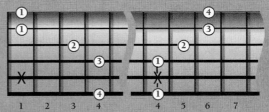

1 2 3 4   4 5 6 7

A♭13 (A flat thirteenth)
Spelling: 1st (A♭) 3rd (C) 5th (E♭) b7th (G♭) 9th (B♭)
13th (F)

(A

th)

Repairs and alterations

GUITARS ARE PRETTY *resilient. Given the torture we sometimes subject them to, they hardly ever seem to break down or wear out. In fact, just like that favorite old pair of shoes, a decent guitar will actually improve with age. Sometimes, however, your guitar may need the occasional surgery to keep it in tip-top working order.*

Following are the kinds of modifications or repairs you might need to undertake in the life of a typical working guitar. Most of them you can do for yourself; some we would suggest are best left to the experts.

Setting the action

Adjusting the action of the guitar – the height of the strings above the frets – is the simplest modification you can make. The higher the action, the greater the pressure that has to be applied by the left hand to fret the notes comfortably. Largely speaking, a low action is more desirable, unless you play a lot of bottleneck guitar. For fast solo work, a low action is more suitable; however, setting the action too low will result in fret buzz – a low action shows up any imperfections in the fingerboard since the frets must be of uniform height.

Measuring the action is a simple matter of taking a steel ruler with fine gradations and placing it on the 12th fret. A reasonably average measurement is likely to be between 0.05 and 0.09 inches for an electric guitar and 0.08 to 0.12 inches for an acoustic instrument. Measure the distance between the tip of the fret and the bottom of the string. Setting the action is not exactly rocket science and is often done by trial and error, selecting the lowest possible action without causing fret buzz.

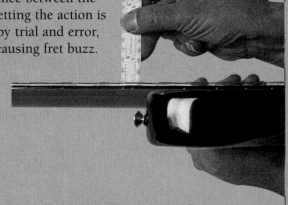

■ **When measuring the action,** *ensure the ruler you use is one where the scale starts at the tip.*

To change the action, you must alter the height of the strings. This is achieved by changing the height of the bridge. On most electric guitars, each string has its own individual bridge saddle which you raise by turning a small screw in a clockwise direction.

Acoustic guitars usually have a bridge saddle made from bone. On some models, screws at the side can be used to raise the entire platform at either edge, which might be sufficient for your needs. To make more refined adjustments to specific strings, you will need to take a fine file to the saddle.

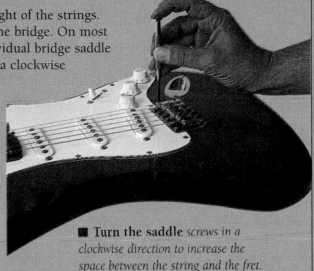

■ **Turn the saddle** *screws in a clockwise direction to increase the space between the string and the fret.*

The nut

For the action to be set perfectly, the nut also needs setting to correct height (if your guitar has a zero fret, this probably won't need attention since it's unlikely to wear out). By trying out this simple test, you will see whether your nut is set correctly. Play the guitar around the first three frets – try an assortment of single notes and chords. Next, fit a capo to the first fret and play the same thing again. If you find the guitar a lot easier to play with the capo fitted, the action at the nut is too high.

To adjust the nut, you simply have to cut the grooves that support the strings a little deeper. Do this in careful, small steps. If you go too deep, you will cause fret buzz, which means you will have to replace the nut.

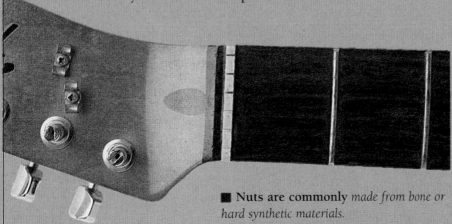

■ **Nuts are commonly** *made from bone or hard synthetic materials.*

Intonation

As you should know by now, intonation refers to how in tune the guitar is with itself. You can tell if the intonation is poor by playing an open string and comparing it to the note you get on the 12th fret. They should be one octave apart and in perfect tune. This is because the distance between the nut or zero fret and the 12th fret should be identical to the distance between the 12th fret and the point at which the string touches the bridge saddle.

If the note you hear when you play the 12th fret is sharp – too high in pitch – this means that the string is too short and must be lengthened by moving the saddle back. Most guitars have individually adjustable string saddles which are usually controlled by an allen wrench or small screwdriver. Turning the screw counterclockwise will move the saddle farther away from the nut, thereby lengthening the string. Carry on with the 12th-fret tests until the intonation is completely correct. If you don't trust your hearing, you can use a guitar tuner to give you a visual cue when you've got it right (see pages 114–115).

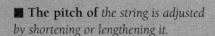

■ **The pitch of** *the string is adjusted by shortening or lengthening it.*

Neck problems

When things go wrong with your guitar's neck, they can be problematic to repair. To be honest, most of the repairs are not worth the time, effort, or potential risk of your performing them yourself unless you really are confident – there are highly skilled guitar technicians out there just waiting for you to pay them a visit. Following are two common neck problems.

Because of the tension coming from the strings, all guitar necks have a very slight curve around the 7th or 8th fret. If this curve becomes too exaggerated, however, the action around the middle of the fingerboard will be significantly higher than at either end of the fingerboard – which is a bad thing. You can control the curve of the neck by adjusting the truss rod – the metal bar that passes through the neck. Depending on the neck design, adjustments are made at either end of the neck. Using a small spanner or allen wrench, turning clockwise tightens the truss rod and reduces the curve.

■ **Check the relief** *of your guitar (the curve along the length of the neck) by holding the string down at the first and last frets and measuring the gap between the bottom of the string and top of the fret.*

If the neck begins to warp, your guitar needs some serious surgery, which may require a brand-new neck to be fitted.

■ **Allen wrenches** *are often used to make adjustments to truss rods at the headstock.*

■ **Adjustments can** *also be made to the truss rods at the body end of the neck.*

Frets

Frets are the one part of a guitar's anatomy that will eventually wear out. Each time you press a string down against a fret, a tiny bit of nickel is worn away from the fret. If you bend the strings, the abrasion will be worse. Eventually, your frets will end up looking like the ones pictured here.

Frets that are too worn will cause the strings to buzz. The only solution at that point is to replace the fret. Removing and replacing a fret is pretty simple, but the fine-tuning and measuring gauges needed to file it to the correct height is best left to a specialist.

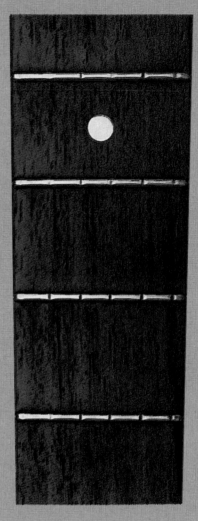

■ **If your frets** *become too worn, then they will need to be replaced.*

Electrical issues

The circuitry found in most electric guitars is so simple that it rarely fails. More likely you'll come across minor faults instead: crackling tone and volume controls, clicking pickup switches, or those pesky loose jack sockets. Most of these problems can usually be solved by spraying switch-cleaning fluid along the contact points. Sometimes, however, you may just have to replace a component.

Although ordinarily we would suggest caution when dealing with electrical matters, the circuitry of a guitar is so simple that anyone who can use a soldering iron should be able to replace any of the individual parts – even if you haven't a clue what they actually do. To be on the safe side, draw yourself a little diagram or mark the wires so you can ensure that they are soldered to the same points on their replacement parts.

Getting to the electrical components depends on the type of guitar you have, although on most it's usually a simple matter of removing a panel at the back of the body.

Supercharging

Some guitarists are never satisfied and are constantly on the lookout for ideas that will improve their sound. One of the most common and simple customizations you can make is to replace the pickups. If you go into a decent guitar store, you will see any number of alternative pickups for sale. These will all sound just a little bit different, but one might be exactly what you're looking for.

Fitting a new pickup is simply a matter of opening the electrics panel, unsoldering the old pickup, and replacing it with a new one. Keep the old one, though. Old pickups always come in handy – and you may want to put it back on if you sell your guitar.

Body repairs and renovations

At some point in its life, no matter how much you care for it, your guitar is going to experience some knocks and scrapes. On solid-body electrics, many of us don't worry too much about this, seeing them rather as battle scars to be worn with pride.

Acoustic instruments are somewhat more delicate, though. A hard knock can make a hole through the body, which can have an impact on the way the guitar sounds. Unless you have a really cheap instrument, we don't recommend that you try to repair cracks to an acoustic guitar on your own – without a workshop full of specialist clamps and glues, that is. This is another one for the big boys.

The subject of refinishing guitars is a thorny one. We've probably all seen our favorite guitarists sporting exotic custom finishes and given the idea at least a moment's thought. A word of warning: Getting your art school pal to air-brush a likeness of your face over your vintage Les Paul might look cool, but it will completely demolish its resale value. If you fancy painting your guitar yourself, you'll need to get some industrial spraying equipment and prepare yourself for a lot of elbow grease. To get something that looks remotely like a professional finish requires the application and buffing of layer upon layer of polyurethane varnish. And hard work like that should be left to the pros.

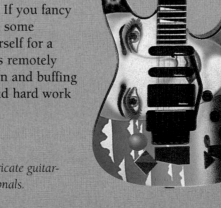

■ **Leave any really** *intricate guitar-decorating to the professionals.*

Web sites

www.bascap.com
Visit this site to register with a mechanical copyright protection or performing rights organization.

www.bmi.com
Find out how royalties are collected.

www.datadragon.com/education/reading/
A great step-by-step introduction to reading music.

www.djprince.net/majorandminor.htm
Find out what makes a chord major or minor.

www.dreamscape.com/esmith/dansm/acoustic/info/strumming.htm
Get into some basic strumming technique on this site.

www.drsdigital.com
Log on and obtain a neat piece of computer software called ChordBook.

www.endprod.com/tab
A basic explanation of how to read guitar tablature.

www.eskimo.com/~ogre/lessons/19961011.html
A very thorough introduction to chord theory, written for beginners, from the Online Guitar College.

www.fender.com
Everything you want to know about Fender guitars.

www.geofex.com
Discover a whole host of effects.

www.gibson.com
Visit the makers of the famous Gibson guitar.

www.glenbrook.k12.il.us/gbssci/phys/Class/sound/u11l5b.html
A simple physics lesson on how guitar strings make sounds, try this page from The Physics Classroom.

www.guitar.about.com
A whole host of information about the instrument.

www.guitar.about.com/entertainment/guitar/library/weekly/a a022000a.htm
For more on playing the same chords in different

places on the fingerboard, check out this site for the major chords.

www.guitar.about.com/entertainment/guitar/library/weekly/a a030800a.htm
This tells you about the minor chords.

www.guitar.about.com/library/howto/htplayleadguitar.htm
"How to play fake lead guitar," and is a little bit amusing.

www.guitar.about.com/msubmenu.htm
Find a huge range of tabulated songs organized in alphabetical order by artist.

www.guitarist.com/cg/cg.htm
The classical guitar homepage

www.GuitarSite.com
This site has everything: Whatever style you're into, you'll find it here.

www.harmony-central.com
Check this out for a list of everything guitar-related you could possibly buy.

www.homerecording.about.com
All about home recording....

www.jamtrack.com
Play over a selection of backing tracks.

www.jazzguitar.com
A site dedicated to jazz guitar.

www.jps.net/kmatsu/
Info. from an amateur luthier on how to build your own guitar.

www.learn2.com/08/0853/0853.php3
How to tune a guitar, and an explanation of what being in tune really means.

www.looknohands.com/chordhouse/
Plenty of chord charts for beginners and advanced players.

www.martin.com
Learn about the history and manufacture of the Martin guitar.

www.mp3.com
Find out more about MP3 files
and how they are compressed and downloaded.

www.music.indiana.edu/som/courses/rhythm/glossary.html
A Rhythm and Meter Glossary.

www.netradio.com/learn/country/index.html
Find out more about the styles that are a part of
this genre.

www.northwestern.edu/musicschool/links/projects/guitar/ele
mentaryGuitarHome.html
Site explains in detail the correct playing posture
for every part of your body, as well as basic stroke
techniques.

www.nwlink.com/~rxg/fsg.html
The history of fingerpicking guitar technique. It
will also put you on the Thumb and Finger Style
Guitar Web Ring.

www.opgc.com/
The website of the Old Pueblo Guitar Company
offers basic lessons, instructions on how to change
your strings, and downloadable sheet music.

www.sound.au.com/project27.htm
This site tells you how to build your own 100 watt
amp that you can modify to suit your own needs.

www.soundwave.com
Professional music industry web site that features
content of interest to recording studios, producers,
musicians, equipment manufacturers and dealers.

www.stagepass.com/tuning.html
For an esoteric but interesting discussion of the
limits of fine tuning, check out this article on Stage
Pass.

www.teoria.com/books/chords/chSevenths.htm
For the low-down on dominant seventh chords,
check this site out.

www.tuckandpatti.com/pick-finger_tech.html
A very comprehensive, easy-to-understand course
on Pick and Fingerstyle Technique.

www.ultimateguitarpage.com/technique
For more information on hammer-ons and pull-
offs, as well as the lowdown on other techniques.

Further reading

The Alternate Tuning Guide for Guitar,
  Mark Hanson (AMSCO, 1991)
Aural Matters, David Bowman &
  Paul Terry (Schott, 1993)
Classic Guitar Technique, Aaron
  Shearer (Franco Colombo, 1963)
The Complete Encyclopedia of the
  Guitar, Terry Burrows (Carlton,
  1998)
The Complete Guitarist, Richard
  Chapman (Dorling Kindersley,
  1993)
How to Make and Sell Your Own
  Record, Diane Sward Rapaport
  (Headlands, 1984)
El Arte de Flamenco de la Guitarra,
  Juan Martín (United Music, 1982)
Electric Blues Guitar, Iain Scott (East
  River, 1998)

The Fender Book, Tony Bacon &
  Paul Day (IMP, 1992)
Flat-pick Country Guitar, Happy
  Traum (Oak, 1973)
The Guitar, Harvey Turnbull (Bold
  Strummer, 1991)
The Guitar Handbook, Ralph Denyer
  (Pan, 1992)
Home Recording for Musicians, Craig
  Anderton (AMSCO, 1978)
The Home Recording Handbook, Chris
  Everard (Virgin, 1985)
How to Read Music, Terry Burrows
  (Carlton, 1999)
Improvisation, Derek Bailey
  (Moorland, 1980)
The New Harvard Dictionary of
  Music, Don Randall (Harvard
  University Press, 1986)

1000 Great Guitarists, Hugh Gregory
  (IMP, 1992)
Play Country Guitar, Terry Burrows
  (Dorling Kindersley, 1995)
Play Electric Guitar, Terry Burrows
  (St. Martin's Press, 1999)
Play Rock Guitar, Terry Burrows
  (Dorling Kindersley, 1995)
Rock, Jazz and Pop Arranging, Darryl
  Runswick (Faber and Faber, 1992)
Studio Recording for Musicians, Fred
  Miller (AMSCO, 1981)
Thesaurus of Scales and Melodic
  Patterns, Nicolas Slonimsky
  (Scrivener's, 1947)
Total Guitar Tutor, Terry Burrows
  (Carlton, 1998)
The Ultimate Guitar Book, Tony
  Bacon (Dorling Kindersley, 1991)

Further listening

IF YOU LOCK *half a dozen guitarists in a room to discuss the most important guitar albums ever made, you're likely to end up with a hugely divergent list. Here is one such offering. Not definitive by any means, this list is merely your humble author's view of some of the best, most noteworthy, and interesting guitar music around.*

When entries are listed by band name, the guitarist is also named in brackets. Truly outstanding albums are highlighted with a star. Happy listening!

Rock and pop

The Allman Brothers Band (Duane Allman and Dickie Betts)
The ultimate twin-guitar band. Duane Allman was a master of bottleneck technique who, in spite of his untimely death at the age of 24 in 1971, is still widely revered. His fiery playing was counterbalanced by Dickie Betts' countryish leanings. Allman also famously out-soloed Eric Clapton on Derek and The Dominoes' classic track "Layla."
The Allman Brothers Band (1969) ✶
At Fillmore East (1971)

The Beatles (George Harrison)
Although The Beatles are, arguably, the most significant band in pop history, George Harrison's role as main guitarist is all too frequently overlooked. And yet many of the most interesting developments in guitar music were popularized by The Beatles: "I Feel Fine" features feedback, the first time such a sound had hit the charts; the use of the Rickenbacker 12-string electric guitar influenced a generation of players; the driving guitar sound of "Paperback Writer" was "the first heavy metal record," claimed John Lennon; the psychedelic studio trickery of "Tomorrow Never Knows" was innovative.
Revolver (1966)
The Beatles ("White Album") (1968)
Abbey Road (1969)

Beck
Not necessarily a particularly noteworthy guitarist in his own right, Beck Hansen has shown how different guitar styles – from acoustic slide to indie thrash – can be melded to produce something uniquely contemporary.
Odelay! (1996) ✶
Midnite Vultures (1999) ✶

Jeff Beck

More admired by fellow musicians than by the general public, Jeff Beck represents everything of good taste in rock guitar. His solo on Stevie Wonder's "Lookin' for Another Pure Love" (*Talking Book*, 1972) is blissful.
Truth (1968)
Wired (1976)

Captain Beefheart (Jeff Cotton and Bill Harkleroad)

Under the names Antennae Jimmy Semens and Zoot Horn Rollo, Cotton and Harkleroad were responsible for the twin guitars that battled throughout the legendary *Trout Mask Replica*, arguably the greatest album ever made – and certainly a milestone in modern music. A collision of traditional blues with avant garde European classical tradition and free jazz, this album is important listening for any guitarist.
Trout Mask Replica (1969) ✳

The Byrds (Roger McGuinn)

Few bands have created such an immediately characteristic sound as The Byrds – a mixture of sumptuous, gentle folk harmonies and Roger McGuinn's jangling Rickenbacker 12-string electric guitar.
Mr. Tambourine Man (1965)
Turn! Turn! Turn! (1966)

Larry Carlton

L.A. session superstar Larry Carlton's pure, clinical tones can be heard backing artists as diverse as B. B. King, Steely Dan, Bobby Bland, and Joni Mitchell. He was also a member of jazz-funk masters, The Crusaders.
Southern Comfort (1974) (with The Crusaders)
Aja (1977) (with Steely Dan)

Chic (Nile Rodgers)

Nile Rodgers' superb rhythm guitar combined with Bernard Edwards' definitive bass lines will get anyone out on the dance floor.
Les Plus Grands Succès de Chic (1979)

Eric Clapton

A blues purist who came to the notice of record buyers as a member of The Yardbirds and with John Mayall's Bluesbreakers. Worldwide success came in 1966 when he formed Cream, creating the very first rock power trio. Widely viewed as the "god of the guitar" by the end of the 1960s, Clapton was sidetracked during much of the 1970s fighting a long battle against heroin addiction. Since the early 1990s, he has enjoyed massive success throughout the world.
Bluesbreakers – John Mayall with Eric Clapton (1965) (with John Mayall)
Disraeli Gears (1966) (with Cream)
Layla and Other Assorted Love Songs (1970) (with Derek and The Dominoes)

Eddie Cochran
Not only was he one of the great stars of the rock 'n' roll era, Eddie Cochran was also rock's first bona fide guitar hero. He recorded avidly between 1957 and his premature death in a car crash in 1960, often overdubbing all the parts himself. He penned such great hits as "Summertime Blues," "Somethin' Else," and "C'mon Everybody."
The Legendary Eddie Cochran (compilation 1957–60)

Country Joe and The Fish (Barry Melton)
Country Joe MacDonald was a San Francisco protest folkie who went electric with some success. Barry Melton is one of the great psychedelic guitarists.
Electric Music for the Mind and Body (1967) (Country Joe and The Fish) *

Steve Cropper
The king of rhythm guitar, as a member of The Mar-Keys and then Booker T and The MGs, Steve Cropper was part of the house band that played on the greatest hits of the Stax and Volt labels in the 1960s – artists such as Otis Redding, Sam and Dave, Rufus, and Carla Thomas – the list is endless. Cropper brought the art of space to the guitar and is as worthy of study as Jimi Hendrix. And you can dance to the music.
The Complete Stax/Volt Singles 1959–68 (1991) *
Booker T and the MG's Greatest Hits (compilation 1959–68) (1974) *

Dick Dale & His Del-Tones
The undisputed king of surf guitar. Using lightning-speed alternating pick strokes, Dale created a unique staccato sound that, when smothered in a heavy spring reverb, simulated the rhythm of riding the surf.
King of the Surf Guitar: The Best of Dick Dale & His Del-Tones (compilation 1961–64) (1989)

Deep Purple (Richie Blackmore)
These 1970s British heavy rockers created famed rifferamas like "Smoke on the Water" and "Black Night." Guitarist Richie Blackmore went on to front his own band, Rainbow.
Deep Purple in Rock (1970) (with Deep Purple)

Duane Eddy
The king of the "twang," Duane Eddy's worldwide hits such as "Peter Gunn" and "Raunchy" made him the best-known guitarist of the late 1950s. His formula was basic: a simple tune played on the bass strings of a Gretsch Chet Atkins guitar. Eddy probably influenced more kids to take up the guitar than just about anyone else.
Because They're Young (compilation 1958–65)

Gang of Four (Andy Gill)
UK politico-indie-funk band of the early 1980s, Gang of Four's aggressive sound was shaped by the sharp, slashing chord work of Andy Gill – a kind of Wilko Johnson (of Dr Feelgood) meets Nile Rodgers. Their recordings are probably difficult to track down, but worth the effort.
Entertainment (1980) *

Jimi Hendrix
In an all-too-short life, Hendrix took the art of rock guitar on to a totally new plane. Every guitarist should own the trio of albums he cut with The Jimi Hendrix Experience! Try to catch video footage of him playing, too – marvel at

how he makes the most complex techniques look easy.
Are You Experienced? (1967) ✳
Axis: Bold As Love (1968) ✳
Electric Ladyland (1968)

King Crimson (Robert Fripp)
King Crimson was one of the most interesting progressive rock bands of the 1970s. The band's sound was defined primarily by Robert Fripp's measured, yet unpredictable, fretwork. The early 1980s incarnation of Crimson saw Fripp partnering Adrian Belew – another superb guitarist – to great effect. He also conceived the "Frippertronics" system with fellow experimenter Brian Eno – a system that involved looping magnetic

tapes across the heads of two linked tape recorders, enabling the creation of lush soundscapes over which Fripp could then play solo parts.
In the Court of the Crimson King (1969) (with King Crimson)
No Pussyfooting (1973) (with Brian Eno)
Discipline (1981) (with King Crimson)

Little Feat (Lowell George)
Little Feat was the best of the Southern Boogie bands to emerge in the United States in the early 1970s. Leader Lowell George's playing displayed a mastery of a wide variety of country and blues styles.
Dixie Chicken (1973)

Yngwie Malmsteen
This high-speed metal star came to prominence with rock band Alcatrazz. His solo work is much given to classical-tinged rock instrumentals, most of which are executed with finesse.
Rising Force (1984)
Inspiration (1996)

Harvey Mandel
Widely traveled session player Mandel is noted for pioneering a two-handed finger-tapping system at least a decade before Eddie Van Halen popularized the technique.
Shangrenade (1976)

Led Zeppelin (Jimmy Page)
The most influential rock band of them all. Featuring former session guitarist and Yardbird Jimmy Page, Zeppelin created an awesome "heavy" riffing blues that made them one of the biggest-selling bands of the 1970s.
Led Zeppelin I (1968) ✳
Led Zeppelin IV (1971)

Scotty Moore
As Elvis Presley's original guitarist, Scotty Moore's crossing of rhythm and blues with country picking defined the "rockabilly" guitar sound. The tracks compiled for *The Sun Sessions* album represent a genuine turning point in the history of popular music.
The Sun Sessions (compilation 1954–55) (1987) (with Elvis Presley) ✳

Nirvana
At the forefront of the Seattle grunge movement, Nirvana – fronted by 1990s icon Kurt Cobain – played a major role in returning the guitar to the forefront of rock music. Their masterstroke was the 1992 worldwide hit "Smells Like Teen Spirit."
Nevermind (1992) ✳
In Utero (1993)

Pere Ubu
This classic U.S. art-rock band cut some of the most intriguing music of the post-punk era, including the magnificent and disturbing single "Thirty Seconds Over Tokyo."
New Picnic Time (1979)

Pink Floyd (Syd Barrett and David Gilmour)
Pink Floyd has had two influential, if very different, guitarists pass through its ranks. Original guitarist, songwriter, and singer Syd Barrett was the ultimate 1960s acid casualty. His inspired use of echo, fuzz, and feedback took the electric guitar into uncharted territory, creating the floating, spaced-out soundscapes that dominated the early, psychedelic Pink Floyd. When Barrett's taste for LSD became uncontrollable, he was forced to quit the band. His replacement was David Gilmour whose altogether more measured style helped overhaul the Floyd sound, turning them into one of the biggest-selling bands in rock history.
The Piper at the Gates of Dawn (with Syd Barrett) (1967) ✳
Dark Side of the Moon (with David Gilmour) (1973) ✳
Wish You Were Here (with David Gilmour) (1975)

The Police (Andy Summers)
Massively successful in the early 1980s, The Police championed a sparse, white-reggae sound. Guitarist Andy Summers filled the spaces with his delicate, reverbed, echoed, and chorused arpeggiated chords. It sounded deceptively easy but required the deft touch of a master craftsman to pull it off.

Regatta de Blanc (1979)
Synchronicity (1980)

Queen (Brian May)

A unique phenomenon, Queen mixed Zeppelinesque riffs with vaudeville, cod-opera, and (later) lumpen disco, and somehow became massive the world over. Always well to the fore was Brian May's nifty fretwork, especially his hallmark harmonized guitar "orchestras" which were built up one track at a time in the studio.
Sheer Heart Attack (1974)
A Night at the Opera (1975)

Radiohead (John Greenwood and Ed O'Brien)

Arguably one of the most important rock bands of the late 1990s, Radiohead captured the angst of the period with a sophisticated sound forged around the interaction of two outstanding and gifted guitarists.
The Bends (1995) ✳
OK Computer (1997) ✳

Rage Against the Machine (Tom Morello)

This U.S. "agit-prop" band created a powerful hybrid of heavy rock and rap. Harvard graduate Morello's style is strongly influenced by the triggered, sampled sounds of early hip-hop.
Rage Against the Machine (1992)

The Ramones (Johnny Ramone)

The band that kick-started punk rock and convinced thousands of kids that you didn't need a music degree to make great guitar music.
Ramones (1976) ✳
Leave Home (1977)

The Rolling Stones

In a career now pushing 40 years, the Stones have earned the reputation as the Greatest Rock 'n' Roll Band in the World. Although fine lead players such as founding member Brian Jones, Mick Taylor, and Ron Wood can be heard on their numerous albums, the Stones' sound is defined by the masterful rhythm guitar work of Keith Richards, whose playing provides myriad lessons to novice rockers.
Beggars Banquet (1968)
Let It Bleed (1969)
Exile on Main Street (1972) ✳

Santana (Carlos Santana)
Merging blues-based psychedelic rock with Latin rhythms, in the late 1960s Carlos Santana managed to create a genuinely innovative sound which – like the sustain and overdrive that characterizes the guitarist's playing – is still immediately recognizable.
Abraxas (1970)
Santana (1970)
Caravanserai (1972)

Joe Satriani
Former teacher of Steve Vai (and Metallica's Kirk Hammett), Satriani is also a technician par excellence – arguably the greatest in the rock world.
Surfing With the Alien (1987)

The Shadows (Hank Marvin)
Britain's most popular instrumental group of all time, The Shadows' simple chords strummed out on acoustic guitars support a superb guitar melody embellished with tremolo, echo, and reverb. Hugely influential.
The Shadows (1961)

The Smiths (Johnny Marr)
Johnny Marr was one of the few credible guitar stars to emerge in the 1980s. His style is characterized by a subtle hybrid of rhythm and lead that made extensive use of neatly picked arpeggios.
The Queen Is Dead (1986)

Sonic Youth (Thurston Moore and Lee Renaldo)
A major influence on bands of the early 1990s, Sonic Youth became known as the "godfathers of grunge." Both players make extensive use of prepared guitars (both worked with Glenn Branca in their youth), altered tunings, discord, and feedback. Their early material remains the most interesting and uncompromising, if less accessible.
Confusion Is Sex (1982)

The Stooges (James Williamson)
Fronted by Iggy Pop, The Stooges were the godfathers of punk rock. Their debut remains a timeless masterpiece.
The Stooges (1969)

Television (Tom Verlaine and Richard Lloyd)
Emerging from the New York new-wave scene, Television produced a couple of classic albums and then split up. "Marquee Moon" (from the album of the same name) is one of the all-time great guitar singles.
Marquee Moon (1977) ✶
Adventure (1978)

Steve Vai
The ultimate guitar pyrotechnician, Vai's albums are of interest mainly for the astounding technical skills on display.
Passion and Warfare (1990) ✶
Sex and Religion (1993)

Van Halen (Eddie Van Halen)
Eddie Van Halen was the most influential guitarist to emerge during the 1980s. He is best known for popularizing the two-handed finger-tapping technique that characterized his soloing. It can be heard to great effect on his guest spot for Michael Jackson on the 1983 hit "Beat It."
Van Halen (1978)
1984 (MCMLXXXIV) (1984)

Velvet Underground (Lou Reed and Sterling Morrison)
Barely acknowledged outside of the hippest circles during their active life (1966–72), VU is now recognized as an important influence on the development of alternative rock. Much of their influential collage-of-noise sound was based on the combined drone and feedback of Reed's and Morrison's guitars.
The Velvet Underground and Nico (1967) ✳
White Light/White Heat (1968) ✳
The Velvet Underground (1969)

The Who (Pete Townshend)
The Who was one of the seminal guitar bands of the rock era. Creative light behind the band, Pete Townshend penned classic us-against-them youth anthems such as "My Generation" and "Won't Get Fooled Again," and

created ambitious concept albums such as *Tommy* and *Quadrophenia*. An influential guitarist, he was more likely to be heard executing lightning-fast power chords than lengthy solos.
The Who Sell Out (1967) ✱
The Who Live at Leeds (1970)

Wire (Bruce Gilbert)
This classic art-house band emerged from the U.K. punk scene to offer the guitar as a tool of sheer energy. Albums from the mid-1980s are more keyboard-based.
Pink Flag (1977) ✱
Chairs Missing (1978)

Link Wray
Wray's place in the history books revolves around one great guitar instrumental, "Rumble," released in 1958.
There's Good Rockin' Tonite
(compilation 1957–65)

The Yardbirds
This legendary English beat band of the mid-1960s saw Eric Clapton, Jeff Beck, and Jimmy Page pass through its ranks. It eventually evolved into The New Yardbirds and finally Led Zeppelin.
Roger the Engineer (1966)

Neil Young
Hallowed as one of the great songwriters of the 20th century, Young's electric work is peppered with fretwork of wild and unpredictable energy. *Rolling Stone* magazine called him, appropriately, an "abstract expressionist of the guitar."
Rust Never Sleeps (1979)
Weld (1991)

Frank Zappa
Both alone and with his band, The Mothers of Invention, Zappa's music was always uncompromising. His body of work traverses pop (if done with tongue in cheek), rock, jazz, and contemporary classical.
We're Only in It for the Money (1967)
Shut Up 'n Play Yer Guitar (1981)

Country, folk, and ethnic

Chet Atkins
The greatest virtuoso guitarist that U.S. country music ever produced, as well as being a master of picking styles, Atkins was crucial in the development of the "Nashville sound" which emerged during the mid-1950s.
A Legendary Performer (compilation 1952–64) (1977)

Martin Carthy
Carthy was a pivotal figure in the English folk movement whose fingerpicking style combined American folk with indigenous Celtic music.
Martin Carthy (1965)

Nick Drake
In a tragically short life, Drake recorded three sublime albums that were largely ignored by the public. Although his singing and songwriting form the core of his ever-increasing reputation, the unique atmosphere of his albums is created by his subtle, bluesy fingerpicking. The 4-CD compilation box *Fruit Tree* contains nearly all of Drake's known recordings.
Fruit Tree: The Complete Works of Nick Drake (compilation 1969–73) (1986) ✳

John Fahey
A unique and uncompromising player, Fahey's steel-string instrumentals traverse the boundaries of country, blues, and folk. His music is, without exception, passionate, exhilarating, and uplifting.
Dance of Death and Other Plantation Favorites (1964) ✳
Blind Joe Death (1967)

Lester Flatt
The most important figure in the early years of country guitar, Flatt established his reputation working with bluegrass maestro Bill Monroe. Flatt is widely credited with having invented his hallmark linking of chords by simple bass-line runs on the bottom two strings of the guitar. Listen to classic numbers he cut with Earl Scruggs in The Foggy Mountain Boys such as "Foggy Mountain Breakdown" and "Flint Hill Special."
The Original Bluegrass Band (with Bill Monroe: compilation 1945–49) (1969)

Danny Gatton
Another "guitarists' guitarist," this time in the realm of country music, Gatton blends Chet Atkins-style country-picking with blues and jazz influences. His albums are recommended for those in search of state-of-the-art country playing.
New York Stories (1992)

Richard Thompson
Thompson was a key figure in the crossover between British folk and rock as a member of Fairport Convention (1967–71), in his career with ex-wife Linda Thompson (1972–82), and as a solo artist.
Shoot Out the Lights (1982) (Richard and Linda Thompson)
Daring Adventures (1986) (solo)

Jazz

Laurindo Almeida
Brazilian jazz and classical guitarist
Laurindo Almeida introduced the bossa
nova in 1962 and assured his place in
music history.
Viva Bossa Nova (1962)

Derek Bailey
British free-jazz player Derek Bailey did
his most interesting work with
saxophonist Evan Parker, but it's difficult
stuff for most mainstream ears. He also
wrote *Improvisation* – a book that all
creative musicians should read.
The Topography of the Lungs (1970) (with
Evan Parker)
View From 6 Windows (1982)

George Benson
Well known to mainstream audiences
as a soul singer, George Benson is
also a fine jazz guitarist in the Wes
Montgomery mold. He dominated
the mid-1970s jazz crossover market,
the album *Breezin'* laying claim to be
the biggest-selling jazz album of
all time.
Breezin' (1976)

Tal Farlow
One of the great technicians of jazz,
Farlow's trademarks are the deft execution
of extraordinarily fast single-note runs
and the ability to move between chord
positions with amazing agility.
Tal (1956)

Egberto Gismonti
An unusual "new-age" jazz musician,
Brazilian-born Gismonti is a classical
pianist who, after 15 years of training
at the highest level, abandoned his
study in favor of the guitar. His music,
usually played on customized guitars
with additional bass strings, is strongly
influenced by the Xingo tribes of the
Amazon with whom Gismonti lived
for a while.
Danca Das Cabecas (1976)

Jim Hall
One of the most versatile players of
the "post-bop" era, Hall's mellow sound
has been heard with just about every
significant name in jazz – from Ella
Fitzgerald and Chet Baker to Sonny
Rollins and Bill Evans.
The Train & the River (1957) (with
Jimmy Giuffre) ✷
Undercurrent (1959) (with
Bill Evans)

Eddie Lang
Widely credited as the man who invented the guitar solo, jazz man Eddie Lang is as revered in the United States as is his European counterpart Django Reinhardt across the Atlantic.
Jazz Guitar Virtuoso (compilation 1928–32)

John McLaughlin
One of the founding fathers of jazz-rock fusion, McLaughlin's groundbreaking album *Extrapolations* impressed Miles Davis, who drafted him into his band. With Davis he recorded *Bitches Brew*, a double-album set that, for many, established fusion as the next leap forward in the development of jazz.
Extrapolations (1969)
Bitches Brew (1970) (with Miles Davis) ✳

Pat Metheny
Prodigiously talented jazz guitarist Pat Metheny taught at the Berkley School of Music while still in his teens. A master of measured playing, Metheny's soloing is technically complex without ever being excessive. He is also a fine composer.
Pat Metheny Group (1978)

Wes Montgomery
Arguably the most important post-war jazz guitarist, Montgomery has been a major influence on the likes of George Benson, Pat Metheny, Herb Ellis, and pretty much every other noteworthy jazz guitarist of the past 30 years. His hallmark style included the use of his thumb to pick the strings, extensive use of unison octaves, and swiftly executed parallel chording.
The Incredible Jazz Guitar of Wes Montgomery (1960) ✳
Full House (1962)

Joe Pass
A highly technical player, Joe Pass consolidated different jazz styles to great effect. He was at his best when playing unaccompanied, where he was able to encompass the role of the traditional jazz bass and integrate lead lines within his considerable chord vocabulary.
Intercontinental (1970)
Live at Montreaux (1977)

Hans Reichel
About as avant garde as it's possible for a guitarist to get, Hans Reichel is not for the faint-hearted. It isn't really jazz, but what the heck . . .
Table of the Elements: Beryllium (1993)

Django Reinhardt
Along with Eddie Lang, Reinhardt was one of the first great virtuoso jazz guitar soloists. In spite of famously disabling his left hand, leaving only the thumb and first two fingers functioning, Reinhardt developed a technique that enabled him to play lightning-fast single-note solos. There are numerous compilations that feature the many classic recordings he made with the Quintet of the Hot Club of France between 1934 and 1939. Check out his arrangements for "I'll See You in My Dreams" and "Stardust," and his own composition, "Nuages." ✳

John Scofield
Jazz guitarist John Scofield – unlike many in this sometimes sheltered sphere – seems to have drawn on influences from other genres. His spacious style brought him to the attention of Miles Davis.
John Scofield Live (1977)
Grace Under Pressure (1992)

Sonny Sharrock
The founding father and master of "free-jazz" guitar, Sharrock's music may be considered "challenging" by those with mainstream tastes.
Memphis Underground (1968)
Ask the Ages (1991)

Blues

Chuck Berry
One of the most influential guitarists of all time, Chuck Berry's numerous rock 'n' roll classics feature some of the most immediately recognizable guitar riffs ever recorded. His simultaneous fusion of rhythm and lead guitar made a huge impact on the generation of young guitarists who followed.
Hail! Hail! Rock 'n' Roll (compilation 1956–65) (1987) ✳

Blind Blake
The greatest innovator of early ragtime guitarists, Blind Blake cut around 80 recordings between 1926 and his death in 1932. His style is characterized by complex, syncopated right-hand barrel-rolls between the thumb and fingers.
Ragtime Guitar's Foremost Fingerpicker (compilation 1926–30) (1984)

Roy Buchanan
A great blues craftsmen, Buchanan was – sadly – more appreciated by his fellow players than the public at large.
That's What I'm Here For (1974)
A Street Called Straight (1976)

Albert Collins
Texas bluesman Albert Collins frequently used open minor tunings with a capo positioned high along the fretboard. Known as "The Iceman," Collins was taught to play the guitar by his cousin Lightnin' Hopkins.
Truckin' with Albert Collins (1969)
Ice Pickin' (1978)

Ry Cooder
This master craftsman's work encompasses blues, folk, rock, jazz, and pretty much any other ethnic music that takes his fancy. Cooder's albums represent an almost academic study of the guitar in popular music.
Chicken Skin Music (1976) ✳
Music by Ry Cooder (1995)

Buddy Guy
Once a teenage blues prodigy, Buddy Guy took blues guitar to new heights during the 1960s with his recordings for the Chess and Vanguard record labels.
A Man and His Blues (1965)
Damn Right, I've Got the Blues (1991)

Lightnin' Hopkins
One of the masters of country blues, Sam "Lightnin'" Hopkins is widely credited to be the most recorded blues artist in history. The Hopkins sound was characterized by the use of single-string guitar lines that echoed, or counterpointed, the vocal melody.
The Gold Star Sessions – Vol 1: 1950–55 (1990)
The Gold Star Sessions – Vol 2: 1955–58 (1990)

B. B. King
The single most famous blues artist of them all, B. B. King's extensive use of string bending both as a playing device and as an alternative vibrato technique has influenced successive generations of blues and rock players. He famously named his trademark Gibson ES-335 "Lucille."
Live at the Regal (1960)
Best of B. B. King (compilation 1953–59) (1973)

Roomful of Blues
The most vibrant and exciting blues group of the past three decades, Roomful of Blues' everchanging line-up has featured the guitar skills of Duke Robillard, Chris Earl, and Chris Vachon. Robbillard's work is particularly recommended.
Hot Little Mama (1981)

T-Bone Walker
One of the father figures of electric blues and one of the first masters of the electric guitar, Walker was a very important influence.
The Complete 1940–54 Recordings of T-Bone Walker (1990) ✳

Muddy Waters
The man who updated the sound of the Mississippi Delta, Muddy Waters was the first great electric blues guitarist. By introducing the blues to a mainstream white audience, he laid the foundations for blues-based rock music in the 1960s.
Live at Newport (1960)
The Chess Box (compilation 1951–59) (1989) ✳

Classical, flamenco, and ethnic

Ernesto Bitetti
One of the modern-day masters of the Spanish classical tradition, Bitetti's interpretations of the works of Rodrigo have been hailed as definitive.
Concierto de Aranguez (1974)

Glenn Branca
More a composer than a guitarist, Branca's music sounds something like a classical symphony crossed with a thrash metal band. Branca's "orchestras" have primarily consisted of guitars.

Conventional tuning is abandoned and guitars re-strung so that each string is tuned to the same note – although not all of the instruments are tuned to the same note. This creates a very big sound!
The Ascension (1981)
Symphony No. 10 (1994)

Julian Bream
British guitarist Julian Bream has done more than anyone else to carry on the tradition of Segovia. Although a virtuoso musician, Bream's historical importance resides in his broadening of the classical repertoire, either as a commissioner of new works or as a transcriber of pieces written for other instruments.
20th Century Guitar (1967) ✱
Julian Bream 70s (1973)

Sol Hoopii
Along with Gaby Pahinui, Solomon Ho'opi'i Ka'ai'ai was one of the two undisputed kings of the "slack key" Hawaiian lap-steel guitar. Hoopii was the first notable user of the Rickenbacker "Frying Pan."
Sol Hoopii (compilation 1929–37) (1974)

Ketama
Fascinating exponents of Flamenco Nuevo, Ketama produced a mixture of jazz-rock and flamenco that is little known outside of Spanish-speaking world.
Ketama (1992)

Paco de Lucia
This modern-day virtuoso has done more than anyone to popularize flamenco, the music of the Andalucian region of Southern Spain.
Fabulosa Guitarra (1989)

Andrés Segovia
More than anyone before or since, Segovia brought widespread respectability to the guitar and helped the instrument gain acceptance in the elite world of classical music.
Recordings (compilation 1927–39) (1974) ✴
The Master (compilation 1952–58) (1982)

John Williams
Williams is one of the most significant classical guitarists to have emerged since the benchmarks were set by Andrés Segovia during the first half of the 20th century.
John Williams Plays Spanish Music (1970)
Music of Barrios (1988)

Carlos Montoya
Exiled from his native Spain during the rule of General Franco, Carlos Montoya used his newly adopted U.S. home to bring flamenco music to the West, allowing it to be presented in musical surroundings without its traditional singers and dancers.
Suite Flamenco (1966)

Paco Peña
Modern flamenco is presented at its best when performed by Paco Peña.
Fabulous Flamenco (1986)

A simple glossary

Accent A playing effect that places emphasis on a specific note or chord. Accents can be used to create rhythms.

Accidental A series of symbols used in written music to raise or lower the pitch of a note: The sharp (♯) raises the pitch by a half-step or semitone; the flat (♭) lowers the pitch by a half-step or semitone; the natural ( ) is used to cancel a previous accidental. It's also possible to use a double sharp (♯♯) or double flat (♭♭) to raise or lower the pitch by a tone or step respectively.

Acoustic guitar A traditional guitar that can produce sound without the need of any form of amplification.

Action The height between the bottom of the strings and the top of the frets on the fingerboard. The lower the action the easier it becomes to fret notes, although a very low action can cause fret buzz.

ADT Automatic double-tracking. An electronic delay effect that, when used with a guitar, simulates the sound of two instruments playing the same part.

Archtop A type of steel-string acoustic guitar with an arched top.

Arpeggio A succession of chord tones.

Ball end A small metal disk found at the end of a steel string used for attaching the string to the guitar.

Bottleneck A glass or steel bar that can be dragged along the strings to alter the pitch. Also the name given to the technique and style of playing with a bottleneck.

Bridge A device positioned on the body of the guitar that supports the strings and controls their height above the fretboard and their length from the nut or zero fret.

Capo A movable bar that can be clamped at different positions along the fretboard allowing open strings to be played in different keys.

Capstan Mechanism standing out from the headstock to which is attached a guitar string.

Chord The sound of three or more notes played at the same time. Although the sound of two notes can create a chordal effect, this is technically known as an interval.

Chorus An extension of ADT, chorus is an electronic effect that simulates more than one instrument playing the same part.

Clef A symbol that fixes the notes on the staff at a certain pitch.

Compression An electronic effect that can increase the volume of quiet notes in relation to the louder notes. Commonly used in conjunction with distortion effects by rock guitarists.

Concert pitch The note A on a piano keyboard that is measured at a frequency of 440 kHz. Electronic tuners, pitch pipes, tuning forks, and electronic keyboards all adhere to this perfect pitch.

Damping Muting the strings by deadening their natural sustain with the hand. This can be used as a musical effect to create rhythms, or as a means to stop particular strings from ringing.

Delay An electronic simulation of echo effects.

Direct injection (DI) When an instrument is plugged directly into an input channel on a mixing board.

Distortion An electronic effect created by boosting the volume in the preamplifier stage of the amplifier. More commonly achieved using electronic effects pedals.

Dreadnought A large-bodied, steel-string acoustic guitar, first produced by the Martin company. Popularly used in folk and country music.

Electroacoustic guitar A guitar with pickup fitted that can also be played acoustically.

Extended chord A chord that uses additional notes that are over an octave higher than the root note.

Feedback The "whistling" effect created when amplified sound from a speaker causes the guitar strings to vibrate. Can also be harnessed for musical effect.

Finger tapping Playing technique where both the left and right hands are used to play notes on the fretboard. Also called fret tapping.

Fingerboard A piece of wood glued to the top of the neck into which the frets are cut (also commonly referred to as the fretboard).

Fingerpicking Right-hand playing technique where the strings are plucked by individual fingers rather than a pick.

Flat-top A steel-string acoustic guitar that has a flat soundboard.

Flatwound strings Often used on archtop guitars, the steel core in these strings is covered by a flat ribbon of metal giving them a smooth feel.

Free stroke Playing stroke used in classical guitar in which the finger strikes the string in a pulling motion and comes to rest above the adjacent string.

Fret A metal strip positioned across the fretboard to determine a semitone space.

Fret buzz The sound of a string unintentionally hitting frets further up the fretboard as it vibrates.

Fretboard See Fingerboard.

Fuzz box The original 1960s electronic distortion effect.

Groundwound strings A compromise between roundwound and flatwound strings in which the surface of the string is lightly ground down.

Hardware A guitar's metal parts, including the machine heads, pickups, bridge, and tremolo arm.

Harmonic Bell-like tones produced by damping the strings before playing them.

Headstock The top part of the guitar neck, where the machine heads that support the strings are fitted.

Heel The end of the neck which is attached to the body

Humbuckers Twin-coil electronic pickups – as found on Gibson Les Paul guitars – that produce a thick or "fat" sound that is favored by many rock guitarists.

Interval The distance between two notes.

Intonation Setting the intonation correctly ensures that the guitar remains in tune along the entire fretboard.

Inversion From the bass note, the order of notes in a chord.

Ledger line A line that places notes above or below the staff.

Linings The continuous piece of ribbed wood in a guitar that joins the soundboard to the back.

Luthier A person who makes guitars.

Machine head Mechanical device mounted on the headstock that controls the pitch of a string. Sometimes called a tuning peg.

Metronome A device for sounding a specific number of beats per minute.

Mixing board A unit that connects, edits, and then outputs sounds from a microphone or instrument.

Multiple-effects module A single unit combining an array of effects.

Nut The string support positioned at the top of the fretboard controlling the horizontal positioning of the strings.

Octave An interval of 12 semitones or half-steps. Doubling the sound frequency of any note increases its pitch by a single octave.

Open voicing Chords formed around the open strings of the guitar.

Pedals Foot-controlled electronic units connected between the output of the guitar and the input of the amplifier, which can be used to create a variety of different sound effects.

Pick Object used for striking the guitar strings – usually made from plastic. Also known as a plectrum.

Pickups Electro-magnetic transducers that convert string vibrations into electrical impulses. When they are amplified the original sound can be heard through a speaker system.

PIMA The letter names for the right-hand fingers.

Plectrum See Pick.

Rasgueado Method of strumming used by flamenco guitarists.

Rest stroke Playing stroke used in classical guitar in which the finger strikes the string in a pulling motion and comes to rest on or against the adjacent string.

Riff A repeated sequence of notes.

Roundwound strings Most commonly used strings on electric and acoustic guitars and made from conventionally shaped wire.

Sampler A piece of hardware that can take digitally recorded audio and reprocess it.

Scale A series of related notes that follow a set pattern of intervals when played in sequence from a specified note to the octave above.

Scratchplate A plate (usually plastic) fitted to the soundboard to protect the body of the guitar.

Soundboard The front face of the guitar on which the bridge, pickups, and scratchplate are mounted.

Soundbox The body of an acoustic guitar.

Soundhole A normally circular hole cut out to allow sound to emanate from the soundbox.

Sustain The length of time a note lasts before it fades away.

Tablature An alternative to regular musical notation that provides specific fretting instructions.

Tempo The speed of a piece of music.

Time signature Symbol at the beginning of a piece of music indicating the number of beats, and their value, within a bar of music.

Top block The heel slots into the top block in the body of the guitar.

Tremolo A playing technique where a left-hand finger is used to create a minor fluctuation in pitch. Also the name given to a mechanical device that can alter the pitch of a string while it is ringing. Technically, this effect is vibrato rather than tremolo, but the incorrect terminology seems to have stuck.

Triad Most basic chord types containing three notes.

Truss rod Metal rod that passes through the full length of the neck underneath the fretboard; this reinforces the neck against string tension.

Vibrato An effect used to enhance the sound of a note.

Wah-wah pedal Foot-operated effect unit that can either be used as a tone control or moved back and forth to produce a characteristic "wah" sound.

Waist The inward shape near the middle of the guitar body.

Whammy bar Mechanical device fitted to the bridge of a guitar to alter the pitch of a note.

Wolf note Certain notes on a guitar's fretboard that have very little sustain.

Zero fret Fret found on some guitars directly in front of the nut that controls the height of the strings at the headstock end of the neck.

Index

A

accidental 213
acoustic guitars 34, 36, 39, 72, 101,
  archtop 34, 52, 54, 67
  changing string 92
  construction of 53, 54–57
  electro-acoustic 66
  f-holes 34
  flat-top 34, 52, 54, 67
  how to play 52
  nylon-string 284
  recording 348
  resonator guitar 57
  steel-string 33, 34, 54, 57, 66, 72, 92
  strings 67–69
  tuning 124
  types of 52
acoustics 345
action 75
  raising 263
adagio 140
ADAT 342
ADT 314, 315
Africa 247
Aguado, Dionisio 42–43, 290
allegro 140
American Ovation Company 64
amplifiers 69
  choosing 71, 77–79
  combo 77, 297
  construction of 300–01
  controls on 301
  early 300
  head 301
  input socket 300
  solid state 302
  sounds from 303–05
  types of 302
  valve 302
andante 140
anular 168
archtop guitars 34, 37, 52, 54, 67, 68
arpeggios 182
Asia 28, 38, 244
Atkins, Chet 45, 49, 269
augmented fourth, intervals 219
augmented triads 226
auxiliaries 334

B

Babylon 28, 39
Bach, Johann Sebastian 287, 294
background noise 336, 342
ballad 279
Balladeer guitar 64
banjo 34
  tuning 246
bar
  beats in 192–96
  definition of 141
  double 173, 180
  lines 192
bar chords 174–83
Barth, Paul 35
bass controls, amplifier 303
bass lines 274–75
  strum rhythm 274, 279
bass guitar
  construction of 62–63, 65
  electric 64, 65–66, 317
  stick 64
bass notes 268
B. B. King 234, 237
Beatles, The 46, 49, 53, 228, 327
Beauchamp, George 35
Beck, Jeff 46, 314
Beethoven, Ludwig van 43

Benson, George 140, 280
Berry, Chuck 46
Beta Band, The 338
Bigsby Merle Travis 36
Bigsby, Paul 36, 39, 271
bindings 54
Blind Lemon Jefferson 46, 239
block 91
bluegrass 45
blues 46, 49
  12-bar structure 238
  boogie 240–41
  pentatonic scales 244–45
  rhythm 239–45
  shuffle 240–41
Blur 342, 343
bossa nova rhythm 284
bottleneck (see also slide) 246, 262–63
B.P.M. 140, 192
bracing 54, 56
Brazil 281, 284, 285
bridge
  acoustic guitar 54
  bass guitar 62
  cleaning 83
  electric guitar 58,
  electroacoustic guitar 66
  pins 54
  saddle 57
  string fixtures 88, 91, 92
British Vox AC30 300
bronze-wound strings 68
Brooks, Garth 45, 266
buzz 332
Byrd, Billy 277
Byrdland 277
Byrds, The 45

C

Cajun 45
Californian National
  Company 35

Acknowledgements

The author would like to thank the following people for their help with this project:
Valerie Buckingham, Sean Moore, Bridget Hopkinson, and David Tombesi-Walton at
Dorling Kindersley; Polly Willis at the Foundry; Hugh Schermuly; Nick Kaçal for
helpful hints; Jim Barber; Chrys&themums; Richard Chapman; Ralph Denyer; Joachim
at JAR Music; Stewart Mason at Flamingo in New Mexico; R. Stevie Moore, king of
home-brewed pop; sticksmeister supreme Andy Ward; Vladimir of the Mumz; Atomdog;
Dave Gregory (late of XTC); Pipefish; SJ and JSJ; Los Bros Dillingham; Mark at Digital
Village; and, above all, Junior.

CD recorded and produced by The Orgone Company.
Terry Burrows: guitars, bass and keyboards. Andy Ward: drums and percussion

Picture credits

All pictures courtesy of the Dorling Kindersley Picture Library except:
Art Archive: Musée du Louvre, Paris, 28
Christie's Images: 29(tl), 186, 190
Greg Evans: 77, 87, 125(b), 224, 337(r), 360, 362(b), 367
Foundry Arts/Nick Wells: 312, 363, 365
Gibson: 34(r)
Jazz Index: 48(t), 416
Lebrecht Collection: 42(br)
Pictorial Press: 45, 46, 47, 50, 97(l), 99, 138, 198, 210, 234, 236, 239, 266, 280, 313,
    343, 348(t), 354(b), 358, 359(b), 407, 408, 409, 411, 412, 414, 418, 419, 420
Popperfoto: 26
Redferns: Fin Costello 359(t); Ian Davies 336, 355; Ian Dickson 354(t); James Dittiger
    335; Patrick Ford 70; Suzi Gibbons 333(bl); Tom Hanley 337(l); Mick Hutson 298,
    326, 352; Andrew Lepley 315; Michael Ochs Archives 48(b), 285, 327(l); David
    Redfern 261; Simon Ritter 248, 412; Ebet Roberts 94, 172; Nicky J. Sims 112, 118,
    322, 325, 345, 347, 361; Jon Super 310
Shure: 346
Tascam: 341, 342
Topham: 18/19, 24, 40, 44(l), 53, 96, 97(r), 109(l), 116, 126, 137, 140, 142, 151, 171,
    286, 316(bl), 344(b), 356, 362(t), 364(b), 404, 406, 410, 415, 420, 421, 422
Yamaha-Kemble Music (U.K.) Ltd: 349